SHAKING the GATES of HELL

Further praise for Shaking the Gates of Hell—

"*In this book, Delgado offers a truly incarnational theology from the heart of her social location, clearly discerning the 'signs of our times'—environmental devastation, economic domination, and violence—while reminding us of the power of biblical hope. This is a handbook for the next generation of grassroots social-change activism.*"

—**Ched Myers,** activist, theologian,
and educator with Bartimaeus Cooperative Ministries

"*Delgado names and then unmasks the myths, laws, and practices that sustain global corporate reach and suck the moral fiber out of well-meaning Christians.... Reflecting on her participation in nonviolent direct resistance against these powers, and describing movements for global justice, Delgado prepares Christians for faith-led resistance as a way of life.*"

—**Carol S. Robb,** Professor of Christian Social Ethics,
San Francisco Theological Seminary

SHAKING
the GATES
of HELL

FAITH-LED RESISTANCE TO CORPORATE GLOBALIZATION

Sharon Delgado

Fortress Press • Minneapolis

Cover design: Brad Norr
Cover image: copyright © Getty Images, Royalty Free
Book design: Tim Parlin

Library of Congress Cataloging-in-Publication Data

Library of Congress-Cataloging-in-Publication data available.

ISBN 978-0-8006-6220-2

The paper used in this publication meets the minimum requirements for American National Standard for Information Sciences—Permanence of Paper for Printed Library Materials, ANSI Z329.48–1984.

Manufactured in the U.S.A.

11   10   09   08   07   1   2   3   4   5   6   7   8   9   10

I dedicate this book to Guarionex,
my husband, partner, lover, and friend,
and to our grandchildren and all the earth's
children to the seventh generation.

"Give me a hundred preachers . . . who fear nothing but sin and desire nothing but God, and I will shake the gates of hell and set up the Kingdom of God on this earth."

—John Wesley

Contents

PART ONE: THE GATES OF HELL: UNDOING CREATION

PART TWO: CORPORATE GLOBALIZATION: THE SYSTEM IS DESIGNED FOR THE RESULTS IT IS GETTING

PART THREE: SHAKING THE GATES OF HELL: FAITH–LED RESISTANCE

Preface

We are living at a time when humanity and the earth itself face unprecedented danger. The current form of corporate-dominated globalization is escalating the plunder of the earth's riches, increasing the exploitation of workers, expanding police and military repression, and leaving poverty in its wake. The most powerful nations in the world support and promote this growing momentum, which pays off handsomely for a few wealthy individuals, giant corporations, and the politicians whose coffers they fill.

The destructiveness of the global economic system presents a moral challenge to all people of faith and conscience, especially those of us whom this system benefits. People who live in richer nations, especially the United States, bear particular responsibility. Our government dominates key global institutions that affect the daily lives of millions. Our military-industrial complex enforces a form of globalization that harms the poor, benefits U.S.-based corporations, and seeks to ensure unfettered access to the world's resources. Our patterns of over-consumption lead to increasing poverty, inequity, and environmental degradation. Our action and our inaction affect others, for our lives intermingle with the lives of people around the world and with the whole web of life.

In this pivotal time the world desperately needs people who are willing to speak and act clearly, with power and integrity, to move us in the direction of hope. Although I write from a Christian perspective, many of the ideas I present have a universal application. This book is a call to people of faith to bring all the resources of the world's great spiritual traditions to bear upon the current global crisis, together with the growing numbers of people of conscience around the world who are resisting the forces of destruction and creating alternatives that sustain life. Only by tapping into these spiritual traditions and connecting with the wisdom of the earth itself will we have a spiritual and moral foundation strong enough to carry us through this time of crisis, when the earth and all its creatures are "groaning in labor pains" (Rom. 8:22).

The book is divided into three sections. The first chapter in each section presents a theological framework through which the issues in that section are developed. The theological analysis expands as new themes are presented, culminating in a call to hope and action.

The theme of part 1, "The Gates of Hell: Undoing Creation," is based on the following William Stringfellow quote: "The work of the demonic powers in the Fall is the undoing of Creation."[1] Chapter 1 addresses the nature of God in relationship with creation, the value of all the diverse parts of creation, and the role of the human in relationship with the rest of the community of life. The chapters that follow provide an overview of the major elements of the current global crisis: loss of biodiversity, climate change, toxic pollution, harmful technologies, growing inequity, poverty, social disruption, violence, terror, and war. Each of these threats is presented in the context of the theology of creation. In each chapter I show how the growing power of corporations aggravates these problems, leading up to the issues addressed in part 2.

Part 2, "Corporate Globalization: The System Is Designed for the Results It Is Getting," addresses the question, What are the forces behind the accelerating ecological destruction and growing human misery that I have described? I argue that the global economic system that is wreaking such havoc is not an accidental phenomenon driven by abstract and irreversible forces, but is designed, supported, and enforced for the results it is getting, that is, the production of wealth, even at the expense of our human future and the earth itself. Chapter 8 expands the book's theological framework by presenting a theology of the institutional "Powers." Chapters that follow in this section describe the structure, ideology, and functioning of the global economy, describe the growing rights of corporations, show how the rule-making institutions of the global economy develop and defend those rights, and describe how police and military institutions enforce the global system. I use a contemporary science-fiction metaphor to illustrate and bring to life the system that has come to be called "corporate globalization," and I describe "Market Fundamentalism," the ideology that supports this system.

Part 3, "Shaking the Gates of Hell: Faith-Led Resistance," answers the questions, Where does hope lie, and what can people of faith do about the global crisis? Chapter 15 builds on the theological understanding of creation and the Powers as developed earlier and culminates in the theology of resistance and transformation that is the foundation of this book. This chapter points to Jesus, who lived in resistance to the dominant institutions of his day and who demonstrates the way to both personal and global transformation. Chapters that follow describe how to organize locally and globally in ways that are both sustainable and just, and suggest concrete actions that engender personal and social change. The overall theme of this section is the power of faith-led resistance and hope for personal, institutional, social, and global transformation.

I am grateful to the congregations and leaders of the California-Nevada Annual Conference of the United Methodist Church, who have taught me much about Christian love, commitment to peace and justice, and the institutional challenges of local church life. Without the encouragement of a clergy sister, Pam Coy-Armantrout, I may never have undertaken this project. My bishops and colleagues enabled me to stay connected as an active member of the clergy while writing and serving through a specialized ministry that my husband and I founded, Earth Justice Ministries, which has provided a vehicle for my work on the issues presented in this book.

I am indebted to the International Forum on Globalization and the following authors and activists for deepening my understanding of corporate globalization and related issues: David Korten, Maude Barlow, Naomi Kline, Vandana Shiva, Anaradha Mital, Martin Khor, Jerry Mander, Kevin Danaher, Walden Bellow, Antonia Juhasz, Lori Wallach, elmira Nazombe, Arundhati Roy, William Greider, Richard Barnett, Bill McKibben, Helen Caldicott, Jared Diamond, and Sandra Steingraber.

I am indebted to many theologians who have influenced my theology, my work, and my way of seeing the world, including: Thomas Berry, William Stringfellow, Jürgen Moltmann, Walter Wink, Dorothee Soelle, James Douglass, Carol Robb, Michael Lerner, Catherine Keller, John Cobb, Bill Wylie-Kellerman, Jim Wallis, Ted Peters, and Rosemary Radford Ruether, who read and critiqued an early draft of my chapters on theology.

My friend and colleague Elaine Schwartz read and edited a later draft. Gary Gardner, research director for WorldWatch Institute, read the manuscript and gave me helpful feedback. Their input was invaluable. I am grateful to Editor-in-Chief Michael West for his support of this project, and to David Lott, Tim Larson, Lynette Johnson, Bob Todd, and the entire staff at Fortress Press for helping bring this work to fruition.

My family, including my grown children and grandchildren, provided emotional support and a welcome change of focus, always reminding me of why I was writing this book. My son Luke "turned to the local," planted a vegetable garden, and helped feed me in body and soul. My sister Kathie Kline gave unwavering support from afar.

My husband, Guarionex Delgado, was my primary support through the process of writing this book. I treasure our conversations, including those that took place at various coffee shops where we wrote, and where he shared his poetry and I shared initial writings for this book. He helped me go deep, and I could trust him to be rigorously honest in both appreciation and critique of this work. While dealing with complex and sometimes painful topics, our walks on the beach and in the woods always brought me back to earth, and our Salsa dancing brought me back to my body and to the joy of life.

I am deeply grateful for those who have publicly modeled nonviolent resistance, including Kathy Kelly, Medea Benjamin, Louis Vitale, Daniel Ellsberg, Daniel and Phillip Berrigan, Judi Bari, Julia "Butterfly" Hill, and so many others. My appreciation extends to my colleagues at the Resource Center for Nonviolence and the extended peace and justice community of Santa Cruz, where I lived and worked most of the time I was writing this book. I am indebted to indigenous people and people in communities everywhere who struggle to resist corporate globalization, and to all who organize courageous campaigns and creative demonstrations, including the colorful and lively festivals of resistance that have shown me that "in resistance is the secret of joy."

Finally, I gratefully acknowledge the Holy Spirit, who motivated and supported me in the writing of this book. To God be the glory.

INTRODUCTION
A Moment of
Profound Choice

In December 1999 I was arrested during the World Trade Organization (WTO) meetings in Seattle. Lying on my bunk in King County jail, wrapped in a thin blanket, alone in the cold cell under lockdown, I felt time pass slowly. I could hear vague sounds of drumming and chanting; supporters were gathered outside. Kaleidoscopic images went through my mind: people marching and chanting together, colorful costumes, banners and giant puppets, police in riot gear, rubber bullets and tear gas, injured protestors, people singing, people crying.

Songs I had been singing with other protestors came to mind, including an old Malvina Reynolds song:

It isn't nice to block the doorways, it isn't nice to go to jail.
There are nicer ways to do it, but the nice ways always fail.
It isn't nice, it isn't nice; you told us once, you told us twice,
But if that is freedom's price, we don't mind.[1]

Having nothing better to do, I added two new verses based on my recent experiences:

It isn't nice to breathe in tear gas or be doused with pepper spray,
To be shot with rubber bullets or to hear their sound grenades.
It isn't nice, it isn't nice; we told you once, we told you twice,
But if that's the price of justice, we don't mind.

It isn't nice to be beat up or be dragged away to jail,
To spend long hours in holding tanks or lockdown without bail.
It isn't nice, it isn't nice, but if that is the price
To save the earth from dying, we don't mind.

As I lay there hour after hour I experienced a sense of triumph, solidarity, divine presence, and joy. I had come to Seattle expecting to participate in nonviolent demonstrations that were purely symbolic.

But just two days before, through nonviolent direct action, we had actually succeeded in shutting down the first day's meeting of the WTO, one of the most powerful and, as I will demonstrate, dangerous institutions the world has ever seen.

TEAMSTERS AND TURTLES, TOGETHER AT LAST!

How amazing it had been, being one of over fifty thousand people who came to Seattle to protest the harmful effects of the WTO's work. Environmentalists dressed as endangered sea turtles marched side by side with labor unionists to oppose corporate globalization. Together we protested with other advocates for a peaceful, just, and sustainable world.

Seattle churches were highly visible in the demonstrations. As an ordained United Methodist minister, I was proud that First United Methodist Church of Seattle was a central meeting place for nongovernmental organizations (NGOs). First United displayed a sign reading, "NGO Central"; hosted teach-ins, planning meetings, and worship services; and was a beginning point for various marches throughout the week.

Jim Wallis of Sojourners Community preached at a glorious service of Christian worship at St. James Cathedral lifting up "Jubilee 2000," a worldwide movement calling for the cancellation of the debt of the world's poorest nations. Sweet Honey in the Rock sang at an interfaith service filled to overflowing. It was followed by a march to the Kingdome, where the opening gala of the WTO was being held, and where thousands of us joined to form a human chain that encircled the arena. There we held a candlelight vigil calling on WTO delegates to consider the victims of corporate globalization and to use their influence to cancel the debt that is starving the poor.

Rising early on the morning on November 30, I put on my clergy collar and went to First United Methodist Church, where my "affinity group" huddled to make final plans. We then walked toward the convention center where the WTO meetings were scheduled to begin. I sat down on the sidewalk in front of the convention center at the intersection of Union and Sixth Streets, linking arms with my eighty-three-year-old friend Ruth Hunter on my left and a trembling young woman on my right. About fifty of us sat blocking the entrance, surrounded by hundreds of supporters.

After two hours, the police put on their gas masks and suddenly began to attack. I felt the pain of hard rubber bullets hitting my back, felt the sting of pepper spray, heard loud explosive sounds of concussion grenades, and gasped in suffocating clouds of tear gas. When I could no longer breathe, I struggled to my feet and helped drag Ruth away. Similar actions were taking place in other intersections around the perimeter of the convention center. Though some have portrayed the Seattle protests as "riots," they were not. The vast majority of demonstrators were peaceful and well disciplined, though police treated many brutally. But despite the pepper spray and tear gas, rubber bullets and concussion grenades, people continued to come back again and again, determined to prevent the WTO from advancing its "free trade" agenda. Suddenly, cheers went up around the city as we got word that the WTO officials had given up. The first day's meetings had been canceled. We had shut them down.

In order for the meetings to go on, the city government suspended civil liberties. On the second day of the meetings, hundreds of individuals and groups were arrested simply for walking into downtown, which had been declared a "No Protest Zone." I was among them.

The Seattle protests marked a turning point. Resistance to the current form of globalization, dominated by corporations, could no longer be ignored. The movement for global justice had emerged on the world scene.

CORPORATE GLOBALIZATION

When people use the term *globalization*, they usually mean global economic integration, that is, free trade and investment across borders, without trade barriers, without government interference. Globalization also means cultural integration, complete with Western-style development, media, marketing, and technology. New York Times columnist Thomas Friedman, a leading proponent of globalization, points out that this process is broadly perceived as the "Americanization of the world."[2]

The term *corporate globalization* is a way of describing the current situation, in which transnational corporations dominate key social, economic, and political institutions and steer human culture, government policies, and international trade and investment in ways that prioritize corporate profits above all else. For it is not really American culture that is being exported. Rather, corporate culture is being superimposed over the varied cultures and traditions within the United States as well throughout the rest of the world. Some call it "the McDonaldization of the world."[3]

This situation has also been called "empire," a new form of colonialism dominated by the United States, which uses its political, economic, and military power to extend free-market capitalism around the world. Others call it "corporate rule".

One of this book's foundational theological concepts is the idea of the Powers, based on William Stringfellow's analysis of the powers and principalities referred to in the Bible (Eph. 6:12). The Powers, as the term is used in this book, refers to the institutions in which human beings function and the larger, interlocking systems of which they are a part. This work primarily focuses on the dominant institutions and systems of our age, referred to in colloquial terms as "the Powers that be."

Most institutions are created to enhance life, but an institution can take on a life of its own, so that its primary purpose becomes maintaining its own survival, growth, and extension of power. When this happens, people are dehumanized. They become like cogs in a machine, serving the needs of the institution, rather than the institution serving the needs of living beings.

With transnational corporations, this problem is compounded. Though corporate charters are supposedly granted for the public good, in practice the primary purpose for which corporations exist is to generate profits for their shareholders. Their survival and extension of power depends upon their continuing generation of wealth. This goal is generally (and legally) more important to a corporation than the well-being of its workers, consumers, the communities in which it operates, the general public, or the earth itself.

Because of their wealth, political influence, and global reach, huge transnational corporations drive the accelerating movement toward corporate globalization. They are expanding their reach and accelerating the pace at which they exploit the world's resources as they seek to integrate all of humanity into the global marketplace. Governments are getting out of their way by eliminating regulations that constrain corporate activity. The mainstream media, dominated by corporations, promotes programming and commercials that implant a specific worldview into people's minds.

The point is not that all corporations are bad (though some are), nor that we need to eliminate them (though some corporations should be disincorporated), but that their proper role is to be servants, not dominators, of life. Corporations should not have the power to make decisions that harm human beings or the earth for the sake of generating private wealth. But this is precisely what is happening.

If corporations continue to amass greater wealth and power, poverty and inequity will also grow. More and more people around the world will be deprived of the basic necessities of life. Communities that have been self-sustaining for generations will continue to disintegrate, as local artisans, small businesses, and small farmers lose out to competition by transnational corporations. Native peoples will continue to be driven off their lands. Jobs will continue to be lost, and labor standards will spiral downward. Places of beauty and diversity will continue to be devoured to create wealth for the few. The resulting social upheaval will require increasingly repressive police forces and ever more jails and prisons. Rich nations, especially the United States, will continue to enforce the corporate colonization of the world through military power. These patterns are already well underway, and are leading to growing poverty, social upheaval, repression, terrorism, war, misery, and ecological collapse.

In short, if we do not turn things around, we face a living hell, a hell on earth. The gates of this hell are open and looming before us.

This is a matter for the soul, for corporate domination is pervasive. It is hard to see beyond the corporate culture in which we live. In reality, it is not just around us, but also within us. So in a very real way, we are it!

Looking at the spiritual aspects of this crisis can help us find ways to face it squarely and to address it in creative and positive ways. Though there are powerful forces at work that threaten life, we need not fear. We can meet this challenge with courage if we are deeply grounded in our relationship with God.

A SPIRITUAL STRUGGLE

This book proposes a way for people of faith to respond to the growing power of corporations and their domination of the world's cultures, governments, and global institutions. Our response must have both an inner and outer dimension, since the commercialization of culture and the commodification of life affect our inner lives as well as the outer world. Our bodies, minds, spirits, and relationships are affected by corporate globalization and by the ideology that accompanies it.

How can we respond creatively and effectively to the challenges posed by corporate globalization in ways that leave us feeling inspired and spiritually energized, rather than depleted and hopeless? The response that I propose is faith-led resistance to the current global order, resistance that involves every aspect of our lives.

The title of this book, *Shaking the Gates of Hell*, is based on the quote by John Wesley that appears as the book's epilograph: "Give me a hundred preachers, and I care not a straw if they be clergy or laity, who fear nothing but sin and desire nothing but God, and I will shake the gates of hell and set up the Kingdom of God on this earth."[4] John Wesley taught that personal spirituality and social concern must be linked. Concern for one's own soul and concern for the world are two related and inseparable aspects of faithfulness to God. Wesley also taught that personal faithfulness can have profoundly positive effects in the world. These concepts are foundational to the faith-led resistance I point to in this book. Radical faithfulness to God will give us the clarity, energy, compassion, and courage we need in this critical time.

When Wesley speaks of fearing nothing but sin and desiring nothing but God, he is speaking about two different but related aspects of faithfulness. Desire for God is at the heart of the spiritual journey, a journey that is also characterized by the struggle with sin and evil. Even Jesus had to struggle alone in the depths of his soul to overcome the temptation to be less than God was calling him to be. He felt the lure of status, wealth, and worldly power, but chose instead to live out the values of what he called the kingdom of God. The spiritual struggle against such temptation is no small thing, and for those who seek to be faithful, it is a struggle that needs to be fought again and again throughout life. These inner struggles equip us for struggles in the outer world.

The temptations with which we struggle, however, do not arise in a vacuum. They are related to external forces that diminish life. There are powerful social, political, and economic forces at work in the world that are harming God's good creation, leaving environmental destruction and human wreckage behind. These forces tempt us. They influence us. We participate in them. Our inner lives mirror the outer world as microcosms of the whole.

Today, society's dominant institutions promote a worldview that reinforces corporate globalization, supported by a market-based ideology that is so widespread, systematic, and influential that it has been called a religion. Most economists, government officials, and the general public accept this pervasive ideology unquestioningly. And yet, as we will see in later chapters, this ideology is based upon assumptions that contradict common sense and upon values that are directly opposed to the compassion and wisdom of the world's great spiritual traditions. To the degree that we internalize, accept, or give in to the dominant worldview, we participate in and further the reach of corporate rule, to the detriment of our souls.

For hell is not a place. Like heaven, it is a state of being that we can experience here and now. The Powers do not simply threaten the future, they oppress and extinguish life today. Rather than living in the hell of psychological bondage and spiritual oppression, we can claim our freedom as children of God, and allow the heavenly reality of divine grace to break in upon our lives. We can live according to the values that Jesus proclaimed, embodying those values with our lives. Together with people around the world who are awakening to this historical crisis, we can "shake the gates of hell," resisting the horror of a barren, violent, and poisoned future, while creating new and viable alternatives for human life in society and in communion with all life.

A MOMENT OF PROFOUND CHOICE

We are at the beginning of a new era in the earth's history. Humanity has reached a crossroads, a moment of profound choice between two incompatible futures. One direction seems almost inevitable: the world's dominant institutions and prevailing ideologies are driving at an ever-accelerating speed toward a market-based future dominated by corporations. The billboards along this multilane freeway advertise the benefits of where we are headed: toward a wonderland of accumulated wealth and general prosperity, technological achievement, economic and cultural integration, and peace through U.S. military domination. Most people are simply going along or being forced along for the ride. But increasing numbers of people around the world are choosing to get off the main road, to walk to the side and off the pavement to find another path, one that leads toward a global future of equity, justice, ecological and cultural diversity, and peace through mutual respect and cooperation. People are defending or changing their lifestyles, working within their communities, and creating alternative institutions. Some are even hiking back up to the main road and blocking it with their bodies, linking arms with others, trying to prevent the tragic consequences of a world given over to greed.

Who will decide which road will be taken? We will. We must. This is our right and our responsibility as human beings. We can refuse to take on the responsibility and allow the institutional Powers to make these decisions by default. Or we can exercise our freedom by refusing to collude, by resisting the Powers that would lead us to destruction, and by embodying life-giving alternatives here and now. This is a profound spiritual choice, since it involves shaking off spiritual domination by the Powers.

At this critical moment in earth's history each of us is called to exercise our human freedom, to choose whether to go along the broad road that leads to destruction or the narrow path that leads to life. As we open ourselves to the Spirit, we create an opening through which change can happen in the world. As we choose, we are part of humanity's choosing. We are a part of the earth's passion for life.

RESISTANCE AS HOPE

It has been said that great evil requires great resistance. Struggles for justice have always required people who were willing to stand up with courage and to step out in faith.

Will we be successful in stopping the global consolidation of corporate power and the empire it supports? No one knows what the outcome of this struggle will be. But as Gandhi said, "You may never know what results come from your action. But if you do nothing, there will be no results."[5]

In addition, the movement for global justice is strong and growing. People who have been working passionately on various issues for years are seeing their causes converge. They are coming together in the struggle to resist global annihilation and to develop creative alternatives for a hopeful future. People are rising up. This is a global movement, largely nonviolent and deeply democratic. As a popular book on the topic proclaims, "We are everywhere."[6]

Jürgen Moltmann says that Christian hope is "hope that the world will be different."[7] The seeds for an alternative, hopeful future are being planted even now by individuals and groups around the world who are working for a world in which each person's work contributes to the common good and provides dignity and a living wage, everyone has the right to basic necessities of life, corporations are accountable, widespread use of poisons is prohibited, nuclear weapons are dismantled, and wilderness is protected as a common heritage of all creatures. The seeds for widespread spiritual, social, economic, and political change are being planted as people participate in nonviolent resistance and develop alternative ways of living, often modeled on indigenous and traditional ways of life. We are living at a pivotal time of the earth's history, and this is a worthy struggle, a struggle for the very body and soul of the earth itself.

It is my conviction that God is working on behalf of life through every person who is engaged in this work. The question for Christians is, where will the church be in this global movement for change? Will we give spiritual and moral support, provide leadership, and share our resources, as happened in Seattle? Or will we work against change or sit on the sidelines and be left behind as irrelevant? Will the church, through sins of omission or sins of commission, be complicit in transforming the blessing of God's world of beauty and abundance into the curse of a world plagued with desolation and misery? Or will we work with others to help bring about the vision of a compassionate, just, and sustainable world, as God created it to be?

THE EARTH IS RISING, THE TIDE IS TURNING

Alone in my jail cell in Seattle, I had no contact with the outside world, no way of knowing what was going on. I was as yet unaware that police violence had increased, that they were using military-grade tear gas in residential neighborhoods and arresting residents and protestors alike. I had no way of knowing that ongoing protests on the streets of Seattle were putting pressure on President Clinton to stand up for labor and environmental standards and were empowering WTO delegates from developing nations to stand firm against the patenting of life-forms, privatization of services, and other injustices in spite of the coercive tactics of industrialized nations. I did not yet realize that the official meetings of the WTO were headed toward failure and that the success of the protests would be beyond my wildest dreams.

But as I lay in my cell I did know that I had been witnessing a different kind of globalization in the teach-ins and worship services, as well as in the streets: a worldwide network of citizens joining together not for the sake of profit but for the sake of a shared vision of a just and sustainable world. I did know that I was part of an amazing, historic movement of kindred spirits coming together to demand fair trade rather than free trade, to promote peace with justice and environmental sanity, supported by the prayers and hopes and hurts of the world, sustained by the presence and love of God.

And it seemed clear to me then, as never before: no matter how entrenched are the Powers that seem to rule the world, they govern only through the will of the people. If the people withdraw their consent these ruling institutions will collapse like a house of cards. And I felt deeply grateful to the One who is "far above all rule and authority and power and dominion" (Eph. 1:21), the Creator of the universe in all its splendor, who is on the side of justice and love, as Jesus was.

As Paul says in Romans 8:24, "Hope that is seen is not hope." For years, I had been preaching, teaching, and acting out of hope that I could not see. But once in awhile we are given a glimpse of what is possible. Now I could see that there is not just hope, but possibility for amazing and positive change in the world. And opportunity. Vast opportunity. In the words of a song that we sang on the streets and in the jails in Seattle:

Rising, rising, the earth is rising.
Turning, turning, the tide is turning.
Si, se puede

Si, se puede! It can be done! With God's help, we can do it. It's happening now.

PART ONE
THE GATES OF HELL
Undoing Creation

"The work of the demonic powers in the Fall is the undoing of Creation."
—William Stringfellow

CHAPTER ONE
The Earth as Primary Revelation

The gospel is written not in the Bible alone, but on trees and
flowers and clouds and stars.

—Martin Luther[1]

Part of my spiritual practice is to spend time in the wild. I
used to jog each day on the paths in the woods behind my home in
Nevada City. I often saw deer, sometimes a fox or bobcat. Once I
saw a Great Horned Owl and stood looking up at it in awe for over
an hour.

One morning in the spring of 1988, as I went jogging down the
path in the woods behind my home toward Deer Creek, I was reflecting on what I had read earlier in Richard Foster's book, *Celebration of
Discipline*. It was advice from John Wesley about fasting: "'Let our
fasting be done unto the Lord, with our eye singly fixed on Him. Let
our intention herein be this, and this alone, to glorify our Father who
is in heaven. That is the only way we will be saved from loving the
blessings more than the Blesser."[2] I had fasted and practiced other
spiritual disciplines, but I had never thought about fasting in this way.
Wesley's words were a mystery to me.

On my way back up the path, I stopped in my favorite sacred
grove. The dogwood and manzanita were exultant, showing off their
blooms. The pines, firs, and cedars seemed to raise their branches in
praise, creating a beautiful canopy of varied greens sparkling with the
rays of the morning sun. Birds of all kinds sang their own unique
songs, joining together in an amazing chorus of joy. The soft mat of
pine needles invited me to stop again and pray, to open my eyes, ears,
and heart to the splendor and magnificence of God's creation, of
which I now felt so gratefully a part.

As I rose and started toward home I reached a spot where the
sun was breaking through the trees. It seemed at that moment like
heaven itself was shining down, illuminating the earth. In the beam-
ing, radiant light I felt a God of infinite love showering me with all the
blessings of creation.

Standing in this light I suddenly remembered Wesley's words about loving the blessings more than the Blesser and it dawned on me: I had been like a child at Christmas opening present after present, saying "thank you" and then looking around to see what was next. I had been "grateful" and had prayed my thanks. But I had forgotten or had never really known what I only then realized: the God of Creation, the Spirit of Love at the heart of the universe, loves each of us deeply, desires the best for us, wants life to flourish and blossom, and through the creation showers us with evidence of self-giving love.

Just a few months later I would experience a powerful call to ordained ministry. I would be propelled into a new and ongoing adventure in which the Spirit of the universe calls forth new gifts that emerge from my own desires and inner promptings and from the needs of our time.

UNDOING CREATION

> Take up weeping and wailing for the mountains, and a lamentation for the pastures of the wilderness, because they are laid waste . . . both the birds of the air and the animals have fled and are gone.
>
> —Jer. 9:10

The woods where I used to jog behind my home in Nevada City, California, are mostly gone now. A developer subdivided "his" ninety acres of second-growth forest that led to Deer Creek and built thirty big new houses connected by a wide road, complete with speed bumps. When I walk there, I look for signs of the forest that I knew and loved so much, but I lose my bearings. The paths were bulldozed. Manicured lawns have replaced the pine needles on the forest floor. Most of the birds and the other wild creatures are gone. The canopy is no more.

This kind of destruction is taking place everywhere. Industrial development, toxic pollution, and the mining of resources are destroying ecosystems all over the world.

Overall, humanity is not doing so well either. The gap between the rich and poor is growing in the United States and around the world. Poverty is on the increase. Violence, terrorism, war, and ecological destruction threaten our very survival. Misery abounds. What we are experiencing on a global scale is the "undoing of creation." The abundance of the earth, the heritage of future generations, our hopes for human life are being destroyed.

Meanwhile, large corporations and a few wealthy individuals are accumulating profits like never before. The gifts of God's good creation and the labor of God's beloved children are being been turned into commodities to be bought and sold. Anything without monetary value, whether human beings or uncut forests, does not count in the global economic system. The world's dominant institutional Powers enforce this destructive system through economic and political coercion and by military force, supported by an ideology that ignores the intrinsic value of creation and the place of human beings in the whole. This ideology has enthralled multitudes into believing that the market is sacred and into accepting violence and domination as social norms. But this ideology is based on a faulty worldview that is leading us down a road to destruction.

"A Multivalent, Mysterious Treasure"

We have shrunk our vision. . . . We have covered up our sensitivities in a drastic way. . . . I call everything a multivalent, mysterious treasure . . . because we find ourselves in a realm that after five billion years has not stopped unclothing itself and revealing yet another splendor. . . . And yet, in our conviction that we know what it is, namely, material to make into throwaway products, we are destroying it. We are destroying it because we are not aware of its infinite depths.

—Brian Swimme [3]

How we understand the universe has a huge effect on our actions. If we see the earth as a "multivalent, mysterious treasure," we are likely to preserve it with care. If we see the earth simply as dead matter, as resources for human beings to use, as "materials to make into throwaway products," we are more likely to be careless and exploitive. As Swimme writes, "We have shrunk our vision. . . . We have covered up our sensitivities in a drastic way."

Christianity, for its part, has often ignored the earth. In dominant forms of Christianity, especially since the Reformation, creation has been seen primarily as a backdrop or stage upon which the real drama of human salvation takes place. This perspective devalues God's creation and supports its exploitation.

With growing ecological awareness, people of various faiths are looking to their scriptures and traditions and finding spiritual support for caring for the earth. The Hebrew Scriptures stress that God creates and sustains the earth and all life (Genesis 1–2, Psalm 104), that humans are to be stewards of creation (Gen. 2:15), and that all creatures reveal God and join together in praising God (Psalm 148). Many of Jesus' parables demonstrate the value of the natural world in expressing spiritual truths—for instance, when he speaks of the lilies of the field and the birds of the air (Matt. 6:25-33). Many biblical passages speak of the intrinsic value of creation, including the first creation story in Genesis 1, when God declares each part of creation "good." Creation-affirming themes are woven into the dominant Christian tradition. St. Francis, for instance, has been called "the patron saint of the environmental movement."[4] Martin Luther wrote, "The gospel is written not in the Bible alone, but on trees and flowers and clouds and stars."[5] John Wesley said, "The world around us is the mighty volume in which God hath declared himself."[6] Such passages from Scripture and tradition support creation-affirming theological understandings that are emerging in light of the ecological crisis and our new understanding of the universe.

Recent scientific discoveries have shattered our previous conceptions of the universe and its origins. Throughout history, people in the world's varied cultures have passed on their creation stories from generation to generation. Only now is one shared story of the origin and nature of the universe emerging, an incredible cosmic story (or cosmology) that has the potential to unite humanity.

Ironically, this new cosmology is emerging through the empirical observations of science, the very discipline that brings us modern technology and our industrialized world. In so many fields—astronomy, quantum physics, biology, genetics—science is revealing to us that the universe is an evolving, glorious splendor that reveals qualities of diversity, interiority, and communion at its very core.[7]

The universe is primary—we come into being as part of the universe story. We humans, together with plants and animals and all the rest of creation, are part of an incredible process of evolution. All that has gone before, the whole unfolding story of the universe, has brought us to where we are today. We are a part of the whole. Wherever we are, here and now, in this moment, in this very place, we are participating in the great adventure of the universe.

Where is God in all this? Christian understanding has often focused on God as transcendent, that is, God as Creator, above and beyond the earth and human beings. That is one aspect of God, as I experienced in the woods behind my home that morning. But Scripture, tradition, and human experience witness to a God who is also immanent, within all things. The creation itself "groans in labor pains" (Rom. 8:22), and as we pray, the Holy Spirit "intercedes with sighs too deep for words" (Rom. 8:26).

There is an inner dimension to the natural world, a spiritual depth that lies at the very heart of matter. How can we doubt this reality? The "interiority" of creation is expressed in so many ways: in the songs of whales and birds, in flowers as they radiate beauty and fragrance, attracting bees, birds, and butterflies, in human love. In the words of Thomas Berry, "The natural world is subject as well as object."[8] There is a profound spiritual mystery at the heart of the created world that expresses and reveals the divine.

This mystery is not contained in the world of matter, but rather encompasses it, for "in God we live and move and have our being" (Acts 17:28). God is not limited or contained by matter, nor is God separated from matter. This understanding of God as being both within and beyond the world of matter has been called panentheism. God both encompasses and fills the whole created universe.

A Sacramental Universe

Ever since the creation of the world [God's] eternal power and divine nature, invisible though they are, have been understood and seen through the things [God] has made.
—Rom. 1:19-20

When people have the opportunity to share about their spiritual experiences they often speak of experiences that take place outside: when they were at church camp as a child, on a backpacking trip, at the top of a mountain, in a forest, by a lake or river, at a beach. Places of natural beauty can trigger experiences of awe, and can put into perspective who we are in relation to the universe and what is really important in life. At such times, the natural world reveals something of the nature of God.

We live in a sacramental universe, a universe that is an expression of the divine. A sacrament is an "outward and physical sign of an inward and spiritual grace."[9] The inward and spiritual grace at the heart of creation is revealed by its outer and physical manifestations. The ongoing creation reveals God as its source. God's beauty and love, power and energy are mediated through the natural world.

Global capitalism knows nothing of the sacramental value of life or the intrinsic value of God's creation. Its view is purely utilitarian, based on turning plants, animals, land, and even water into commodities so that they can be bought and sold, reducing their value to the economic value of the bottom line. This ideology desacralizes life and creates a framework that allows creation to be exploited for the sake of human beings.

But does this view of the natural world merely as natural resources to be exploited actually improve the quality of human life? In later chapters, we will explore how a degraded environment affects human beings. But for now, let it suffice to say that no matter what the benefits of such an ideology might be, they are not worth the cost of living life "in the absence of the sacred."[10]

Passionist priest Thomas Berry claims that the earth itself is the "primary revelation" of the divine.[11] He writes: "The natural world is the life-giving nourishment of our physical, emotional, aesthetic, moral, and religious existence. The natural world is the larger sacred community to which we belong. To be alienated from this community is to become destitute in all that makes us human. To damage this community is to diminish our own existence."[12]

Berry also makes a potent and eye-opening case about our human responsibility to care for creation. He points out that since God's glory is revealed and mediated through the natural world, when we degrade the earth's bounty or turn its natural beauty to ugliness, it changes how we experience God.

> Our exalted sense of the divine comes from the grandeur of the universe, especially from the earth in all the splendid modes of its expression. Without such experience, we would be terribly impoverished in our religious and spiritual development, even in our emotional, imaginative, and intellectual development. If we lived on the moon, our sense of the divine would reflect the lunar landscape. Our imagination would be as desolate as the moon, our emotions lacking in the sensitivity developed in our experience of the sensuous variety of the luxuriant earth. If a beautiful earth gives us an exalted idea of the divine, an industrially despoiled planet will give us a corresponding idea of God.[13]

When the earth is diminished, its ability to mediate God to us is diminished, and thus our experience of God is diminished as well.

The Christian sacraments of Baptism and Holy Communion involve the use of water, bread, and wine to symbolize the sacred in the ordinary elements of life. What would baptism mean if the water is polluted? Could polluted water symbolize healing, blessing, cleansing, renewal? What would it mean to celebrate the eucharist by serving pesticide-laden wine or bread made with genetically modified grain? Could we still claim that it is the bread of life and the cup of salvation? Thomas Berry says, "If the water is polluted, it can neither be drunk nor used for baptism. Both in its physical reality and in its psychic symbolism, it is a source not of life, but of death."[14] The same would be true for the elements of Holy Communion.

God has given the physical and spiritual blessings of creation to all creatures and all generations. If we diminish creation's ability to show forth God's glory, we diminish the opportunities for God to touch people through creation. We prevent the earth's blessings from being received by those for whom they are intended. Destroying the beauty of God's creation is a spiritual and moral issue. To despoil the earth, pollute the air, and contaminate the waters is desecration and sacrilege. To knowingly and willfully do so is sin.

A WORLD OF RELATIONSHIPS

> **Human beings are not the web of life, but only a strand in it.
> Whatever we do to the web, we do to ourselves.**
>
> —Chief Seattle[15]

Discussion of Christian ethics has mainly focused on human relationships with God and with other human beings. Our ethical responsibility to the rest of creation has often been ignored. But we are in relationship not only with God and with each other but also with the other life forms that inhabit this planet and with the earth itself. We are part of the web of life.

This may not always be obvious in the midst of shopping malls and parking lots, gated communities and megachurches. We may be under the illusion that our human-constructed "world" sits on top of nature, somehow insulated and separated from the forces of nature that we have tamed through technology. But this view is as artificial as our constructions.

John Wesley said, "Sin is the refusal to acknowledge our dependence on God for life and breath and all things."[16] In spite of our incredible cultural and technological accomplishments, we are still created beings, dependent on the God who created us and interdependent with the rest of creation: plants and trees, mountains and rivers, stars and swirling galaxies.

What we do affects the whole web of life, and the condition of the whole affects us. Poisons released into the air and waters come to lodge in our tissues, as well as in the tissues of the other creatures with whom we share the earth. The loss of other species depletes the biological diversity from which medicines and food sources for human beings are developed, while also diminishing the whole. Ozone depletion causes skin cancer and cataracts in people as well as in other animals. Climate change brings floods and super-hurricanes, changes disease patterns, destroys ecosystems, and threatens to submerge whole islands, including populated ones. In the words of theologian Jürgen Moltmann: "Human beings . . . belong to nature and are dependent upon nature. Human civilizations can only develop in equilibrium with the cosmic conditions of the earth's organism, which provide their framework. If civilization destroys these, human civilization itself dies."[17]

In the following chapters we will take a closer look at the direction that the Powers are taking us, and at the hell on earth they are preparing for future generations. These topics are painful. As the awful truth of our current situation dawns on us, it becomes clear why many would rather stay in denial. But we can't afford that luxury; time is too short. Besides, the path of denial leads to darkness and spiritual death. It also leads us further along the path of complicity with evil and destruction. If we are willing to have eyes that see, ears that hear, and hearts that understand, God will surely give us the capacity to face reality, no matter how painful, to process what we learn, to see where hope lies, and to gain a more complete understanding of our calling as people of faith in the world.

Furthermore, the future has not yet been determined. The interrelated network of institutional Powers that dominate the world is not absolute, and the direction that they are taking us is not inevitable. The dominant global system continues only with the willing conformity and active compliance of people who support it, either knowingly or unknowingly. Without this support, it cannot go on. If enough of us nonviolently resist, refuse to go along, and instead choose another path, there is yet hope for the earth. As people around the world join together to resist global domination by the Powers and to develop life-giving alternatives, hope becomes more real and creative change becomes possible.

OPENING TO THE PAIN AS WELL AS THE GLORY

> But ask the animals, and they will teach you; the birds of the air, and they will tell you; ask the plants of the earth, and they will teach you; and the fish of the sea will declare to you. Who among all these does not know that the hand of the Lord has done this?
> —Job 12:7-9

How can we face the multifaceted global crisis without falling victim to apathy and despair? One way is to spend time in the natural world. Creation's beauty helps to put things in perspective, to make us humble, to remind us of who we are in relation to the universe: children of God, children of the earth. Wendell Berry's poem, "The Peace of Wild Things," points to the renewal that we can find in the wild:

> When despair for the world grows in me
> and I wake in the night at the least sound
> in fear of what my life and my children's lives may be,

I go and lie down where the wood drake
rests in his beauty on the water, and the great heron feeds.
I come into the peace of wild things
who do not tax their lives with forethought
of grief. I come into the presence of still water.
And I feel above me the day-blind stars
waiting with their light. For a time
I rest in the grace of the world, and am free.[18]

We can open ourselves to creation's glory, whether in wild nature or a city park or our own backyard. We can also go to places where the earth has been harmed and open our hearts to creation's pain.

I often walk on the road behind our family home where I used to jog. I watch and listen for signs of life. Birds still come to nest in the trees near the houses. Except for a few brave skunks and raccoons, most of the wild animals are gone. Foxes and deer, coyotes and quail do not coexist very well with dogs, cats, and people. I have not yet fully grieved this loss.

There are a few places, though, off the road, where I go to remember. Sometimes I kneel down and pray. I still have a sense of relationship with that place. In the words of a song by Leanne Hinton,

The land knows you're there
The land knows you're there
And the rocks and trees and rivers
Give you friendship and care.[19]

Even though the forest is gone, this place still calls to me.

No matter where we are, even in cities, we are connected with the earth, even if we don't realize it. For, as Hinton's song continues: "Underneath the concrete / The land is living still."

No matter where we are, we can ground ourselves in our bodies, in our breath, in our senses, for this is where we connect in an intimate way with the rest of creation. The wind blows where it wills (John 3:8); God makes the sun to shine on the just and unjust and sends rain on the righteous and the unrighteous (Matt. 5:44-46). The wind, rain, and sun on our skin can remind us of God's love and of our place in the universe. The Word of God is in the waters (Psalm 29), enabling us to deeply touch the Spirit, if only we have ears to hear. The birds of the air that make nests in the branches (Matt. 13:32) or "pigeons roosting on the only possible ledge below the tiny overhang during the downpour"[20] can remind us of our relationship to the rest of the natural world if we open our eyes both to creation's joy and pain.

Being alive is sensual. We are intimately connected to the earth through our senses, and through our senses, the earth can awaken us from apathy or despair. The earth, as primary revelation, has power to call us back to life.

ASHES TO ASHES, DUST TO DUST

It's this radical humility that is absolutely essential to our time.
—Brian Swimme[21]

As we consider the destruction of the earth and the suffering of our fellow creatures, both human and nonhuman, two primary responses seem appropriate: repentance and humble acceptance of our mortality. In Christianity ashes are used to symbolize these two themes on Ash Wednesday, the beginning of Lent. In Ash Wednesday services the imposition of ashes is a way of showing our repentance, our intention to turn away from harmful actions and to turn back toward God. As we consider the damage to the earth we are called to repent of our own violence, greed, and over-consumption, our participation in ecological destruction and human misery. We are called to repent of our complicity in the harm caused by the institutions and systems of which we are a part.

We are also called to a humble acceptance of our place in the universe: "Remember, O mortal, that you are dust, and to dust you will return." Ashes symbolize our mortality, reminding us of who we are: human beings, made up of the dust of the earth. Humus, human, humility—these words all have the same root. Our bodies are made up of the same elements that make up the earth's crust. For that matter, we are made up of the same elements that make up the stars. We are, quite literally, star dust. We participate in the great unfolding journey of the universe, and our role is to celebrate in mystery and awe. And yet we are mortal. Ashes to ashes, dust to dust.

T. S. Eliot's poem "Ash Wednesday" brilliantly portrays the dual Lenten focus on repentance and acceptance of our mortality. It expresses a sense of dust and ashes, of hopelessness, of powerlessness to change. These feelings resonate with many people facing the pain and challenges of the world today. But then, in the poem, surprisingly:

> The lost heart quickens and rejoices
> for the lost lilac and the lost sea voices
> and the weak spirit quickens to rebel
> for the bent goldenrod and the lost sea smell
> quickens to recover the cry of quail
> and the whirling plover.[22]

The earth has the power to call us back to life, through the divine Spirit that moves through creation. In some mysterious way, the earth can provide us with an antidote to despair and can renew our spiritual connection with what is deepest within our souls. It is our context, our "ground of being," through which the Spirit touches us, reminding us of what is real and important, who we are, and with whom we are connected.

Teach us to sit still,
even among these rocks,
our peace in His will.
And even among these rocks,
Sister, Mother, and spirit of the river, spirit of the sea
Suffer me not to be separated,
And let my cry come unto Thee. [23]

CHAPTER TWO
Deforestation Is Hell:
Loss of Biodiversity and Ecosystem Destruction

If the animals were gone, humans would die of a great loneliness of spirit.

—Chief Seattle[1]

In 1999, soon after my husband and I moved to Scotts Valley, our nine-year-old grandson, Jimmy, visited us. I wanted to show him nearby Carbonero Creek, with its sloping banks covered with big ferns and beautiful trees, including redwoods.

When I invited him, his eyes opened wide. He jumped up and quickly put on his shoes. He then went into the kitchen, began rummaging around in the cupboards, and finally pulled out a large cottage-cheese container with a lid, which he proceeded to poke full of holes. "It's for frogs," he said eagerly. He partly jumped, partly ran down the stairs. I followed closely behind.

Jimmy was my guide. I followed him along the creek, walking on whatever path we could find, crossing on big rocks and getting our shoes wet. "Where would they be?" he asked several times, trying to figure out where frogs would be hiding, using a stick to sir up the water under overhanging roots and moss-covered rocks. As we made our way down the creek, I began to get the eerie feeling that we were not going to find any frogs.

"Maybe they aren't here this time of year," I finally said, trying to hide my sense of unease. But nine-year-olds know a few things about frogs. "This is the perfect time for them to be out. They should be looking for food."

Onward he strode, still eager and hopeful, looking for "frogs or salamanders" now. "Amphibians," I said, thinking about their worldwide decline. "Yes, amphibians," said Jimmy. Now I was looking as hard as he was. With a sense of foreboding I noticed that there were no signs of life in the creek at all, just a few water skippers on top.

I finally suggested that we head back home. On the way we

noticed some orange sludge in a few spots, which Jimmy stirred up with his stick. As we climbed up the hill, he found a few banana slugs, but he was still puzzled and disappointed about the frogs. We later learned that the creek had been polluted and could not sustain life. Human beings, by nature, feel a deep connection to other species. We evolved together over eons, as coinhabitants of the earth. Chief Seattle said, "If the animals were gone, humans would die of a great loneliness of spirit." After searching for frogs, I could sense that loneliness of spirit in Jimmy—and in myself.

THE REMARKABLE VARIETY OF LIFE ON EARTH

> Let them praise the name of the Lord, for [God] commanded and they were created. . . . Mountains and all hills, fruit trees and all cedars! Wild animals and all cattle, creeping things and flying birds! . . . Young men and women alike, old and young together! Let them praise the name of the Lord.
> —Ps. 148:5, 9-11, 13

Life is precious. In our solar system, only the earth has life. Plants, animals, and other species fill every niche in the earth's mountains, deserts, plains, forests, oceans, rivers, and other ecosystems, creating a remarkable variety of life on earth. This biological diversity is a treasure, a source of delight, inspiration, and awe.

How many species are there? No one knows, since most have not yet been catalogued. So far, scientists have identified 1.7 million species; they estimate that in total there may be thirteen or fourteen million.[2] Each of these life-forms is a unique expression of the genetic diversity of life. Each has value in and of itself—intrinsic value. For people of faith, each species is precious simply because it is created by God.

The earth's biodiversity benefits humans, since we are interrelated with the rest of creation. Many small species help keep us alive by purifying water, fixing nitrogen, and recycling nutrients and waste. Fish and animals of many kinds have provided food for humans since the days when most of us were hunter-gatherers. Birds and small animals help disperse nuts and seeds of plants and trees. Bees, hummingbirds, and bats pollinate flowers, including the flowers of fruit trees and other agricultural crops. Plants absorb carbon dioxide and breathe out oxygen. Through this process, forests offset some of the of the greenhouse gases that cause climate change.[3] Wild relatives of cultivated crops help ensure food security in case of major crop losses resulting from insect infestations or disease. The earth's varied species offer a wealth of sources for medicines as well.

Preserving the variety of life on earth is essential for human well-being, including spiritual well-being. Our relationships with other creatures and our experiences in the wild can delight us, inspire us, and fill us with awe. Since God is revealed through the creation, each species reveals something of the divine. But it is in the totality of the creation with all its diverse parts that the Creator is revealed most completely. As Thomas Aquinas noted:

> The divine goodness could not be adequately represented by one creature alone. . . . He produced many and diverse creatures, that what was wanting to one in the representation of the divine goodness might be supplied by another. For goodness, which in God is simple and uniform, in creatures is manifold and divided; and hence the whole universe together participates in the divine goodness more perfectly, and represents it better than any single creature whatever.[4]

Earth's many and diverse creatures together represent and participate in the divine goodness. Creation's incredible diversity reveals the magnificence of the Creator.

THE GREAT DYING

There is no faithfulness or loyalty, and no knowledge of God in the land. . . . Therefore the land mourns, and all who live in it languish; together with the wild animals and the birds of the air, even the fish in the sea are perishing.
—Hos. 4:1b, 3

It is sad that there are no frogs in Carbonero Creek, that it has been poisoned and can no longer sustain life. A greater tragedy is that this is not just happening in Scotts Valley, but all over the world.

A mass extinction is taking place.[5] Species are being lost at an accelerating rate around the world. Plants and animals are being lost at the rate of fifty species each day.[6] Many species disappear before they are discovered because habitats are being destroyed so quickly. Many of the best-loved animals that are seen in zoos are listed as endangered. Some are already extinct. This loss is being called "the Great Dying."[7]

Why are so many species being lost? Plants and animals are being endangered by rising human population, pollution, invasive species, industrial agriculture, climate change, and over-harvesting of resources. Some species and local subspecies are hunted to extinction, such as the grey wolf in England and the California grizzly bear.

Black-market trafficking in endangered species is taking its toll, in spite of international laws banning such trade. Invasive species take over native plants, animals, and whole ecosystems. Although global climate change threatens to dwarf all other factors, the primary cause of species extinction until now has been the destruction or fragmentation of habitats upon which they depend for survival.

Around the world, whole ecosystems are being destroyed. More than a third of U.S. rivers and about half of its lakes and estuaries are too polluted for swimming or fishing.[8] The world's oceans are suffering environmental damage, including loss of coral reefs and the appearance of giant "dead zones" that are too low in oxygen to sustain fish or other aquatic life.[9] Around the world, wetlands, prairies, forests and their watersheds, and fragile desert ecosystems are being degraded and destroyed. As they disappear, so do the species who depend upon them for life, along with indigenous and other peoples who have lived sustainably for generations. As a protest sign in the midst of a clearcut forest proclaims, "Deforestation is Hell!"

In 2006, the World Conservation Union listed 15,589 species known to be at risk of extinction, but this greatly underestimates the true number, since only forty thousand species were assessed.[10] Up to one-fifth of all living species could disappear within thirty years.[11]

The ocean's largest fish species have plunged 90 percent due to industrialized fishing.[12] Species threatened with extinction include one in seven flowering plants, one in three amphibians, almost half of all turtles and tortoises, one in five sharks and rays, one in eight birds, and a quarter of all mammals.[13] Nearly half the world's nine hundred species of waterbirds have declined in population in the past five years.[14] One third of primates are at risk of extinction,[15] including all the great apes—gorillas, chimpanzees, orangutans, and bonobos (pygmy chimps).[16] Populations of all African predators are plummeting. Lions are "close to extinction," with their populations just 10 percent of what they were twenty years ago.[17] This grim overview of endangered species could go on and on. These are simply examples of the tragic decline in the earth's biodiversity due to human activity.

This widespread destruction is supported by an economic system and ideology that promote industrial development at the expense of the natural world. But we are destroying the very earth that sustains us, and the ecosystems of which we human beings are a part! The loss of so many species is a warning sign that the earth upon which we depend for life is being degraded. Widespread death of other species is a bad sign for humans, too.

Although we tend to forget, we human beings are part of the created world, interrelated and interdependent with the rest of creation. We are not separate, even in our human-constructed environments. The damage we inflict on the web of life will catch up with us, or with future generations. If we relinquish our responsibility to live as responsible members of the community of life, our children will inherit a wasteland. They will bear the burden of our environmental debt, impoverished, with a degraded earth, with fewer frogs and songbirds and butterflies and mammals, with fewer plants for medicines or for the food supply.

The accelerating pace of species loss and ecosystem destruction is not just an ecological issue. It is also a spiritual issue. We are permanently eliminating life-forms created by God, degrading God's creation, and diminishing human hopes for the future.

SHE'S ALIVE TODAY BECAUSE OF THIS FLOWER

The earth is our mother.

—Chief Seattle[18]

I have a poster in my home that celebrates the U.S. Endangered Species Act. On the poster, a beautiful little girl holds a bright pink flower. The caption reads: "She's alive today because of this flower." Human life today and our quality of life in the future are inextricably linked with the fate of the myriad of other species with whom we are connected: with frogs, forests, fish, and flowers.

The United States has stronger environmental laws than do many other countries. We have the Endangered Species Act, the Clean Air Act, the Clean Water Act, and other laws that help protect the natural world from some of the worst abuses. These have brought many successes, such as the restoration of some species, the clean-up of the Great Lakes, and improved air quality in many cities. Most of these laws are in place because people became aware, concerned, and organized. But many of our environmental laws are too weak, they are often not enforced, and they are in danger of being weakened even further. Several have been challenged and some found illegal according to the rules of free-trade agreements, which limit what governments can do to protect the environment.

Public participation is needed even to enforce existing laws, both in developed and developing nations. Timber, mining, and other extractive industries contribute large sums of money to elect political representatives of their choice, and to lobby for deregulation, corporate subsidies, and laws that favor these industries. They spend millions to defeat environmental initiatives that grassroots groups have organized, often by putting alternative initiatives on the ballot to confound the voters. They contribute to industry front-groups that identify themselves as the "Wise Use Movement." These groups challenge scientific findings, promote private property rights as absolute, and use a cost-benefit approach to environmental protection, considering only financial, not environmental, costs.

These tactics confuse people until many are overwhelmed with what William Stringfellow calls "overtalk": too much noise and too many conflicting "facts" overlaid one upon another until people become numb and confused and simply turn off. This is one way that the Powers get people to back off from involvement in the public sphere. The amazing thing is that people around the world have persisted through grassroots struggle to create and defend environmental laws that do protect the earth. This is a tribute to people's stamina, courage, faith, hope—indeed, to their humanity.

Environmental groups often find themselves in a kind of triage situation, defending particular ecosystems that they have identified as particularly vulnerable, diverse, or beautiful. If such groups are internationally known and respected, they may even be invited into negotiations with government and business leaders. This process is seductive, because compromise is expected, so environmental groups at times participate in crafting agreements that seem politically realistic, but that bring further harm to the earth. This mentality of compromise was the basis for the formation of Earth First!, with its slogan, "No compromise in defense of Mother Earth."

Truly, the earth is our mother. Through the earth, God creates, nourishes, and blesses us. We are formed from her very body. From her we emerge, by her we are sustained, to her our bodies return. The earth is not a stage or backdrop at all, but the key to who we are—embodied, natural, physical, as well as spiritual beings who have evolved together with other species on a living planet to participate in the great adventures of an evolving universe. To care for the earth is to care for ourselves.

Local, state, and national laws protecting earth's biodiversity must be strengthened and enforced, as must international treaties such as the Convention on Biodiversity and the Protocol on Biosafety. Trade agreements must protect the global commons, the natural heritage of all creatures. Economic systems must include environmental costs in their calculations. Corporations must be restrained. Their extraction of profits must never supercede the rights of present and future generations to enjoy and be nourished by the gifts of the earth. For it is God who gives true wealth to humanity and all creatures: fresh air, pure water, glorious forests, fragile deserts, fertile plains, diverse species, abundant life.

Throughout this book we will consider principles that can support a shift to a more hopeful future. One of these principles is *diversity*. Corporate globalization promotes uniformity through imposing a single model of industrialized development that encompasses agriculture, energy systems, manufacturing, transportation, and culture. Alternative institutions and operating systems will need to support biological, cultural, economic, and political diversity if they are to be sustainable.

Such changes will only come about through grassroots organizing, through widespread resistance to the dominant institutions that keep the current systems in place, through adopting alternative lifestyles and alternative social structures. Such major systemic transformation will only be possible if there is a great change in worldview, a shift in priorities on the part of many people from different cultures and walks of life, a spiritual awakening, if you will, to the value of the earth in all its diversity.

Such a change of consciousness will require humility, a dawning awareness of who we are as creatures in relationship with God and the rest of creation. It will require repentance, a change of heart, and willingness to turn around, to eliminate old and harmful patterns and to initiate new and life-sustaining ones. The good news is, it is happening now! As eco-philosopher Joanna Macy says, "A revolution is underway because people are realizing that our needs can be met without destroying our world. . . . Future generations, if there is a livable world for them, will look back at the epochal transition we are making to a life-sustaining society. And they may well call this the time of the Great Turning."[19]

We will explore these developments later in this book, and explore how we can contribute to this changing paradigm. But few will be willing to change course radically until it becomes clear that we are headed for disaster. So stay with me during this first section of the book as we explore the direction the human race is currently headed. Look with me a little longer through the gates of an ecological hell on earth, where children wander through barren dust that used to be forests, where they see rivers but cannot swim in them, streams but cannot drink from them, where an occasional frog or bird or butterfly reminds them of the stories they have heard about a time when life was abundant. Look with me into a stolen future of toxic pollution, global warming, runaway technologies, poverty, inequity, violence, terror, and war. This is the direction we are headed—it is already well underway. The Powers are moving things in this direction, and we, with God working in and through us, are the only ones who can stop it.

The way out of fear, guilt, denial, and powerlessness is through courage, the courage that comes when we allow the Spirit to open our eyes, ears, and hearts to the suffering of the world and the reality of what is happening. Grounded in the earth, open to the will of the Creator, in communion with Christ and with generations past and future, we can find courage to face the truth, see what is at stake, and work with others to create a more hopeful future. We can be part of the Great Turning.

CHAPTER 3
The Heat Is On:
Our Changing Atmosphere

Talk about weather has lost its innocence . . . the casual [has] become apocalyptic.

—Catherine Keller[1]

In the summer of 2000 my family had its annual camping trip in Lassen Volcanic National Park. One pleasant, sunny morning the whole extended family set off to hike to the top of Mt. Lassen. We drove to the foot of the mountain and began the long, winding uphill trek. The beginning of the hike was not too challenging. Before long we could look down on the parking lot and two small nearby lakes and up at the clouds that shroud the peak. We had a long way to go and I was already winded, but that's not unexpected at my age. I had to pace myself.

Two of my teenaged grandsons, JP and Jerry, were hiking way up ahead. Their T-shirts were already off, and they likely hadn't put sunscreen on their backs, in spite of the sunscreen ritual we went through in the parking lot, and in spite of the shoulder-to-shoulder scar on JP's back where a surgeon had excised a Stage 2 malignant melanoma just six months before. But they were out of sight now. As with so many other dangers and life challenges, especially with teenagers, all I could do was let go—and pray.

But soon, two of the younger teens, Jimmy and Sophia, were having trouble. They stopped frequently to catch their breath, sitting on rocks as other hikers passed by. They pulled their inhalers out of their backpacks, but in the thin atmosphere they couldn't get much relief. Their asthma wouldn't let them go on.

I volunteered to hike back down the trail with them. We walked down, spent a little time throwing rocks into a nearby lake, and drove back to camp. When the others returned, we listened to the stories of how it felt, what it looked like, and how long it took each of the others to hike to the top of the mountain.

This wasn't my first experience with Lassen Peak. I remember the sense of awe and triumph I felt hiking to the top when I was fourteen. I have a picture my mother took of me at the top of the peak, bedraggled and exhausted, but I made it! At the time, I didn't even know anyone with asthma, and I had never heard of skin cancer. Was I just uneducated or out of touch with people who suffered from these ailments? Perhaps. But the fact is that both asthma and skin cancers are on the rise. And both are related to human-created changes in our atmosphere.

According to the World Health Organization, asthma rates have risen worldwide by over 60 percent since the early 1980s, and asthma related deaths have doubled to five thousand a year.[2] According to the U.S. Center for Disease Control, asthma rates among children in the United States have more than doubled since 1980. Asthma now affects an estimated 6.5 million children under age eighteen, nearly one in ten children.[3] This dramatic increase in asthma is related, at least in part, to pollution in the atmosphere.

Skin-cancer rates are also rising 4 to 5 percent each year[4], and have been described as epidemic. The incidence of melanoma, the most deadly skin cancer, has risen worldwide, especially among Caucasians. In the United States, the incidence of melanoma has more than tripled in the white population during the past twenty years[5]. There are now more than eight thousand deaths from melanoma in the United States each year. In the past twenty years, cases of pediatric melanoma have increased more than 100 percent.[6] A significant cause of the overall increase in skin cancer is the thinning of the ozone layer in the upper atmosphere and the resulting exposure to harmful ultraviolet (UV) rays from the sun.

While ozone is harmful in the air we breathe at ground level, a natural layer of ozone in the upper atmosphere protects us from the harmful UV rays of the sun. But the protective ozone layer is thinning, due to the release of chlorofluorocarbons (CFCs) into the atmosphere from air conditioners, aerosol cans, and other industrial products. CFCs attack the ozone in the upper atmosphere, causing a hole three times as big as the continental United States to open up in the ozone layer over New Zealand and part of Australia. The hole also breaks off and creates a general thinning of the protective ozone shield around the earth. Scientists estimate that the ozone layer has thinned over the whole world by almost 10 percent in the past forty years. For every 1 percent decrease in ozone, there is a 2 percent increase in UV radiation bathing our skin and a 4 percent increase in skin cancer.[7] Many other parts of the natural world are harmed by excessive exposure to ultraviolet radiation as well.

Fortunately, in the 1980s the nations of world signed the Montreal Protocol, which phases out emissions of CFCs. Although CFCs that have already been released will continue to harm the ozone layer for years, there are some indications that the ozone layer is healing. Some scientists say that if current trends continue, the global ozone layer should be restored to 1980 levels sometime between 2030 and 2070. This is hopeful for future generations, and is an example of the positive environmental effect that concerted global efforts can have.[8]

GLOBAL CLIMATE CHANGE

> They come to the cisterns, they find no water, they return with their vessels empty. They are ashamed and dismayed and cover their heads, because the ground is cracked. Because there has been no rain on the land, the farmers are dismayed; they cover their heads. Even the doe in the field forsakes her newborn fawn because there is no grass.
>
> —Jer. 14:3-4

Sadly, international efforts to address global climate change have been far less successful, in spite of the fact that many scientists say that the threats from climate change may dwarf all other environmental concerns. The United States, which has released the greatest percentage of greenhouse gases that cause climate change, refuses to sign the Kyoto Protocol, the international treaty that would limit such emissions to the levels from the year 2000. Although many countries, and even some states within the United States, are changing laws and rising to the challenge posed by global warming, U.S.-based oil, gas, and car-manufacturing corporations have succeeded in their decades-long efforts to block the raising of federal fuel-efficiency standards and other laws that would limit their impact on the atmosphere.

Corporate globalization is speeding up the release of fossil fuels into the atmosphere. Ships and planes from various countries cross paths carrying luxury goods, manufactured components, basic foodstuffs, and even water around the world. Many of these good are packaged in plastic, a substance derived from fossil fuels.

Earth's climate is changing due to human activity. Scientists on the Intergovernmental Panel on Climate Change have found that human activities are altering the earth's atmosphere, and that global warming is already underway.[9] The earth has been warming most rapidly during the past twenty-five years. Nine of the ten warmest years have all occurred since 1980.[10] As of this writing, the 2006 heat wave compares with temperatures in 2005, the hottest year in recorded history. This year, 2007, threatens to be even hotter.

These high temperatures are consistent with computer-generated models, which also predict increasingly severe and frequent heat waves, more violent hurricanes, melting ice caps, global sea-level rise, extreme droughts, increased ranges of disease-carrying insects and rodents, crop failures, heavy rains and flooding, ocean temperature increases, forest fires, migration of bacteria and change in disease patterns, destruction of coral reefs, drying up of wetlands, acceleration of species loss, change in the patterns of seasons, serious social and economic disruption throughout the world, and environmental refugees. Many of these patterns are already well underway.[11] *New Scientist* writer Fred Pearce says:

> Climate change is with us. A decade ago, it was conjecture. Now the future is unfolding before our eyes. Canada's Inuit see it in disappearing Arctic ice and permafrost. The shantytown dwellers of Latin America and Southern Asia see it in lethal storms and floods. Europeans see it in disappearing glaciers, forest fires and fatal heat waves. Scientists see it in tree rings, ancient coral and bubbles trapped in ice cores. These reveal that the world has not been as warm as it is now for a millennium or more.[12]

Many of the changes brought by climate change are unpredictable. Some rivers are evaporating, while melting glaciers cause others to flood. Diseases are spreading. In some areas crop yields are harmed by drought, while in other areas crops grow faster. Hurricanes are becoming stronger and more frequent. Melting Arctic sea ice is creating fear of a shutdown of ocean currents that moderate Europe's climate.[13]

Global climate change may have already had catastrophic effects. After the devastating heat wave in Europe in the summer of 2003, which killed at least thirty thousand people, a study showed that greenhouse gas emissions due to human activity at least doubled the risk of such an event.[14] Likewise, scientific studies done after Hurricane Katrina show "dramatic new evidence" that human-induced climate change has significantly affected the level of hurricane destructiveness. The ocean's temperatures have warmed over the past forty years, and hurricane strength is directly proportional to the warmth of the waters that feed the storm.[15]

With shifting weather patterns, the devastation caused by Hurricane Katrina, and increasingly public concerns, the public is becoming more aware of the dangers of climate change. The reality is hitting us. As Catherine Keller points out:

> You exchange pleasantries with a stranger and find a casual allusion to the weather—for instance when it is unseasonably warm, or cold, or when the weather weirdly bounces—rudely insinuating the end of the world. The foreboding feeling of irretrievable and unforeseeable damage reverberates in the brief silences, as we nod and shake our heads, break eye contact, change the topic. . . . Talk

about the weather has lost its innocence. . . . The casual
has become apocalyptic.[16]

Why then do U.S. tax incentives and government subsidies continue to promote the consumption of fossil fuels? Why haven't we
moved toward conservation and renewable resources? The technology is there. Why does the United States, the country that has released
the largest volume of greenhouse gases, refuse to sign the Kyoto
Protocol, to the dismay of the rest of the world? Why did our government institute a WTO grievance against Japan, challenging its fuel-
efficiency standards? Why this stubborn refusal to take action to prevent the global upheaval that is likely to occur with climate change?
These questions can only be answered by looking at how oil and automobile corporations influence U.S. energy policy.

THE CORPORATE CONNECTION

**A twenty-first century based on petroleum . . . may well mean
that we all surf the oil pipeline right into a stormy and turbu-
lent greenhouse world.**

—Joseph Karliner[17]

In the United States, big oil and automobile companies have
focused their efforts over the years toward development based around the
car. In 1936, General Motors, Standard Oil, Firestone Tire and Rubber
Co., B. F. Phillips Petroleum, and Mac Manufacturing formed a holding
company called National City Lines. They bought up local trolley lines
and tore up the tracks throughout the United States. By 1949 they had
converted more than one hundred electric transit systems in forty-five
cities to diesel-powered buses. By 1995, 85 percent of city streetcars had
been destroyed,[18] thus paving the way for suburbs, strip malls, huge parking garages, and other development geared toward the automobile.[19]

Large oil and automobile corporations lobby directly and fund
right-wing think tanks to lobby on their behalf.[20] Meanwhile, they
engage in "greenwashing," using their right to free speech to fund
tax-deductible commercials that profess how environmentally sensitive they are. Convincing the federal government to reject the Kyoto
Protocol and stricter fuel-efficiency standards and to allow oil
drilling in the Arctic Wildlife Refuge are just their most recent successes. According to Joseph Karliner: "The Climate Convention continues to be stymied by a powerful corporate lobby and foot dragging
by those nations up to their necks in oil. Consequently, oil production and consumption are expanding unhindered, in tandem with
economic globalization."[21]

In addition to direct oil subsidies, U.S. foreign policy protects access to oil reserves. U.S. wars in Iraq, Afghanistan, Colombia, and other countries in the Middle East, Central Asia, and Latin America have been called "resource wars,"[22] fought largely to protect U.S. access to water, oil, and other resources. "No blood for oil" is a decades-old slogan that continues to be seen at antiwar rallies. Motivation for war is, no doubt, multidimensional—geopolitical as well as economic. Nevertheless, as Kevin Danaher points out, "We wouldn't be in Iraq if their primary export was broccoli."[23]

I will return in later chapters to the topic of corporate influence in politics and government. For now, it is enough to acknowledge that corporations influence government policies on climate change and that governments protect the "rights" of corporations to continue releasing greenhouse gases into the atmosphere.

This must change. It is crucial that we begin to shift society's resources to operating systems, including transportation systems, that are ecologically sustainable. This will require personal, cultural, institutional, and systemic conversion to the principle of *ecological sustainability*. Our institutions and systems must enable people to meet their genuine needs while preserving the earth's biodiversity and its ability to support future generations. Without ecological sustainability, we diminish life on earth, damage the foundation of life, and destroy hope for future generations. For, in the words of Karliner: "Unless there is a fundamental transformation away from fossil fuels, the petroleum companies that have generated oil's wave of power and prosperity and ridden it throughout the last century will send the Earth spinning into a terrible wipe-out—one that could leave us gasping for breath."[24]

FACING THE FUTURE

> While there are other parts to this story—the depletion of the ozone, acid rain, genetic engineering—the story of the end of nature really begins with that greenhouse experiment, with what will happen to the weather.
>
> —Bill McKibben[25]

No doubt some of the disruptions that we are already experiencing due to climate change are irreversible, and there are more disruptions to come, since global warming is a gradually unfolding process. But human activity or inactivity on this issue will influence the extent of the damage and what harm can be mitigated.

With our tax dollars, consumption patterns, and lifestyles we are participating in and giving our consent to the destruction of the earth, yet we often feel powerless to stop it. The threat of global warming seems so vague, so amorphous, so hard to tackle, that we are tempted to simply look the other way.

But let us look again at events that we know climate change may cause or aggravate. Let us listen to the cries of displaced and bereaved people who suffered through Hurricane Katrina, to people in Africa who suffer from drought and desertification, to Pacific Islanders who fear that their islands are being gradually submerged by rising seas. And let us consider the effects on God's nonhuman creatures: Emperor Penguin chicks who have to jump off melting ice floes two weeks early into the icy Antarctic Sea, pregnant polar bears whose range is so reduced that they have to dig their dens on land instead of on sea ice,[26] butterflies, birds, and other species who must adapt to a shift in their ranges or perish.[27]

The threat of global climate change is far beyond our ability to calculate or control. In humility, we can accept that we are not strong or wise enough to reverse it by sheer effort alone. The irony is that when we face the extent of our own powerlessness and the pain and fear within and around us, we discover a source of power and wisdom far beyond our own, a spiritual power that works within us and through us. God has not abandoned us or left us without recourse. The Holy Spirit is still a very real presence and, if we are willing, will comfort, guide, and motivate us to take action for change.

We can say yes to God and no to apathy. Even small actions can be actions of resistance and can slow the momentum toward destruction. Each time we install an energy-efficient light bulb, it can be an act of faithfulness. Each time we ride our bike or take less-polluting forms of public transportation, it is a spiritual victory. Each time we plant a tree, it is a sign of hope for the future.

These personal actions are necessary, but they are not sufficient. We must also work for systemic change, for a massive shift in resources away from polluting and dangerous industries, investment in sustainable sources of energy, and aid to developing nations that will enable them to "leap frog" over more polluting sources of power. The technology is there. What it will take is political will.

This is where we come in. We have a big job ahead. But each time we struggle to bring the necessary changes to our church, our community, our nation, or our world, we engage in action that can lead to change. Each time we make decisions that will lead to a better world for a grandchild or niece or nephew, it is an act of faith in the God who raised Jesus from the dead and who, through the power of the Holy Spirit, can work through us even today to bring about God's future. In these ways we do our small part in helping to preserve God's creation, for the sake of the people we love, for the sake of the whole, for the sake of future generations, for the sake of our souls.

CHAPTER 4
A Toxic Future?
The Environment and Human Health

Only in a viable natural world can there be a viable human world.

—Thomas Berry[1]

Karen was a vibrant and youthful lay leader in one of the churches I served as pastor. Her daughter and little granddaughter lived nearby. We celebrated Karen's fiftieth birthday together, and soon after that we shared another joyous occasion—the five-year mark after her mastectomy. After that significant milestone, she took a trip to Hawaii to celebrate. A few months later she got word: she had a malignant tumor in her other breast. She and her family were devastated. She went through another surgery, chemotherapy, and radiation.

As Karen's health declined, I was in the process of moving to another church. This was hard, since I had been a primary support for her through her illness. She told me that she wanted me to be with her and her family when she died.

A year later, I happened to be in the area, and I had a strong sense of needing to see Karen. I knew she was declining and that it might be my last chance to visit her. I called her husband Hank, who said that she was near death and that her hospice worker was on her way. Hank had not been able to reach their daughter by phone, but somehow she got the message. She and I arrived at the same time.

Although Karen was extremely weak and emaciated, she was lucid, positive, and full of faith. She died peacefully in her family's arms, surrounded by love and supported by the prayers of all who loved her. She was buried in the beautiful pink dress she had worn at her fiftieth birthday party.

I could tell many other similar stories. So could people in any faith community. So many women are dealing with breast cancer, men with prostate and testicular cancer, couples with infertility, elders with neurological disorders, children with various forms of cancer. Each of these people and each of their families has a story they could tell. People have prayed for them. They have prayed for healing for themselves. They have asked, "Why me?" "Why my family?" "How can God allow this to happen?" "Can this be the will of God?"

All of these diseases cause physical, emotional, and spiritual suffering for families, congregations, and communities. All of them are linked to exposure to toxic chemicals. And all of them are on the rise.

THE GLOBALIZATION OF TOXIC POLLUTION

We all live downstream.

—Bumper sticker slogan

Medical advances have eradicated many illnesses that used to be deadly, and have made many more of them treatable. Breakthroughs in medical technologies have extended many lives. But there is also an alarming increase in the incidence of diseases that are linked to exposure to toxic chemicals.

Toxic pollution has become a global problem. In the mid-1980s scientists gathered samples of breast milk from Inuit women in the Canadian Arctic, expecting to find their milk relatively free of toxic chemicals, pure enough to be used in controlled studies of breast milk from other populations. Instead, they were alarmed to find that the breast milk of the Inuit women was as contaminated as the milk of women who had been exposed to industrial accidents.[2]

Scientists have found that the hydrologic cycle serves to disseminate pollution globally. As water evaporates from polluted land or waterways, the water vapor forms clouds and is carried by winds around the world. In the Arctic it is deposited as toxic rain or snow.[3] The Arctic has become the "resting place for volatile persistent chemicals."[4] Persistent chemicals accumulate to ever-higher concentrations and can be magnified millions of times as they travel around the world and up the food chain.[5] Scientists also discovered high levels of toxic chemicals in seals and polar bears in the Arctic region.[6] Polar bears are at the top of the food chain. So are humans.

Today there are more than 73,000 synthetic chemicals circulating in our environment, most of which did not exist before World War II. Only a fraction of these have been tested for toxicity.[7] Some are persistent toxic chemicals, including metals such as lead and mercury, industrial wastes such as dioxins, and pesticides such as aldachlor and atrazine. Many of these chemicals resist breakdown and accumulate in our food and water, as well as in our bodies, exposing us to risk of disease. These chemicals also interact with each other, multiplying and intensifying their effects.

Wildlife studies, experiments with laboratory animals, and studies of human exposures show that many of these chemicals disrupt the body's endocrine system by mimicking, blocking, or distorting the intended messages of hormones.[8] There has been a sharp increase in hormone-related health problems among human beings, including infertility, endometriosis, miscarriages, and depressed immune systems. There has been a marked decline in sperm counts around the world.[9]

Studies link exposure to hormone-disrupting chemicals to the rising incidence of various forms of cancer, especially hormone-related cancers.[10] The incidence of breast cancer has gone from one in twenty women in 1960 to one in eight today.[11] The global incidence of testicular cancer has tripled in the past thirty years, and the incidence of prostate cancer has doubled in the past twenty years.[12] Cancers of the brain, bone marrow, and lymph nodes are also rising.[13]

While cancer death rates among children have decreased by 50 percent, the incidence of children's cancers has risen by one-third since 1950.[14] The rate of leukemia and brain cancer among children is rising.[15] One in four hundred children in the United States will contract cancer by the age of fifteen.[16]

Toxic pollution often brings the greatest harm to the most vulnerable people. Pregnant and nursing women and their unborn children and infants are at higher risk. Chemicals such as dioxin can be transmitted across the placental wall, increasing the danger of fetal abnormalities.[17] Breast milk may also contain high levels of dioxin and other chemicals, which are passed on to nursing infants during a time when they are most vulnerable.[18]

Young children are also at increased risk of harm from the many toxic chemicals to which they are exposed each day, an amount that is often greater than most adults encounter. They eat more than adults in proportion to their body weight, including fruits and juices that may be laced with pesticides, while their growing bodies absorb substances at a much faster rate. In parks, schoolyards, vacant lots, or in their own backyards, children play on or around lawns, gardens, and sidewalks that may be treated with pesticides and herbicides. They may play on carpets or floors that are treated or cleaned with toxic compounds. Children handle things and put things in their mouths more often than adults. In neighborhoods where hazardous materials are present or areas where streams are polluted, children may be exposed to extremely hazardous levels of pollution.

As the numbers of chemicals released into the environment continue to increase, children of today will be exposed to more chemicals during their lifetimes than are today's adults. Today's exposures pose a threat not only to their health, but to future generations. Animal testing, wildlife studies, and studies of exposed human populations show that endocrine-disrupting chemicals can affect several generations. Because of the long lifespan of human beings relative to many other species, it will be many years before it is known how our exposures to these "hand-me-down poisons"[19] affect our descendents. As the scientists who wrote *Our Stolen Future* state: "The danger we face is not simply death and disease. By disrupting hormones and development, these synthetic chemicals may be changing who we become. They may be altering our destinies."[20]

GLOBAL POLLUTION, GLOBAL INJUSTICE

> Shouldn't the World Bank be encouraging MORE migration of the dirty industries to the LDC's [less developed countries]? . . . I've always thought that under-populated countries in Africa are vastly UNDER-polluted.
>
> —Lawrence Summers[21]

The globalization of toxic pollution, like other aspects of globalization, does not mean that its risks are evenly distributed. The concept of environmental racism is an acknowledgment that people of color are disproportionately affected by toxic pollution in every country, including the United States. The poorest countries and the poorest people in every country bear the greatest risk and pay the highest price in terms of human health and safety.

Global trade highlights the problem of environmental racism and injustice. Hazardous and polluting industries move to countries that offer cheap labor and less stringent corporate regulations, including environmental regulations. This is especially obvious on the Mexican side of the U.S.-Mexico border, where U.S. corporations operate several thousand factories, often called *maquiladoras*, where products are assembled on a duty-free and tariff-free basis to be "exported" back to the United States. These factories have created an "environmental disaster zone" of pollution that has been linked to a variety of health problems, including birth defects.[22]

U.S. high-tech industries are also "going global," moving their supply chains to "pollution havens" in developing countries where regulation is lax. Many electronics industries are now served by suppliers in Southeast Asia, where workers and communities are exposed to highly polluting processes, such as those employed in the making of semiconductors.

The global toxic trade includes the trading of hazardous wastes, especially from industrialized nations to poorer nations in the developing world. After several shocking incidents, many countries established laws to prohibit the dumping of hazardous chemicals within their borders. The Basel Convention, an international treaty, was also established to prohibit such dumping, but the waste trade continues, as industries seek to find ways to dispose of the hazardous by-products of industrialization. "Waste traders" have moved their business to Southeast Asia and eastern Europe as Africa and Latin America shuts them out.[23] Some function illegally as "waste mafias."[24] Many waste disposal operations that are labeled "recycling" carry hazardous materials such as batteries or computers to poor nations, where they are disassembled, melted down, or otherwise disposed of, exposing workers and communities to contamination.[25]

Some countries continue to produce harmful substances that in other places have been banned. Canada still produces asbestos, 96 percent of it for export. Because a growing number of European bans on asbestos threaten its industry, Canada has lodged a complaint with the World Trade Organization challenging France's law that bans the production of asbestos domestically, that is, in France. Canada claims that the French ban breaks trade rules because it was instituted with inadequate scientific evidence of adverse health effects of asbestos.[26]

Industrial nations often produce and export toxic products that are illegal for domestic use. The global trade in pesticides is an especially sinister example. Over the past fifty years, pesticide use has increased fifty times over. Over ninety countries have banned the domestic use of various poisons, including harmful pesticides such as DDT and chlordane,[27] but the practice of producing and exporting pesticides that are illegal for domestic use is rising. For instance, the extremely toxic pesticide DBCP, known to cause sterility in farm workers, was banned in the United States in 1979, but it has been exported over the years to Costa Rica, the Philippines, and ten other countries for use on banana plantations owned or operated by Del Monte, Dole, and Chiquita.[28] Foods (for instance, bananas) imported from these same countries create a "circle of poison" that affects the health of people in exporting and importing countries alike.[29]

In short, we are living in a global "chemical soup." Complete studies of the effects of these chemicals on human health are impossible, since there is no control group. Every animal on earth now carries synthetic chemicals in their bodies, including human beings. The synergistic effect of most of these chemicals is as yet unknown. We are the lab animals in a massive, uncontrolled, dangerous experiment that is affecting all life on earth, and will affect future generations.

ACCEPTABLE RISK?

No one can quantify what the loss of a creek means to a child in Tennessee or measure the grief of parents who must forbid their son or daughter from exploring along its banks. But I think we can say with assurance that the transformation of a popular swimming hole into a cancer hazard and child's play into a cancer risk factor is a terrible diminishment of our humanity.

—Sandra Steingraber[30]

Current regulations are vastly inadequate for protecting the public from exposure to dangerous chemicals. Regulations are based on risk-benefit and cost-benefit analysis, which means they are not based on safety concerns but on so-called "acceptable risk".

Pesticides are among the most toxic chemicals in use today. The World Health Organization (WHO) estimates that twenty-five million agricultural workers in the developing world suffer pesticide poisoning each year, resulting in twenty thousand deaths.[31] There is no way to determine scientifically whether there is a safe level of exposure to these "designer poisons."[32] Pesticide regulations are based on tests in which laboratory animals are given fatal doses; "safe" levels for humans are extrapolated from such tests.

Chemicals are allowed to stay on the market unless they are proven to be dangerous.[33] Many chemicals that are known to be toxic are still in circulation. Each year 2,400 new chemicals are introduced into the environment, most of them without being tested.[34]

In other words, chemicals are considered innocent until proven guilty. This situation highlights the conflict between the rights of corporations to release toxic pollutants and the rights of people to avoid toxic exposure.

The chemical industry generates $558 billion annually. Large chemical corporations use their vast wealth and political power to influence public opinion and regulatory processes in significant ways, while people who are most vulnerable to the harmful effects of the chemicals these corporations produce have much less economic and political clout. Industry-funded groups lobby for regulations that will benefit corporations. When threatened with more stringent regulations, these groups react by developing "studies" and commentaries that confuse and obscure scientific facts. The chemical industry makes large campaign contributions and lobbies to keep harmful products on the market, even known carcinogens.[35] Some of the corporations that manufacture cancer-causing chemicals also manufacture pharmaceuticals used to treat cancer.[36]

When considering the cost-benefit and risk-benefit approach, we need to ask, "Who benefits from such policies?" (the corporations), "Who pays the greatest cost? Who is at highest risk?" (the most vulnerable people), and "Who gets to decide?" It is not right for people to be exposed to toxic chemicals without their consent. In the words of Sandra Steingraber: "Chemicals are not citizens. They should not be presumed innocent unless proven guilty, especially when a verdict of guilt requires some of us to sicken and die in order to demonstrate the necessary evidence."[37]

Many are calling for laws that would introduce the *precautionary principle* as an operating basis for society. This principle would mandate precaution in the manufacture and sale of synthetic chemicals and other potentially hazardous products. Indication of harm, rather than proof of harm, would be sufficient to keep potentially dangerous products from being released. Instead of citizens being required to prove that products cause harm, corporations would be required to prove their products safe if such products had the potential to cause grave or irreversible harm, even in the case of scientific uncertainty. By instituting this principle society would be safer and corporations would have the incentive to develop nontoxic alternatives as well as alternative uses for products already known to be safe.

The scientists who wrote *Our Stolen Future* issue a warning: "Nothing . . . will be more important to human well-being and survival than the wisdom to appreciate that however great our knowledge, our ignorance is also vast. In this ignorance we have taken huge risks and inadvertently gambled with survival. Now that we know better, we must have the courage to be cautious, for the stakes are very high. We owe that much, and more, to our children."[38]

As We Heal the Earth, the Earth Heals Us

Nothing is more important for health than our learning to live with more love for this planet and all of God's creation. Only thus can we save it as a healthy place for all of us.
—Shantilal P. Bhagat [39]

The special vulnerabilities and higher exposures of people of color, the poor, women, and children have led churches that have traditionally worked for social and economic justice to now work for environmental justice as well. Environmental justice is based on relationships: relationships between various societies around the world, relationships between present and future generations, and relationships between human beings and all the other parts of God's creation. Our challenge today is to stop toxic pollution at its source, to contain the pollution that already exists, and to let the earth begin the process of cleansing itself.

Ministry to the sick has always been an important part of Christianity and of other faith traditions. As people of faith, we continue to be called to ministries of healing, to visit and pray for those who are sick, and to work for the well-being of the whole. Our health and the health of future generations depend upon the health of the whole planet. As we work to heal the earth, the earth heals us. As we care for the earth, the earth cares for us. This is a holistic view of health, a vision of shalom, a promise of abundant life for all creation.

CHAPTER FIVE
Engineering the Future: Techno-Utopia or Techno-Hell?

> The road to hell is paved with good intentions.
>
> —Samuel Johnson[1]

I love spending time with my three youngest grandchildren. What beautiful and unique little beings they are! Nikayla, two and a half, high-spirited and sensitive, with light brown hair and her daddy's clear, blue eyes. Her sister Malina, one year old, with my daughter's dark skin, hair, and eyes, highly social, determined to win over everyone she sees with her smile and her first word, "Hi." Alex, my son's firstborn, almost two, dark hair and eyes like his father, very verbal, who lives in glee much of the time. Each one is so different, so unique; each an irreplaceable gift from God.

One morning, after enjoying these beautiful children, I sat down with a cup of coffee and the newspaper. I read a small headline: "Stanford gets OK to try human cells in mouse brain." I continued reading:

A Stanford University researcher has gotten a preliminary go-ahead to create a mouse with a significant number of human brain cells—as long as the creature behaves like a mouse, not a human. . . . A university ethics committee studied a provocative project that transplants human neurons into the brains of mice where, surprisingly, they settle in and feel right at home. The research team, led by Stanford biologist Irving Weissman, has no immediate plans to build a mouse with an entirely human brain. But it remains a theoretical possibility. . . . The federal government does not regulate the creation of such chimeras, named after the mythical Greek creature that is part-man, part-animal. So Stanford asked where it should draw the line. It is the first university in the nation to tackle the philosophical question: When does a chimera stop being an animal and start becoming a person, suggesting that research should end?[2]

As I read, I felt a deepening sense of foreboding as I considered the world in which my grandchildren will grow up. What will such experiments lead to in twenty years? What will become of our sense of relatedness to other creatures? What kind of animals will there be? What kind of people?

Modern technology has brought with it many benefits. The Internet enables us to communicate, invest money, organize and mobilize interest groups, start up and expand businesses, promote products, and transfer money in ways that used to be impossible. Modern transportation systems facilitate global travel and trade. Medical technologies bring ongoing breakthroughs in treatment for many diseases. Building technologies enable people to create homes that are not just shelters and family centers, but also warehouses for the many consumer goods made possible by technology. Food and clothing from around the world are available to anyone who can afford them.

Many technologies were developed with the best intentions—to alleviate human suffering and improve the quality of human life. Some have succeeded in doing so. But modern technologies come with tremendous environmental and social costs and bring risks unlike any that our species has faced before, "manufactured risks"[3] that may have grave consequences for future generations.

The same computers that facilitate globalization through the Internet pollute groundwater in the construction of their components and create hazardous waste in their disposal. Santa Clara County, at the heart of Silicon Valley, has 179 toxic "hot spots."[4] The same transportation systems that facilitate global travel and trade, since most are based on fossil fuels, pollute the air and contribute to climate change. As global trade continues to expand, these environmental effects will intensify.

Our globalized food production and distribution systems depend upon industrialized agriculture and large-scale food processing, which come at the cost of soil fertility, seed diversity, and small and subsistence farmers around the world. Factory farming creates immeasurable suffering among our fellow creatures, and hardens our hearts as such suffering becomes commonplace.

Even common technologies create hazards. Everyday appliances, including microwave ovens, cell phones,[5] and baby monitors,[6] create electromagnetic fields that are linked to various diseases, including leukemia, lymphoma, and cancer of the nervous system. Plastics, including those found in baby bottles, pacifiers, and children's toys, shed hormone-disrupting "phthalates." Television actually changes the brain waves of the person watching.[7] So do video games.[8]

Technology's costs and risks are disproportionately borne by the most vulnerable people. As discussed previously, children, the poor, and people of color are at most risk of harm from toxic contamination, one of the by-products of technology. Technology's benefits are also unevenly distributed. The wealthy, especially those in developed nations, have the greatest access. Laws that protect intellectual property and trade secrets, while motivating investment and technological innovation, also prevent widespread distribution and access to technologies by those who cannot afford them.

Global institutions such as the International Monetary Fund (IMF), World Bank, and WTO uphold and strengthen patent laws and other corporate rights that grant richer nations continuing dominance in global markets and control over access to technology, and its price, to poorer nations. For example, India is one of the world's most vital sources of generic drugs, and is a major producer of antiretroviral medicines used to treat AIDS patients in developing nations. India recently changed its patenting laws to comply with a WTO ruling that prohibits it from developing generic drugs from new products. Nevertheless, Novartis and other pharmaceutical companies are threatening legal action if India does not add even further restrictions.[9]

The prevailing view is that the market drives technology—companies will research, develop, and make available those products that are most in demand. Those who put their faith in the market argue that the market itself will create consumer demand for environmentally sound technologies, such as solar and hydrogen-based energy, and that this demand will make them cost–effective. This argument ignores the fact that many technologies are heavily subsidized. Until government and social priorities shift, the majority of subsidies will continue to favor industries that currently dominate the political process.

Many argue that the current form of globalization is driven by technology and is therefore inevitable. The Internet, which enables instantaneous electronic exchange of information and money across borders, will continue to extend its reach. As global transportation systems improve, human travel and the global transportation of goods will continue to expand. Since these and other technologies will continue to improve, it is argued, the continuing process of global economic and cultural integration is assured. Since technology itself drives globalization, and the market drives technology, there is nothing we can do to stop it. We human beings are simply passengers on the globalization train.

We will return to this argument later in this chapter. For now, let's turn our attention to new and emerging technologies, and see just where this train is headed.

GENETIC ENGINEERING

> Hidden behind complex free-trade treaties are innovative
> ways to steal nature's harvest, the harvest of the seed, and the
> harvest of nutrition. . . . Food security is in the seed.
>
> —Vandana Shiva[10]

Genetic engineering is the scientific process of manipulating plant, animal, or human DNA. It often involves transplanting genetic material from one species to another.

The public has been told that genetically modified (GM) foods will provide more abundant and nutritious food for a growing world population. But most GM crops are modified to tolerate herbicides or resist insects. In other words, a lot of it is about poison. Seventy percent of GM crops are altered to be herbicide tolerant, so that the companies that develop them can use their herbicides more freely. Monsanto developed its "Roundup Ready" soybeans from toxic-eating bacteria that were discovered living on waste outside the factory where their herbicide, Roundup, was being produced. (This gives a whole new meaning to the phrase "You are what you eat.") Twenty-five percent of GM crops are modified to be insect resistant. In other words, the plants themselves contain pesticides, posing a danger to beneficial insects. Larvae of monarch butterflies have died from eating the pollen of genetically modified Bt corn. This raises the question of how such crops might affect human beings.

How healthy, in general, are GM foods for human beings? Many people have had allergic reactions to GM foods that contain certain genes (for instance, from peanuts). Other effects on humans are still largely unknown, since no long-term studies have been done.

Most processed foods on supermarket shelves in the United States are made from GM crops. By contrast, Europeans have largely rejected what many call "Frankenfoods" and have imposed a five-year moratorium on GM foods. The United States, Canada, and Argentina challenged the moratorium at the WTO. The European Union (EU) is a signatory to the Biosafety Protocol, an international treaty that permits countries to prohibit GMO products. Nevertheless, in October 2006, the WTO ruled the moratorium on GM foods to be illegal, in effect overruling the treaty.[11] If the EU does not change its law it may have to add to the millions it already pays every year to maintain its ban on U.S. hormone-fed beef.[12]

GM crops pose environmental risks. Pollen from transgenic plants can cross-pollinate crops in other fields, even fields planted with organic crops. GM "super plants" could become invasive, outcompeting other crops and native plants and taking over whole ecosystems. GM trees, designed to grow quickly and to be harvested as crops, pose similar environmental risks.

Genetic technologies are facilitating the corporate takeover of global food production. A handful of transnational corporations now dominate the world's seed supply. They are designing seeds, initiating lawsuits, and lobbying governments for even stronger patent protections at the domestic, regional, and global levels. Monsanto recently sued a farmer in Canada for illegally benefiting from its GM seed, even though he had not planted the seed in his field. The farmer alleged that his crops had been contaminated by cross-pollination or "drift" from a nearby crop.[13] Nevertheless, Monsanto won. Monsanto also has many lawsuits pending against farmers for saving their seed, instead of buying it anew each season, including nine hundred farmers in the United States.[14] Environmental activist Vandana Shiva points out that saving seeds has been considered a sacred duty for generations in cultures around the world.[15]

As corporations consolidate their control over the development, marketing, and use of GM seeds, local seed varieties and traditional methods of planting continue to give way to seeds designed for industrial agriculture, that is, for large fields planted with single crops (monocultures) that need chemical fertilizers and pesticides. If seeds are not planted, their fertility is lost. When our food supply depends upon technologies that are controlled by a few powerful corporations, it is a dangerous situation indeed.

Furthermore, powerful corporations are scouring the globe, often in sensitive areas like rain forests, seeking new genetic resources, and with them, indigenous wisdom upon which they can base new products. For instance, who should "own" basmati rice, developed and used by people in India for thousands of years? RiceTech, a Texas company, now owns the patent.[16] Activists from the developing world call for laws protecting the "genetic commons" from such "bio-piracy," where corporations exploit the genetic resources of poor nations and, through patent laws, deprive the people of these nations of benefiting from their own resources.

At the time of this writing, genetic engineering of animals is barely regulated. Animals may be altered with DNA from bacteria, plants, or animals, resulting in cross-species animals, that is, "chimeras." Human genes are used in some of these cross-species transfers of DNA. Some say that developing such creatures violates the integrity of life on earth, which took millions of years to evolve in all its intricacy and interrelatedness. Also of concern is the fact that these species are being developed for commercial exploitation. Global biotech corporations are rushing to patent these so-called "inventions", which are actually living beings.

Patent laws are also an issue in debates about genetic technologies related to animals and human beings. The U.S. Patent Office issues patents not just for drugs or particular inventions, but for life-forms themselves. It awards patents on specific plants, animals, and even human genes, cells, organs, and embryos, and treats them as human inventions. Some have not even been genetically altered. The question becomes: who "owns" life? And by what authority?

Human genetic technologies promise incredible benefits, especially in the field of medicine. If genetic therapies could be developed for heart disease, stroke, Alzheimer's, or even birth defects, we could eliminate much suffering. Some genetic therapies are already available. Somatic genetic engineering provides GM-based treatments or drugs to individuals. Germline genetic engineering, however, changes not only the genetic makeup of the individual who was treated, but of his or her offspring. It thus involves tampering with human evolution by trying to engineer "bad" genes out of the gene pool, although there is no way to predict the generational effects.

If parents are given the opportunity to genetically modify their children before they are born, what choices will they make? If parents decide to eliminate the gene that predisposes their fetus to heart disease, why not also eliminate the gene for left-handedness? Why not add a gene that would increase creativity or raise intelligence or make the child more beautiful? In his book *Enough: Staying Human in an Engineered World*, Bill McKibben warns:

> In widespread use [these technologies] will first rob parents of their liberty, and then strip freedom from every generation that follows. In the end, they will destroy forever the very possibility of meaningful choice. . . Faced with a challenge larger than any we've ever faced—the possibility that technology may replace humanity—we need to rally our innate ability to say no. We will be sorely tempted to engineer our kids, but it's a temptation that we need to resist as individuals, and to help each other resist as a society.[17]

A POST HUMAN WORLD?

This horrid vision of the human being made in the image of the machine cries out for resistance, for visions of life other than the predominating ones. . . . We need to remind ourselves that there was once a time when genetic technology did not determine the beginning—and nuclear technology the end—of life.

—Dorothee Soelle[18]

Another emerging technology, nanotechnology, refers to technology that takes place at the molecular level.[19] Nanotechnology is quickly transforming medicine, biotechnology, manufacturing, and information processing. It is being promoted as having the potential to bring revolutionary breakthroughs in medicine, as well as solutions to pollution and the energy crisis. It is also the basis of science fiction doomsday scenarios, such as Michael Crichton's bestseller *Prey*, in which molecular-sized robots seek to destroy the entire human race. Will nanotechnology be a blessing or a curse? As with other technologies, it may be mixed. But as technologies become more advanced, the stakes grow ever higher, creating risks never before faced by humankind.

In addition to transforming life through genetic engineering and nanotechnology, progress is being made in developing robots and computers with artificial intelligence. Scientists working on the cutting edge of these technologies point to a "post-human" future, when genetic modification and technological implants will have created super-human beings, even transhuman chimeras, enhanced with animal genes, and when robotics and artificial intelligence technologies will have created nonbiological, superintelligent machines. Such beings, supposedly, will even be able to "self-bootstrap," that is, change themselves "in ways that limited human minds can't even start to understand."[20] For some this may seem like a techno-utopia; for others it sounds like a techno-hell.

Since technology has such a tremendous impact on the direction of society, many are calling for widespread public discussion about the potential benefits and risks of particularly dangerous technologies before they are approved. There are few avenues for public discussion, debate, or input into the decision-making process, but we the people have as much authority to speak out about these things as scientists do.

Citizen groups are promoting the precautionary principle in dealing with emerging technologies. Some scientists point toward "relinquishment," that is, the renouncing of certain technologies because of their extreme risks of harm. Bill Joy, the chief scientist at Sun Microsystems, argues that society should "relinquish" some lines of human genetic research, nanotechnology, and advanced robotics: "These technologies are just too much for a species at our level of sophistication. . . . We are on a course of human destruction. . . . Open access to and unlimited development of [these technologies] henceforth puts us all in clear danger of extinction."[21]

Some argue that enforced relinquishment would infringe upon the rights of scientists and researchers. Others claim that these rights are not absolute, but should be superseded by the rights of humanity, other species, and future generations to be protected from technological risks that that could be catastrophic. Theologian Jürgen Moltmann writes: "We are setting developments afoot that are getting out of control. We are making free decisions through which we lose our own freedom. If these decisions are final, irrevocable, and unrepeatable, then we are not dealing with experiments anymore. . . . This is the point of no return: all or nothing. That means that we are coming to the end of time, and into the presence of what was traditionally called doomsday."[22] Some say that relinquishment is our only hope. Others argue that relinquishment is not possible, or that it is not possible without global totalitarianism, or that we need to develop these technologies if only to find defenses against them. In other words, going forward with the development of these technologies is inevitable.

TECHNOLOGY DRIVES GLOBALIZATION, SO . . . IS IT INEVITABLE?

Technology no longer serves as a tool to improve human life, but is a prostitute to the drive for profits. Greed drives technology as businesses compete to develop new technologies in order to generate more profits.

—Dorothee Soelle[23]

Does technology drive globalization? Is the uncontrolled development of new technologies inevitable? Will technology itself determine the future? Let us not be misled into thinking that technology somehow progresses on its own in a vague process over which human beings have no control. Technology does not create itself, at least not yet. Human beings still participate in decision making about which technologies will be developed and made available for widespread use.

Some argue that market forces determine which technologies are developed. Such economic determinism ignores the fact that the market is not really free at all, but is distorted by laws, subsidies, tax breaks, social costs, and global infrastructure that protect the "rights" and the profits of huge corporations and that keep the overall system going. Corporations decide which technologies to research and develop, based on what will bring profit. They market their ideas to gain funding for research from government, foundations, and research centers. They lobby for national laws and international trade agreements that protect trade secrets and intellectual property and that ban the precautionary principle, which would put public health and safety above corporate power and profits.

For its part, the U.S. government grants strict patent protections for corporate research and development, including, as we have seen, patents on life-forms. The government uses our tax dollars and public universities to support research on cutting-edge technologies and gives corporations the right to develop products based on this subsidized research. An example is a little-publicized government effort to converge nanotechnology, biotechnology, information technology, and cybernetics (NBIC) in order to "engineer the modification and enhancement of human beings." The primary coordinator of the program, Dr. Mihail Roco, stated that "the government investment in this project will be second only to the NASA moon-landing program."[24]

Most government funding for the research and development of emerging technologies, however, is for military purposes. We will return to the topic of war-fighting technologies in a later chapter. For now, suffice it to say that efforts to develop new technologies are not always undertaken with the "best intentions" after all.

It is the dominant institutions of our society, peopled by human beings, which make the development of these technologies possible. These institutional Powers promote specific laws that move potentially profitable or strategic technologies forward quickly, quietly through protection of "trade secrets," and without public participation. These same Powers promote the expansion of corporate globalization.

None of this is inevitable. The development of specific technologies depends upon both political and economic choices. Long-term research and development of new technologies require huge financial investments, directing of resources, and legal protections that could be going toward other priorities, if there were political will.

This is a good time to present another foundational principle for a just and sustainable future: *participatory democracy*. Human beings must become involved at every level in making the decisions about both local and global issues. The debate about these new technologies is broadening, and includes discussion on their ethical, social, ecological, and spiritual effects. The European Union's moratorium on GM foods came about because of the European people's organized opposition to such products. We will explore other successful citizen actions in later chapters of this book. The point here is: the only thing that could make either technology or corporate globalization inevitable is apathy and inaction on the part of the people.

The idea that emerging technologies are moving us forward in an inevitable process is idolatrous and dehumanizing, and therefore demonic. To give technology the power to determine the direction of society is to put it in the place of God. It is to ignore the chilling indictment, "[You] have made offerings to other gods, and worshiped the works of [your] own hands" (Jer. 1:16). This argument also ignores human responsibility for developing and distributing new technologies, and reduces human beings to a position of passive helplessness in accepting the advances of technology, without power to determine which technologies might be helpful or harmful. This hopeless view emphasizes the powerlessness of human beings in relation to technology. It is part of the dominant ideology that keeps people down and leaves them at the mercy of the Powers.

WE HAVE PASSED OVER A THRESHOLD

It has taken the entire course of some fourteen billion years for the universe, the earth, and all its living creatures to attain this mode of presence to itself through our empirical modes of knowing. Such is the culmination of the scientific effort. . . . This has brought us into the far depths of the heavens and into the inner spaces of the atom.

—Thomas Berry[25]

It is ironic that the very science that is enabling our scientists and engineers to create such powerful, creative, and risky technologies is also the science that reveals to us the mysteries of the "new cosmology," the scientific story of the origins and makeup of the universe, with all its awesome implications.

In the mid-1990s, my son Luke attended the University of California at Santa Cruz as a biology major. He took a course on genetics from Dr. David Deamer, whose work was featured in *Discover* magazine[26] about that time. Luke described what happened in class: to show the creativity of genes, Professor Deamer set genetic sequences to music, using the musical notes A, C, G, and D to represent the four different nucleotides. (Since all species share the same DNA, all are made up of different sequences of these four nucleotides.) Using an electronic keyboard, Professor Deamer then played the musical notes in the order assigned to each of the various species. He played the sequence of notes that made up the DNA of "carrot." He played the DNA songs of various plants, of bird species, of frogs, of whales, of chimpanzees, of humans. The songs were incredibly beautiful. The students were in awe—an appropriate response. Luke said that he and others had tears in their eyes.

What will we do with this science and the technologies that it makes possible? Are we mature and wise enough to engineer the future of life on earth? Whose interests would such engineering serve? Will we be arrogant or humble in making decisions about the direction of technology? And who will decide—the people, through an informed, democratic, participatory process, or the Powers?

Thomas Berry warns that we are moving into a new geological age. With the radical disruption of the ecology of the planet and the loss of so many species, the Cenazoic Age, the age of flowering plants and the flowering of life as we know it, is coming to an end. Unlike ever before we humans have a choice as to what the coming age will be. Will it be a "Technozoic Age," with the beauty of the earth reconstructed, engineered, and laid waste by human technologies? Or will it be an "Ecozoic Age," with human beings consciously grounding themselves in, cooperating with, protecting, and living in awe of the interrelatedness and sacredness of the natural world? We have a choice. The responsibility is ours. There is no turning back, for, says Berry: "The earth will never again function in the future in the manner that it has functioned in the past. A decisive transformation has taken place, for whereas the human had nothing to say in the emergent period of the universe prior to the present, in the future the human will be involved in almost everything that happens. We have passed over a threshold."[27]

CHAPTER SIX
Race to the Bottom:
Facing the Abyss

> How much of our traditional consumer values and First World living standard can we afford to retain? I already mentioned the seeming political impossibility of inducing First World citizens to lower their impact on the world. But the alternative, of continuing our current impact, is more impossible. . . . A lower-impact society is the most impossible scenario for our future—except for all other conceivable scenarios.
>
> —Jared Diamond[1]

In July 1993, I was appointed as pastor to a church in a new community. Congregational members welcomed my husband and me with open arms. I preached from the lectionary, and my sermons were generally well received. Several months after I arrived the lectionary passage was Luke 16:19-31, the parable of the rich man and Lazarus:

> There was a rich man who was dressed in purple and fine linen and who feasted sumptuously every day. And at his gate lay a poor man named Lazarus, covered with sores, who longed to satisfy his hunger with what fell from the rich man's table; even the dogs would come and lick his sores. The poor man died and was carried away by the angels to be with Abraham. The rich man also died and was buried. In Hades, where he was being tormented, he looked up and saw Abraham far away with Lazarus by his side. He called out, "Father Abraham, have mercy on me, and send Lazarus to dip the tip of his finger in water and cool my tongue; for I am in agony in these flames." But Abraham said, "Child, remember that during your lifetime you received your good things, and Lazarus in like manner evil things; but now he is comforted here, and you are in agony. Besides all this, between you and us a great chasm has been fixed, so that those who might want to pass from here to you cannot do so, and no one can cross from there to us." He said, "Then, father, I beg you to send him to my father's house—for I have five brothers—that he may warn them, so that they will not also come into this place of torment." Abraham replied, "They have Moses and the prophets; they should listen to them." He said, "No, father Abraham; but if someone goes

to them from the dead, they will repent." He said to him, "If they do not listen to Moses and the prophets, neither will they be convinced even if someone rises from the dead."

As I preached on this parable, I used the movie *Grand Canyon* as a modern-day sermon illustration. The movie is a brilliant commentary on race and class relations in the U.S.A. and the growing inequity in our world. It follows the lives of a black family and a white family who are brought together by a series of events and who end up traveling together to the Grand Canyon. One comment in the movie is especially striking:

> There's a gulf in this country, an ever-widening abyss between the people who have stuff and the people who don't have sh—. It's like this big hole has opened up in the ground as big as the Grand Canyon . . . and what's come out of this big hole is an eruption of rage and the rage creates violence and the violence is real, Mac, and nothing's going to make it go away until someone changes something.

In my sermon, I pointed to the beggar Lazarus as the ultimate picture of human poverty and misery. I spoke about our call to respond to the needs of the wretched and poor and to work for a world that is just, as Jesus called people to do in his day.

I learned later that a few members of the congregation were offended that I brought up issues of race and class so early in my ministry there. Others were grateful. One old-timer defended me: "I've heard pastors preach on that passage my whole life, and it always comes round to the same thing." The honeymoon with the church was over, but our relationship and conversation became deeper. I still had six fruitful years as pastor there ahead of me.

In this book we are not exploring the concept of punishment in a hellish afterlife, as portrayed in the above parable, but the future possibility of a living hell on earth. We are, however, also looking at the spiritual effects of the life-choices we make here and now and at how we respond to the growing challenges of our world. The fact is that many, though not all, of us in the United States and other wealthy nations live sumptuously by world standards, using far more than our share of the earth's resources. In a world of poverty and growing inequity, how we respond to the needy at our gate is a spiritual question, a question posed by Jesus.

We can't just avoid or deny this spiritual dilemma—it will catch up with us. The rich man in the parable bewails his separation from God. There are very real spiritual consequences to hardening our hearts and turning away. For when we shut the door of our hearts to our neighbors, we are shutting out God.

Although Jesus told this story over two thousand years ago, the parable of the rich man and Lazarus graphically portrays today's global situation. Growing inequity is a primary feature of corporate globalization. Everyone agrees that there are both winners and losers in the global economy. How those of us who currently see ourselves as winners treat the losers is both a spiritual and a practical issue.

THE RACE TO THE BOTTOM

When corporations and governments lower costs by reducing environmental protection, wages, salaries, health care, and education, the result can be malignant—a "downward leveling" of environmental, labor, and social conditions. Downward leveling is like a cancer that is destroying its host organism—the earth and its people.
—Jeremy Brecher and Tim Costello[2]

With globalization, corporations are now able to scour the earth, looking for places that offer them the best incentives to set up shop: cheap labor, low or no taxes, lax environmental standards, and strictly enforced security. Countries, regions, and communities, including many within the United States, compete for the dollars these corporations control by relaxing regulatory standards and promising benefits such as corporate tax breaks, subsidized infrastructure, environmental waivers, deregulation, limited worker protection, restrictions on labor's right to organize, guaranteed security, and so on. This pressure to offer the best deal to corporations creates a race to the bottom, for it is clear to all that the chosen countries, states, or communities will be those that most benefit corporations.

It should be no surprise, then, that corporations move high-paying U.S. jobs to low-wage countries like Mexico, and from there to even lower-wage countries like Cambodia or Romania. China now produces many of the consumer items imported into the United States and other developed nations. It has a totalitarian government, an almost endless supply of cheap labor, and a migrant-worker program that has been compared to that of South Africa under apartheid. In Chinese sweatshops, girls as young as eleven typically work twelve- to sixteen-hour days, some with wages as low as six cents an hour.[3] Who can compete with that?

The point is not that we should exclude Chinese workers from the benefits of development, or begrudge China its growing middle class. But free-market capitalism sets workers in one country against workers in all others, and enables corporations to set the terms of employment. Competition for corporate "investment" drives down wages, environmental protections, regulatory standards, worker and other human rights, and the tax base of communities around the world. The resulting contest is a head-over-heels freefall that has no logical stopping place except in the pit of all-encompassing global human misery.

As the market becomes the principle around which societies are organized, people without money are left behind. Public services are sold off to private companies, as more sectors of society are privatized and absorbed into the global economy. As funds for social services are cut, many are deprived of health care, education, public transportation, access to energy, even water and nutritional food. The winners can win big, but the losers can lose everything, even those things needed to sustain life itself.

In the past several chapters we have considered ecological and technological threats to the natural systems of the earth. As we have seen, the extensive damage already inflicted on the earth is causing grave harm to human beings, especially the most vulnerable. In this chapter we focus on additional threats to human well-being. These dangers include social trends directly related to corporate globalization, such as growing inequity, changing work patterns, global migration, the loss of indigenous lands, the breakdown of traditional families and communities, human trafficking, and the spread of diseases such as AIDS. Human well-being is also threatened by the growing scarcity of oil and water, which may lead to grain shortages, waves of refugees, social chaos, and resource wars, such as the war in Iraq. Overpopulation and over-consumption threaten to overwhelm the carrying capacity of the earth itself. Books have been written on each of these topics. I will only touch on them here.

As long as our dominant institutions continue along the current course, such damage will only increase, along with the resulting harm to human beings. These effects will likely be compounded, since none of these things are happening in a vacuum. Furthermore, the system of corporate globalization interacts with the conditions that cause these dangers, often aggravating them and multiplying their effects.

Let me be clear: I am not claiming that the system of corporate globalization caused these problems. The Soviet Communist system left a grim legacy of industrial contamination and human misery throughout eastern Europe. And as Jared Diamond points out in his book *Collapse*, societies with various political and economic systems, both ancient and modern, make decisions that cause them to succeed or fail.

But the global spread of unrestrained market-based capitalism is now exacerbating these problems. More to the point, the institutions and systems that currently dominate our world will not be able to solve them. In spite of globalization enthusiasts' claims to the contrary, market forces and new technologies do not reverse the damage being done. In fact, as corporations consolidate their power, the destruction is increasing, as can be clearly seen. The race to the bottom is fueled by a race to the top among the dominant Powers. Transnational corporations, the engines of global capitalism, compete fiercely in the global marketplace, with their client governments working on their behalf. Institutional pressures drive these entities to seek profit and expansion by any means possible, for this is the only way they can survive and extend their power.

The pace of the race to the bottom is accelerating; we have not yet hit bottom. For the most part, human society is still going down the same path, the path carved out by the dominant Powers. We are heading toward an abyss. Later chapters of this book will focus on the mechanisms of this process, the institutions that keep it going, and alternatives to the current global system. We will explore what a reversal of direction—toward hope—would entail. But here we will look into the abyss that is opening up, into which many, even now, are falling, and which threatens future generations with grave and irreversible harm.

A DIVIDED WORLD

> The world may be going to hell, but there's lots of really neat stuff you can buy.
> —Internet review of *Wired* magazine, 1993[4]

Those of us who have become dependent upon modern conveniences can hardly imagine life without them. Where would we be without our comfortable homes, running water, varied foods, and store-bought clothes? What would life be like without our cars, telephones, televisions, and computers, without modern schools and hospitals, without steel and plastics or the myriad mass-produced consumer products to which we have grown accustomed? Those of us who enjoy these amenities may not realize that the majority of people in the world are still doing without many of them.

The Industrial Revolution brought gains and raised living standards for many around the world. During the twentieth century, life expectancy went up and rates of infant mortality went down. There were gains in nutrition, literacy, and sanitation. Many diseases were controlled or eliminated. Such gains were unequal, but steady.

But in the last twenty-five years, in most poor and middle-income countries, such gains have suddenly slowed, stalled, and in some places, reversed.[5] This slowdown in progress has been linked to several factors, including free-market economic "reforms" promoted under the system of corporate globalization.

Some countries continue to show progress in these areas. During the past twenty-five years, India's economy grew by an average of 3.8 percent. China grew by an average of an astounding 7.15 percent, increasing sixfold in twenty-five years to become the second largest economy in the world.[6] Although these two countries contain almost half the entire population of the developing world, they cannot be held up as examples of the success of free-market capitalism, since their governments retained economic controls that the vast majority of developing nations did not.[7] Even in these countries, there is growing inequity, and many are excluded from the benefits of a general rise in living standards. Some are left destitute, victims of the "creative destruction" of capitalism.

In Africa, per capita income rose 36 percent from 1960 to 1980, but declined 15 percent from 1980 to 2000.[8] Life expectancy plunged, due in part to the HIV epidemic, which has infected over sixty-eight million Africans, killing over twenty-six million.[9] Africa is expected to have twenty million "AIDS orphans" by 2010.[10] If not for the economic collapse, some African nations may have been able to deal with the HIV/AIDS and other health crises more effectively.[11] "Poverty begets disease and disease begets poverty,"[12] since those without access to nutritious food, safe water, literacy, and basic health care are more likely to suffer from disease, and those who are sick cannot support their families.

According to the World Bank, half the world's people live on less than two dollars a day. 1.2 billion people live on less than one dollar a day, over nine hundred million of whom are women.[13] Each day, more than sixteen thousand children die from hunger-related causes.[14]

As the market becomes society's primary organizing principle, people without money become expendable. While many enjoy a rising standard of living and a few grow exceedingly rich, others become destitute. National policies promoted under corporate globalization do not always improve the lives of the majority of people, especially if a country's primary comparative advantage is virgin rainforests or other natural resources, cheap labor, or "right to work laws," that is, laws that restrict union activity. Some governments allow the wholesale destruction of ecosystems for the sake of profit. Some tolerate almost slavelike conditions, including prison labor and child labor, in order to keep manufacturing costs competitive. Many developing nations, strapped by debt and suffering under IMF-imposed austerity measures, have been unable to lift themselves out of poverty. Some countries spend more on debt repayment than on health care and education combined.

As living conditions deteriorate, migration rates increase as people flee from war, environmental devastation, loss of land for subsistence, and hunger. Many migrate for the purpose of finding work. Around the world, people are on the move, both within countries and among countries. People who have subsisted on native lands or small family farms for generations move from the countryside to the cities, hoping to join the ranks of urban workers. In poor countries, many end up in the burgeoning shantytowns growing up around city limits, trying to make it in the underground economy or by scavenging in the garbage dumps of the affluent.

Families from poor countries risk their lives crossing borders to become migrant workers in countries that offer opportunity. Men leave their families behind to become day laborers in order to support their families back home. Women leave their own children in the care of relatives, migrating to countries where they can earn enough to support them by serving as nannies for rich people's children.

In this global workforce, exploitation abounds. Human traffickers, like drug cartels, use modern transportation and communication networks to transport people across borders. This can take the form of human trafficking, even of minors, as indentured servants or as sex slaves. Those who profit from the misery of others usually find their victims in places of extreme poverty. These exploitive networks facilitate the more rapid spread of HIV/AIDS and other diseases.[15]

We live in a world divided between rich and poor, and the gap in incomes between the rich and poor around the world continues to rise. The income gap between the richest 20 percent of the world's people and the poorest 20 percent increased from a ratio of thirty to one in 1960 to seventy-four to one in 1997.[16] By 1997, the richest 20 percent received 86 percent of the world's income, while the other 80 percent made do with the 14 percent. The poorest 20 percent received less than 1 percent of the world's income.[17]

Meanwhile, corporations are accumulating wealth and consolidating their power. Of the one hundred largest economies in the world, fifty-one are now global corporations; only forty-nine are countries. The largest two hundred corporations surpass the combined economies of 182 countries, and have almost twice the economic clout of the poorest four-fifths of humanity.[18]

Inequity is growing not just among countries, but also within countries. In the United States, the model and primary promoter of corporate globalization, the poorest 20 percent own no wealth, the top 20 percent own over 80 percent, and the top 5 percent own more than half of all the wealth.[19] Between 1979 and 2000, the income of the richest 1 percent rose by over 200 percent.[20]

Of the twenty richest billionaires in the world, ten are U.S. citizens.[21] In 2006, for the first time, the wealthiest four hundred Americans are all billionaires. In one year, their collective net worth climbed one hundred twenty billion dollars, to $1.25 trillion.[22]

Corporate profits have never been higher. At the same time, corporate taxes have gone down. In 1945, corporations provided 50 percent of federal taxes; by 2001, they provided 8 percent.[23]

At the same time, the bottom has fallen out for many people in the United States. Jobs that provide a living wage are being lost to mechanization, outsourcing, and the switch to temporary jobs and contract labor. The manufacturing industry has fled the country; office work, data entry, accounting, and information technology are close behind. As good jobs are exported to poor countries, as the quality of public education declines, and as costs of higher education rise, opportunities to create a better future for oneself and one's children are lost.

Real wages fell about 19 percent between the 1970s and 1990s.[24] Many employers have cut pensions and health benefits. The United States has more households with two wage-earners, U.S. workers work 350 hours more per year than their counterparts in other industrialized nations, and they often make do with inadequate day care.

According to the U.S. Census Bureau, the poverty rate continues to rise; it went from 7.6 million (10 percent of U.S. families) in 2003 to 7.9 million families (10.2 percent) in 2004.[25] One in five children lives below the poverty line; of those living with a single mother, over half are in poverty.[26] Although the United States has more neonatal intensive-care beds than many other countries, it has the second worst newborn mortality rate in the developed world.[27]

As more families are thrown into poverty, as public services are cut, and as welfare is eliminated for the poorest of the poor, society as a whole becomes less stable. The breakup of families and the breakdown of communities becomes part of what has been called the creative destruction of unrestrained free-market capitalism, as the middle class shrinks and poverty grows. This is the result of the current global economic system. We are moving toward a world where, in the words of Walter Russell Mead, "The First and Third worlds will not so much disappear as mingle. There will be more people in Mexico and India who live like Americans of the upper-middle class; on the other hand, there will be more—many more—people in the United States who live like the slum dwellers of Mexico City and Calcutta."[28]

This decline in living standards and quality of life is not taking place in a vacuum. As we will see, global institutions such as the International Monetary Fund (IMF), World Bank, and World Trade Organization (WTO) pressure governments, including the United States, to eliminate programs that benefit the majority of people, preserve the environment, and provide a safety net for the most vulnerable. At the same time, their policies encourage governments to maintain order by increasing their spending on police, prisons, and the military. Indeed, the WTO and many free-trade agreements exempt "national security" expenditures from their jurisdiction. In countries around the world, the beneficent function of government is being sacrificed, while the repressive function is becoming paramount.

At the same time, the current darlings (countries or communities) of corporate investors experience economic growth and a rising standard of living, and the wealthy few make a killing. But these global corporations are fickle; these are marriages of convenience. More predator than paramour, always lusting after profits, after ravishing one country or community these corporate giants can easily pull up stakes and move on to the next. (I speak here about the institutions themselves, not about human beings, although they can function only with human complicity.)

Inequity continues to grow. But as we shall see in the next chapter, this growing inequity, while violent in itself, fosters violence at every level. Injustice breeds resentment. Repression breeds dissent. Extreme poverty breeds desperation.

The growing abyss between rich and poor threatens the well-being of us all. As in the parable of the rich man and Lazarus, those with wealth and power dine in luxury, behind locked doors, in exclusive country clubs or gated communities, protected by security guards, "tough on crime" policies, and weapons that threaten all life on earth. But in the long run, such "protection" is just an illusion. Nothing can protect any of us from a growing sea of human misery or from ecological dangers that threaten everyone.

In the parable, the rich man finds himself in hell, and begs for a drop of water to quench his thirst. Declining supplies of fresh water have an impact on the rich as well as the poor, as does the loss of topsoil, depleted fisheries, and shortages of oil and other resources. Global climate change and pollution of our soil, air, and water affects us all, as does poverty, disease, social chaos, massive migration, and violence. All of us have the same basic human needs. We are not protected, ultimately, by our privilege or our wealth. The challenges we face as a human family tie us together, regardless of our class, race, religion, or political perspective. Our futures are intertwined.

In the parable the rich man asks Father Abraham to send someone to warn his brothers. The answer: Moses and the prophets have warned us, again and again. Contemporary prophets are warning us today that the human family faces disaster if we do not turn around.

EARTH'S CARRYING CAPACITY: TOO MANY PEOPLE, NOT ENOUGH PLANET

The problems of all these environmentally devastated, over-populated, distant countries become our own problems because of globalization.

—Jared Diamond[29]

A primary challenge is the carrying capacity of the earth. How many people can the earth support' and at what level of consumption? Population is rising exponentially. In his book *Earth in the Balance*, Al Gore said it well: "From the beginning of humanity's appearance on earth to 1945, it took more than ten thousand generations to reach a world population of two billion people. Now, in the course of one human lifetime—mine—the world population will increase from 2 to more than 9 billion, and it is already more than halfway there."[30]

Population is growing fastest in extremely poor countries where illiteracy, malnutrition, disease, and infant-mortality rates are also high. The majority of the world's malnourished and hungry people live in the Indian subcontinent and in sub-Saharan Africa, where the population is growing fastest. In India, which has one billion people and is expected to reach 1.5 billion by 2050, over half the children are malnourished. In Africa's two most populous countries, Nigeria and Ethiopia, the figures are 27 percent and 47 percent, respectively.[31]

World population is projected to rise to almost nine billion by 2025.[32] By that time, India will add over half a billion people, and will have more people than China. China will add more people than the entire population of the United States.

In weighing the human impact on the earth, we must consider not only population, but also patterns of consumption and related greenhouse-gas emissions and other forms of waste. Corporate advertising in countries rich and poor alike promotes ever-increasing consumption as a path to well-being.

The United States, with less than 5 percent of the world's population, consumes about 25 percent of the world's resources.[33] China, however, has overtaken the United States as the world's leading consumer of resources; it now consumes nearly twice as much meat and over twice as much steel as does the United States.[34] With 1.3 billion people[35] and an economic growth rate of over 8 percent per year,[36] China's increasing levels of consumption will have a severe impact on the earth. If China's *per capita* consumption even approaches that of the United States, we will be in a grave situation indeed. According to Lester R. Brown of the WorldWatch Institute: "The western economic model—the fossil fuel-based, car-centered, throwaway economy—is not going to work for

China. If it does not work for China, it will not work for India, which by 2031 is projected to have a population even larger than China's. Nor will it work for the 3 billion other people in developing countries who are also dreaming the 'American Dream'"[37]

Poor people around the world aspire to higher living standards. As global corporations relocate their offices and supply chains to developing nations, infusions of capital enable those who are fortunate to join the middle class. A few become exceedingly rich. Others are left behind. But even in poor countries, the rich are becoming richer. With rising affluence comes rising consumption. This vast increase in consumption is good for corporate globalization, which depends upon continuing economic growth, but it is very bad for the earth. According to the World Wildlife Fund, at the current rate of consumption of the earth's resources, we will need two planets by the year 2050.[38]

Without expanding markets, the present economic system would collapse. But if current rates of consumption continue to increase, the impact of human behaviors threatens to overwhelm the already strained natural systems of the earth, triggering a global ecological catastrophe that encompasses all creatures, including human beings.

A "LONG EMERGENCY"?

> The so-called global economy was not a permanent institution, as some seem to believe it was, but a set of transient circumstances peculiar to a certain time: the Indian summer of the fossil fuel era.
>
> —James Howard Kuntzler[39]

Some believe that the earth's natural limits will establish themselves sooner rather than later. James Howard Kuntzler predicts what he calls a "long emergency," triggered by oil scarcity and resulting high prices.

Oil is becoming more scarce. The United States reached the peak of its oil production in 1970,[40] and world oil production is expected to peak in the first decade of this century.[41] Many believe that we are at that pivotal point right now. We will know when that point comes only in hindsight, when it becomes increasingly expensive to pump oil from deeper underground. At some point, the cost of accessing ever-scarcer, lower-grade oil will become prohibitive.

When we reach and pass peak oil production, everything will change, since industrialized agriculture and our whole way of life, which so many take for granted, is based on plentiful, easily available, and relatively cheap oil. According to Kuntzler, during the long emergency: "Globalism will wither. Life will become profoundly and intensely local.

The consumer economy will be a strange memory. Suburbia . . . will become untenable. We will struggle to feed ourselves. We may bankrupt ourselves in the effort to prop up the unsustainable."[42]

Market forces alone will not prevent the long emergency that oil shortages may bring about, nor will piecemeal interventions by governments. Kuntzler recommends that the U.S. government undertake a coordinated, massive effort to build the infrastructure necessary for a switch to alternative fuels. Even then, in all likelihood, lifestyles based on excessive energy consumption will have to change if there is to be any hope of supplying the energy needed to raise the living standards of the poor or providing for the needs of the world's growing population.

Clearly, conversion to a just and more sustainable way of life is necessary. The earth simply cannot support current rates of growth in population or consumption. Gandhi's words become increasingly and obviously true: "There is enough for everyone's need, but not for everyone's greed."[43]

WATER SCARCITY

> There is simply no way to overstate the fresh water crisis on the planet today. The alarm is sounding. Will we hear it in time?
> —Maude Barlow and Tony Clarke[44]

All living things depend upon water for life itself. For human beings and many other species, this need can be met only by fresh, clean water, which has been available in abundance on this "blue planet" since the dawn of life.

But now the world faces a severe shortage of fresh water. The earth is drying up. Water tables are falling in countries around the world as aquifers are pumped far beyond their recharge rate. Since 1991, the Ogallala Aquifer in the United States has fallen three feet per year.[45] Water tables on the North China plain, China's breadbasket, are falling five feet per year.[46] Rivers are being dammed, diverted, and overtapped. Many of them, including the Nile, Ganges, Yangtze, and Colorado Rivers, now rarely or never reach the sea.[47] Wetlands are being filled in for development, deforestation causes streams to fill up with silt, large-scale paving prevents absorption into groundwater, global warming dries up the land. Widespread urbanization, diversion of water for industry, and industrialized agriculture consume massive amounts of water, just when conservation is most needed.

Consumption of water is doubling every twenty years, twice the rate of population growth.[48] According to the United Nations, thirty-one countries are already experiencing water scarcity. Over one billion people currently lack access to clean water. Three billion have no sanitation services.[49] Over three million people die each year due to waterborne diseases, mostly children.[50]

As population grows, adding a projected 2.6 billion people to the world's population by 2025, as many as two-thirds will face serious water shortages, and one third will be living with "absolute water scarcity."[51] Demand for water will be 56 percent greater than supply.[52] Ismail Serageldin, vice president of the World Bank, predicted in the late 1990s, "The wars of the next century will be about water."[53]

The Powers that be have a solution to the world's water crisis: privatization. According to the institutions that govern the global economy and to standard economic theory, if you turn water into a commodity to be bought and sold, people will conserve it more carefully.

The IMF and World Bank have imposed water-privatization programs on many countries, including some of the poorest countries in Africa, programs that include fees for service and full cost recovery. The WTO, NAFTA, and other free-trade agreements seek to give transnational corporations the right to buy and sell the water of countries that sign on to these agreements and to sue any countries that stand in their way. Many governments are turning the public control of their water over to global corporations, like Bechtel, that profit from this precious gift of creation. Plans are in the works to create a huge water-export industry, channeling it overland through pipelines and canals or hauling it across oceans in supertankers or in giant plastic bags.

Who will set the global price for water? The bottled-water industry, including Coke and Pepsi, may well lead the way.[54]

In a system where fresh water is captured, channeled, piped, and bottled for profit, who will provide water to wildlife? When the rivers and streams run dry, where will the animals go? How will the poor pay for the water they need to sustain life? How will human need compete with corporate greed in allocation of the world's water? As a resident of the high desert in New Mexico said, when his water was diverted for industry, "Water flows uphill to money."[55] Maude Barlow and Tony Clark write: "What lies ahead is a world where resources are not conserved, but hoarded, to raise prices and enhance corporate profits and where military conflicts could arise over water scarcity in places like the Mexican Valley and the Middle East. It's a world where everything will be for sale."[56]

FOOD INSECURITY

The sector of the economy that seems likely to unravel first is food. Eroding soils, deteriorating rangelands, collapsing fisheries, falling water tables, and rising temperatures are converging to make it more difficult to expand food production fast enough to keep up with demand.

—Lester R. Brown[57]

Meeting our need for food depends ultimately on edible wild species, seeds, sunlight, fertile soil, and the knowledge of farmers passed down in various cultures through generations. Until the Industrial Revolution, generations of subsistence farmers supplied their families' needs and traded or sold their excess crops. Many still do today.

But now market forces are at work, or rather, government policies that support corporations are at work, driving small farmers off the land. Global institutions such as the IMF, World Bank, and WTO pressure governments (1) to privatize land, including communal lands still held by indigenous people; (2) to put precious farmland to work growing cash crops for export instead of basic foods for their own people; and (3) to import basic foods from world markets. In this way, everyone is to become dependent on the global economy for the very sustenance of life itself. This puts human beings in a position of extreme vulnerability, especially those without money or political power.

Throughout the twentieth century, crop yields largely kept pace with the world's growing population, due to a seemingly endless supply of land, water for irrigation, and relatively cheap oil. The availability of these resources made possible modern industrial agriculture, which depends upon fossil fuels for fertilizers and pesticides, for powering mechanized farm equipment, for pumping irrigation water, and for transport of crops, food processing, packaging, and delivery of foods to global markets.

Challenges to our global food supply are many. Cropland around the world is shrinking due to development. Globally, we lose an estimated twenty-five billion tons of topsoil each year due to erosion, deforestation, overgrazing, development, and industrialized agriculture itself.[58] Deserts are spreading at the rate of 2.4 million acres a year.[59] As water tables drop due to the overpumping of aquifers and as oil reserves are depleted, it will become more difficult to produce enough food to meet human need. This will be especially true if people in developed nations continue to eat large quantities of meat, since a meat-based diet requires seven times more land than a plant-based diet.[60]

Water and oil shortages will eventually translate into food shortages. When this happens, food prices around the world will certainly rise. Lester Brown of Worldwatch Institute says that a steep rise in grain prices may well be the first sign of a global food crisis.[61]

Even now, we can see signs of a global food shortage. Since 1984, global grain output per person has fallen by 11 percent. Since 1989, the fish catch per person has fallen by 7 percent, due to depletion from overfishing.[62] By 2003, twenty-nine commercially fished species had collapsed; at current rates, "the world will run out of seafood by 2048."[63] Even as food sources decline, those who are wealthy or able to maintain a middle-class lifestyle continue to increase their consumption, which leads to further inequities. The poor and those in the middle will be squeezed as world population continues to rise.

As food, water, and other resources become harder to obtain, who will have access to them? These are gifts of God, our birthright, freely given to us, to future generations, and to all creatures. But the current global economic system does not recognize such rights and has no mechanism for a just distribution of goods.

Since the market is based on supply and demand, scarcity of any particular product leads to higher prices. Falling water tables and reduced global grain output will stimulate great demand for these goods and will enable transnational corporations to raise prices to whatever the market will bear. (This is the same phenomenon we have seen with oil—rising prices at the gas pump, with record profits for oil companies.)

With so many people now dependent upon world markets for basic foods, a sudden spike in world grain prices, triggered or compounded by shortages of oil or water, could wreak havoc, causing many who are living on the economic edge to slip into poverty, in both rich and poor countries, while many of the poor would slide from poverty to destitution, and without social support systems, to death. This hellish scenario would inevitably trigger social instability, ecological destruction, violence, and massive waves of migration, as desperate people use desperate means to try to keep their families alive. These trends, combined with other ecological challenges such as climate change, not only threaten the system of modern industrialized agriculture, but also present the specter of hunger and starvation on a massive scale.

This vulnerability is part of the price we pay for giving control of our food production, from seed to supermarket shelf, to global corporations. Their control is daunting, threatening food security on a global scale.

As with food, so with water. As we have seen, a few giant corporations are buying up control of the world's fresh water, in order to profit from its growing scarcity. If we allow a handful of profit-seeking transnational corporations to control the global food systems and the world's fresh water supplies, the human family and the earth's nonhuman creation will be in a grave situation, indeed.

The path we are on is unsustainable. We are heading toward more of what we are already experiencing: shrinking of social services, erosion of human rights, loss of jobs and weakening of labor standards, relaxation of health, safety, and consumer protections, hunger and thirst, growing police forces to repress dissent, increasing arms trade and military buildup, the undermining of democracy, a degraded earth. As the ruling Powers consolidate their control over human life and the earth itself, our slide down this slope accelerates, toward the pit of increasing human misery and social and ecological collapse.

GLOBAL COLLAPSE?

Will tourists someday stare mystified at the rusting hulks of New York's skyscrapers, much as we stare today at the jungle-overgrown ruins of Mayan cities?

—Jared Diamond[64]

Jared Diamond, one of our contemporary prophets, portrays today's ecological and societal challenges as urgent and grave. In his book *Collapse: How Societies Choose to Succeed or Fail*, he painstakingly documents several failed societies, both ancient and modern, and warns that we must learn from their mistakes in order to avoid a similar fate. He predicts that the current crisis will be resolved during the lifetimes of the children and young people living today. The only question is whether these problems will be resolved through learning from our mistakes and changing course, or through ecological and social collapse on a global scale.

Diamond's study of Easter Island provides a metaphor for today. Once richly forested, the island is now barren, without a single tree. But gigantic stone monuments, some standing, some fallen, still give tribute to the high chiefs or gods of the islanders who cut the trees to use as logs to roll and maneuver these statues into place. Easter Island also stands as a warning. In Diamond's words: "Today we have over 6 billion people equipped with heavy metal machinery such as bulldozers and nuclear power, whereas the Easter Islanders had at most a few tens of thousands of people with stone chisels and muscle power. Yet the Easter Islanders still managed to devastate their environment and bring their society to the point of collapse. That difference greatly increases, rather than decreases, the risks for us today."[65]

The factors that lead to the collapse of human societies are often interrelated. Ecological destruction may lead to poverty, migration, and competition over scarce resources. Poverty, migration, and competition over scarce resources may lead to social unrest and violence, even war. One problem leads to another, and the damage is compounded.

For example, a combination of factors triggered the genocide in Rwanda. In forty years, its population grew from 1.9 million to nearly eight million, making it the most densely populated country in Africa.[66] Rwanda suffered from extreme poverty, economic inequity, scarce resources (especially land), an unjust political system, the neglect of Africa by the international community, and a history of colonial domination that deliberately separated people who had lived together for centuries into "ethnic groups" (Hutu and Tutsi) based on apparent racial characteristics. None of these factors explain the Rwandan massacre that took place in full view of a paralyzed international community, nor do they explain the depths of the human capacity for evil. But, as Diamond points out, the Rwandan massacre is not an anomaly—it is a modern example of a "collapsed" society. Before the end, Easter Island, too, descended into a living hell of starvation, chaos, and violence, as did other failed societies, due to a convergence of factors similar to those listed above.

If we refuse to turn around as a global community, we face the massive suffering and extreme violence that has accompanied the collapse of individual societies. Will today's global crises be resolved by our conscious choice to establish just and sustainable alternatives to our present system or through lowered quality of life leading to ecological or social collapse?

These challenges bring to mind the principles of *equity* and *common heritage*, both of which are basic to our hope for a peaceful, just, and sustainable world. The current trend toward increasing inequity caused by corporate globilization must be reversed, so that wealth is more equitably distributed both within and among nations. Likewise, the commons must be protected, for all life depends upon the natural heritage of the earth, and all people have a right to share in the cultural heritage of humankind. Furthermore, as we have seen, our futures are interwined.

Fortunately, we still have choices. Alternatives are many, and are being explored in communities around the world. Like societies in the past, we now have to make decisions about values, consumption, governance, and our relationship to the rest of creation, for our choices will determine whether our now global society will succeed or fail.

Diamond raises the question asked by a student in one of his classes: "What could have been in the mind of the person who cut down the last tree?" By association, we must ask: What is in our minds as we participate in systems and lifestyles that are destroying the very earth that sustains us? What can we be thinking? And to what end? To what gods are we offering tribute? If it continues where will such idolatry lead?

CHAPTER SEVEN
The Infernal Whirlwind:
Violence, Terror, and War

> You have plowed wickedness, you have reaped injustice, you have eaten the fruit of lies. Because you have trusted in your power and in the multitude of your warriors, therefore the tumult of war shall rise against your people, and all your fortresses shall be destroyed . . . .
>
> —Hos. 10:13-14

On the morning of September 11, 2001, I was sitting in a coffee shop near my home. Word spread quickly from table to table that the World Trade Center had been attacked. I left quickly, wanting to find out more. I drove to the home of our friends, Jazz and Abdul, a young Afghan American couple who moved here and became citizens ten years ago. Like millions of other people around the world, we sat in front of the television, stunned, watching again and again the twin towers collapsing as people rescued others and tried to escape amidst clouds of dust, smoke, and debris. Jazz and I put our arms around each other and cried.

A month later we were again sitting together in their living room, watching as the United States bombed Afghanistan. Again we wept. CNN didn't interview survivors or show us injured Afghans, but Jazz and Abdul knew where their family members were in relation to the falling bombs. They were especially concerned about Abdul's sister and her family in Kandahar. After the bombing, no one heard from them for over a month.

They also worried about the effects of all this on their sons, Ali and Arya. Arya's kindergarten teacher was concerned as well. She told Jazz that he used to play with the other children, but now he was usually alone, building scenes with blocks and then "bombing" them. I had noticed the change in him as well. When I visited one day, Arya looked at me with his serious brown eyes. "They're bombing my people," he said.

In his work on the Powers, Walter Wink claims that the primary myth of our time is the "Myth of Redemptive Violence,"[1] which has its roots in the ancient Enuma Elish, a Babylonian creation story of the struggle between cosmic order and chaos. The theme of the myth is that order can be brought out of chaos by force and that evil can only be conquered through domination and violence. This story has been played out around the world for generations, and continues to be played out today.

The pervasiveness of violence among human beings brings to mind the ancient biblical story of Cain's murder of Abel and the subsequent multiplication of violence articulated by Cain's descendent, Lamech: "If Cain is avenged sevenfold, truly Lamech seventy-seven fold" (Gen. 4:24). It is this very cycle of violence that Jesus seeks to remedy when he tells his followers that they must forgive even seventy-seven (or seventy times seven) times (Matt. 18:22). Sadly, Jesus' rejection of violence and his embrace of nonviolence, so central to his life and message, have been ignored by many who claim to be Christian. And although it was the political, military, and economic Powers, supported by the religious establishment, that put Jesus to death, much of official Christianity throughout history has supported similar institutions and systems that are based on domination and violence. Walter Wink calls this changing but similarly interlocking network of worldly Powers "the Domination System." Others call it "empire."

Empires, too, function out of the myth of redemptive violence, under the illusion that domination and violence can bring order out of chaos and can conquer evil. Furthermore, empires seek to be ultimate and absolute, demanding people's loyalty and service. Those who resist are seen as enemies and subversives, as Jesus was.

We will look more closely at the interlocking network of institutional Powers that make up the current global empire in the next section of this book. Let us look now at the violence that pervades every level of the Domination System of today.

THE GOLDEN ARCHES THEORY OF CONFLICT PREVENTION

The greatest harm globalization does is to delude us with a make-believe pseudo-unity and universality of humankind.
—Felix Wilfred[2]

Violence has been part of the human story from the beginning, but the scale and scope of modern violence far surpasses that in all other eras of history. In *Unspeakable: Facing Up to the Challenge of Evil*, Os Guinness says: "To anyone who thinks deeper than the morning headlines, the atrocity of September 11 forms part of the wider record of the dark catalog of human evil in modern history and pales beside the worst of the evils. ...Leaving aside the one hundred million human beings killed in the [twentieth] century's wars, more than one hundred million more were killed by their fellow human beings in political repression, massacre, and genocide."[3]

The vast and "unspeakable" violence of the twentieth century should have put an end once and for all to the secular myth of human progress that came out of the Enlightenment, but it has not. Globalization proponents still point toward a future of peace and plenty and environmental balance made possible through technological progress driven by unrestrained market forces.

Thomas Friedman promotes "the Golden Arches theory of conflict prevention," since, he says, countries that have McDonald's don't (generally) go to war with each other.[4] The idea is that countries that are connected through business and financial interests will cooperate with each other, since it is in their best interest to do so. This is a primary argument in favor of free trade. Indeed, globalization proponents present the whole economic globalization project as a gradual, inevitable, unfolding process that leads to greater prosperity, stability, human well-being, democracy, and peace. But as Felix Wilfred points out in an essay entitled "Religions Face to Face with Globalization,"

> If globalization has been really bringing the whole world together, as claimed, it should have by now eliminated weapons of war from the earth. This is far from happening. Instead, conflicts and confrontations have escalated all over the world; small-scale wars are fought everywhere; and there is a growing threat to the whole of humanity and to nature. The poor and the marginalized are more and more excluded from power, freedom, participation and community. All this only uncovers the lie of unity being trumpeted by the acolytes of globalization.[5]

We have explored some of the human and ecological threats that accompany the expansion of global capitalism. We will now look at its violent underside, for violence pervades the global economic system at every level, and the system as a whole depends upon the threat of force. This includes the United States, for global capitalism originates in, proceeds from, and is dominated by the United States, and the U.S. military is the primary enforcer of corporate globalization.

Wealth inequality is a primary feature of our global economic system. As we saw in the previous chapter, corporate globalization, while bringing great fortunes to the few and improving the prospects of many, leaves in its wake vast enclaves of poverty and extreme inequity.

Inequality is clearly linked to violence. Unjust distributions of status, wealth, and power depend upon structures of domination and violence to support them and to control those at the bottom of the economic ladder who might rebel against such inequality. At the same time, extreme poverty and inequity can breed social instability, chaos, and violence. Victims of injustice, excluded from access to necessities, may be driven to violent acts as they seek to meet their basic human needs.

Since the U.S. government dominates the global economic system, many blame the United States for both its good and its harmful effects. People around the world are both drawn to the U.S. lifestyle, as portrayed by the corporate media, and resentful of it, since most people have no opportunity to attain the "American way of life." There is social disruption as traditional values are subsumed by images of graphic violence, commercialized sex, consumer products, and fast foods. People's appetites for consumption are heightened, but for the vast majority of people, these appetites will never be satisfied.

As Ian Barber points out in *Jihad vs. McWorld*,[6] there is a clash of cultures, as consumer culture spreads around the world and is met with impassioned and sometimes violent opposition from Islamic fundamentalists and other traditionalists who seek to protect their way of life from the influx of Western images and values. But these two competing worldviews do not explain the level of hostility toward the United States, which creates a milieu that nurtures and supports terrorists. To understand this degree of antipathy, we must look at U.S. foreign policy.

U.S. FOREIGN POLICY: THE VIOLENCE OF EMPIRE

"All of the kingdoms can be yours," the devil tells Jesus, "if you will just lord your power over others and take up the sword of the nations. Take charge of the biological weapons, deploy some troops, command the implementation of a 'Star Wars' missile defense system. All the kingdoms can be yours—if you will just use the world's means of power: domination and violence."
—Charles Campbell[7]

For many, the only solution to our increasingly violent and unstable world is for the United States, the only remaining superpower, to establish stability through global domination. The United States has been called an empire because of its dominant position among nations and the global reach of its corporations.[8] The United States supports the current global order by dominating the world politically, economically, and militarily. This has been called Pax Americana, loosely translated as "Peace, American–style."

Chalmers Johnson suggests that the United States should try to lead the world through diplomacy and example, not through economic domination and military force.[9] In his book, *Blowback: The Costs and Consequences of American Empire*, Johnson points out the drawbacks to U.S. foreign policy. The CIA first used the term *blowback* to refer to "the unintended consequences of policies that were kept secret from the American people."[10] According to Johnson: "'Blowback' is shorthand for saying that a nation reaps what it sows, even if it does not fully know or understand what it has sown. Given its wealth and power, the United States will be a prime recipient in the foreseeable future of . . . blowback, particularly terrorist attacks against Americans."[11]

Although proponents of corporate globalization claim that U.S. economic, political, and military dominance is positive and necessary for the sake of global security, the U.S. government itself acknowledges the instability caused by the current movement toward globalization. Every five years, the CIA releases a study that projects the greatest threats facing the United States within the following fifteen years. The CIA's 2000 report included the following projections:

> The rising tide of the global economy will create many economic winners, but it will not lift all boats. . . . [It will] spawn conflicts at home and abroad, ensuring an even wider gap between regional winners and losers than exists today. . . . Regions, countries, and groups feeling left behind will face deepening economic stagnation, political instability, and cultural alienation. They will foster political, ethnic, ideological, and religious extremism, along with the violence that often accompanies it.[12]

The CIA's 2005 report, "Global Trends 2020: Mapping the Global Future," reiterates these dangers of globalization and links them with terrorism: "Globalization will profoundly shake up the status quo—generating enormous economic, cultural, and consequently political convulsions. . . . The key factors that spawned international terrorism show no signs of abating over the next fifteen years."[13]

A global empire demands both the means and the willingness to use extraordinary military power. The United States backs up its foreign policy with the threat of military force, supported by the most advanced weapons that our scientists can invent and our tax dollars can buy. These include cluster bombs, land mines, weapons to induce blindness or dysentery, weapons to produce intolerable pain, chemical weapons, weapons based on nanotechnology, biological weapons produced through genetic engineering, and nuclear weapons. When such weapons are used, they create a living hell, reenergize the cycle of violence, and poison the earth for generations. Modern warfare is the most deliberate, immediate, and extreme way for the Powers to "undo creation."[14]

In spite of the all-out war on terror, few claim that the world is more peaceful or secure than it was before September 11, 2001. U.S. weapons have killed hundreds of thousands of Afghan and Iraqi people, mostly civilians. Both countries are in chaos. U.S. service personnel continue to be killed, wounded, and psychologically damaged. Atrocities abound. The cycle of violence continues.

Meanwhile, the danger of nuclear war, while less visible in the public eye than during the Cold War, continues to threaten humanity. The Bulletin of Atomic Scientists has moved the time on its "Doomsday Clock" closer to midnight. The clock now stands at five minutes to midnight, symbolizing the nuclear perils facing the human race. The scientists are concerned about a "Second Nuclear Age" that brings grave risks, including (1) the continuing "launch on warning" status of two thousand of the United States and Russia's twenty-five thousand nuclear weapons, (2) unsecured nuclear materials in Russia and elsewhere, (3) Iran and North Korea's "nuclear ambitions," (4) escalating terrorism, and (5) climate change, which is creating new pressures for civilian nuclear power that could lead to increasing nuclear proliferation.[15]

The United States continues to develop a new generation of nuclear weapons. U.S. nuclear policy is built upon the "plausible threat" of massive force. That is, the United States must convince others of its willingness to use whatever force is necessary, including nuclear weapons, in order for the empire to survive and expand its power.

The need to demonstrate a willingness to use massive force is also behind the logic that supports or turns a blind eye to the use of torture. News about Abu Ghraib, Guantanamo, secret CIA prisons, and terms such as *enemy combatants* and *extraordinary renditions* have brought the public into debates about the finer points of prisoner abuse.

But for followers of Jesus, who was tortured and put to death by the state, should it not be self-evident that torture is always wrong? What could be more dehumanizing for both perpetrator and victim than state-sponsored violence and torture? Violence breeds violence. Where will it end?

The Pax Americana, the so-called peace brought about by U.S. economic, cultural, and military domination, is no more peaceful than the Pax Romana of Jesus' day. Corporate globalization, enforced by U.S. military might, does not bring peace at all, but perpetuates the cycle of violence.

Nevertheless, the U.S. government shows no signs of changing course, but continues to protect corporate interests and promote the expansion of global capitalism through its foreign and military policy. The U.S. government promotes corporate globalization: the U.S. military enforces it.

THAT ONE GIANT, NECESSARY STEP

> Behind the spreading terror of nuclear and ecological catas-
> trophe is a pervasive sense that there is no one in control. The
> demonic has become the everyday policy of national leaders
> trapped in the momentum of a spirituality they can neither
> name nor discern, but which constrains them, against the best
> interests of humanity, toward rationalized suicide.
>
> —Walter Wink[16]

The human capacity for violence, combined with runaway technologies and modern bureaucratic processes, threatens all life on earth
with death and suffering worse than the agonies portrayed in Dante's
Inferno. Yet the ruling Powers of our age support, teach, model,
reward, and perpetrate violence at every level.

Today's system of global domination is idolatrous; it is working
at cross-purposes with God. But it is not inevitable, ultimate, or eternal, although it pretends to be. Empires come and empires go—God
alone is eternal. People of faith are called to put God above mammon
(Matt. 6:24), above the state (Acts 5:29), and above even the threat of
death (Matt. 10:28). This is as true today as ever, even though today's
empire of corporate globalization is the first truly global empire, and
even though it is enforced by the U.S. military, with the most terrible
and destructive weapons the world has ever seen.

The same forces of modernity that have brought us globalization
have magnified the destructive power of violence and the dangers to our
world. Many fear that terrorists will gain access to chemical, biological, or
even nuclear weapons, enabling them to launch massive attacks against
civilians in the United States or elsewhere. The threat of a nuclear confla-
gration continues to plague humanity. We face the danger of collapsed
societies descending into violence, or even global collapse.

Surely globalization has enabled us, through our communication and transportation networks, to be aware of what is going on
around the world. But this ability does not guarantee that aid will be
forthcoming. Sometimes the international community responds to a
crisis with an outpouring of generosity and goodwill, sending in relief
supplies or peacekeepers. Sometime aid does not come, as in Somalia
or during the Rwandan genocide.

We know some of the factors that contribute to violence among
human beings and can seek to alleviate them, but we cannot fully comprehend the human capacity for cruelty and malevolence. We do not
know what it is in the human heart or psyche that makes a Holocaust or
Hiroshima or Rwanda possible. As Os Guinness says, "In the face of such
wickedness, explanations born of psychology, sociology, economics, or

politics are pathetically inadequate."[17] Although faith can help us struggle with the meaning and implications of violence, nothing can "explain" it. Evil is a dark mystery, interpreted theologically through concepts such as original sin or the fall. William Stringfellow describes it thus:

> Violence describes all of the multifarious, inverted, broken, distorted and ruptured relationships characteristic of the present history of this world. Violence is the undoing of Creation. Violence is the moral confusion and practical chaos which, so long as time lasts, disrupts and displaces the truth and peace of Creation, which the Bible denominates as the Fall. Violence is the reign of death in this world and violence is the name of all and any of the works of death.[18]

Much of our history has been written in blood, and unless things change, it looks like it will continue to be. Unless we change course, we create an increasingly violent society and an increasingly dangerous world. We may even grow accustomed to the daily reports of atrocities. Perhaps this is the gravest danger—that we will get used to it. For this is soul-sickness of the first degree.

Modern technologies that make globalization possible enable us to see far more suffering than we can respond to as individuals. We can become so numbed by the scope and magnitude of interpersonal, institutional, and systemic violence that we turn a blind eye to the suffering of fellow human beings, afflicted with what some have called "compassion fatigue" and others have called "apathy" or "numbness." Our hearts become hard. We seem to have little input into the systems and processes that inexorably carry us along, together with the rest of the human family, toward some unknown end. At the back of our minds is a sense of unease, for we know that we are complicit, that somehow, without even wanting to, we give our consent to the present violent and unjust order.

That is why resistance to the dominance paradigm is so vital to faith, for the sake of our own spiritual well-being as well as for the sake of others and the well-being of the whole. A key to maintaining one's humanity is to speak out against evil and to take a stand for truth, compassion, beauty, and love. And that is why resistance must be based in the principle of nonviolence—otherwise it simply perpetuates the vicious cycle of violence at work in our world today. According to Ken Butigan, nonviolent resistance is "a form of embodied social change that actively and persistently challenges violent and unjust conditions, structures, or policies through non-injurious means." He goes on to say, "Nonviolent resistance is a process for challenging violence, but even more deeply it is an embodied practice that helps to free us from our faith in violence. . . . Nonviolent resistance is a spiritual practice and a way of being at the service of conversion, the transformation of ourselves, our communities and our world."[19]

Our only hope as a species is for a deep transformation of worldview and values that extends to our institutions and systems—in short, a spiritual renewal that motivates people to join with others to work for peace and to seek justice for all creation. Is such change possible? No one knows, but we can choose to step out in faith. In the words of Walter Wink: "The image of God, so near to extinction under the suffocating terrors of civilization, still holds out the possibility of change. We will never build a utopia on earth—but will we take that one gigantic, necessary step out of the system of power into a system of human values? The whole creation is on tiptoe, waiting."[20]

PART TWO

CORPORATE GLOBALIZATION

The System Is Designed for the Results It Is Getting

"The gravest effort of the principalities is the capture of humans in their service, which is to say, in idolatry of Death . . . ."

—William Stringfellow

CHAPTER EIGHT
The Powers of This World

> However many evil men hold places in the American establishment, they are far, far outnumbered, by my tally, by those bereft of conscience, so pathetically have they been dehumanized by the principalities and powers for which they are acolytes. [1]
> —William Stringfellow

We live in a world that radiates the grace and power of God, but we are also faced with terrible evil. We are seeing such damaging effects of human activity, grave violations against other human beings and against the natural world: the loss of biodiversity, climate change, toxic pollution, harmful technologies, growing inequity, social disruption, violence, terror, and war. The current global crisis can only be explained by facing the reality of evil.

Although the topic is usually avoided, even in many churches, evil is an obvious and pervasive reality. In addition to incredible beauty and amazing love, we have also received a legacy of sin and brokenness, which, tragically, we pass on to others. We experience God's love and much that is good and valuable in human life and in the natural world. And yet we see, feel, and even participate in attitudes, behaviors, and systems that are destructive. How can this be explained?

Discussion of sin and evil is usually limited to the topic of the personal immorality or sinfulness of individuals or groups of human beings. The primary focus is on specific "sins," that is, personal weaknesses, perversions, moral failings, and deliberate violations of generally accepted standards. People assume that society's evils are simply the combined effects of the personal wrongdoing of many individuals.

But are that many people really that bad? Can this explanation account for the pervasiveness of political corruption, social disruption, economic injustice, and environmental devastation? On the contrary, many people who have high standards of personal morality and who see themselves as kind and generous are deeply, if unwittingly, involved in systems that are moving the world toward destruction.

In the movie *The Remains of the Day*, Anthony Hopkins plays an aging Austrian butler who prides himself on his loyalty to the man he has served for many years. He devotes himself to duty and undertakes each task with exquisite care, whether serving tea, tending to household duties, or giving instructions to the other servants. One evening, in the midst of an elaborate dinner party he has organized, he discovers that the dinner guests are Nazis and that the man he has served all these years has become part of the inner circle of the Nazi elite. Although this butler has always seen himself as honest, hardworking, and dedicated to duty, he realizes now that his service to this man has had an effect on the larger patterns of history. He realizes that he has been participating in evil.

We can practice seemingly virtuous behavior while serving an institution that causes harm, without acknowledging or even recognizing our contribution to the damage being done. "Good" people can participate in destructive systems. All of us, to the degree that we benefit from and support these systems, are implicated in the harm they cause.

Personal morality is an essential aspect of spiritual growth and responsible participation in the world, but how can we determine what is "good?" Standards of morality vary from culture to culture, and are largely determined by religious, economic, and political institutions. What is defined as "good" by a particular society can actually be harmful to certain groups of people, to other societies, or to the world as a whole. This fact is usually obscured by our immersion in the culture in which we live and in the institutions that dominate it.

It can be difficult to determine what is good or evil, helpful or harmful, in many situations. In our globalized world, enmeshed as we are in institutions and systems that have effects that we cannot see, it can seem almost impossible. Still, we are not left in the dark, without help in discerning a positive path. In spite of their shortcomings and historical misuse, the world's great spiritual traditions can help orient us by pointing us toward the living Spirit, who cuts through confusion and gives us light.

John Wesley said, "Sin is the refusal to acknowledge our dependence on God for life and breath and all things."[2] In light of what we now know about the interconnected web of life, we can adapt Wesley's definition of sin in the following way: "Sin is the refusal to acknowledge our dependence on God for life and breath and all things, and our interdependence with the rest of creation." This way of looking at sin seems especially fitting in light of the damage being done to the human family, other creatures, and the earth itself.

Stated positively, we might look at virtue as faithfulness to God and compassionate and just relations with all parts of creation. It is a version of what Jesus said was the greatest commandment: to love God above all and our neighbor as ourselves, extending the idea of neighbor by including our nonhuman neighbors within our circle of care and concern.

But, like the butler in the movie *The Remains of the Day*, it is not enough to weigh our personal behavior without considering how our actions contribute to larger patterns of good or evil in the world. Sin is not simply an individual matter; it is also social. Evil is not just personal; it is also institutional.

SOCIAL SIN AND INSTITUTIONAL EVIL

> For these prophets a spiritual form of life had to include responsiveness to the hunger or anguish of those around us, as well as seeing and resisting the authority of the arrogant and privileged who controlled the kingdom.
>
> —Roger Gottlieb[3]

The prophets of ancient Israel did not usually just focus on individual sinners, but called the whole Hebrew community to account. They challenged not just individuals about their own personal sins, but the whole community for creating and participating in a sinful and unjust society. The prophets particularly challenged the representatives of the people, those in positions of authority: judges, kings, prophets, and priests. Leaders were especially obligated to establish justice and not to lead the people astray, but society as a whole was called to "let justice roll down like waters and righteousness like an ever-flowing stream" (Amos 5:24).

The gravest social sins emphasized by the prophets were idolatry and injustice. The Hebrew people were to love God above all else, to worship and serve God alone, and to create a just society. They were not to worship false gods, place their security in weapons of war, or accumulate wealth at the expense of the poor. They had a duty to provide for the needy and to protect society's most vulnerable members. If they went astray in these areas, the prophets claimed that the society was on the wrong track and needed to repent, that is, change course. Each time the people ignored the prophets' warnings, disaster resulted.

Jesus, too, warned people against idolatry and injustice. He proclaimed a message of justice and liberation, and demonstrated these values in the way he lived. He demonstrated what it means to love God above all else and taught that loving and serving others is a way of loving and serving God. Jesus specifically admonished people not to store up treasures on earth, saying, "You cannot serve God and mammon" (Matt 6:24b, RSV). He challenged the well-to-do and representatives of the established order to be more just in their dealings with the poor and oppressed. He announced the coming of a new order of justice and compassion, and stood against the social sin and institutional evil of his day. In the end, it cost him his life.

WHEN MAMMON BECOMES A GOD

> The Kingdom of Mammon exercises constraint by invisible
> chains and drives its slaves with invisible prods. . . . But
> Mammon is wiser in its way than the dictator, for money
> enslaves not by force but by love.
>
> —Walter Wink[4]

Social sin and institutional evil can have a deep impact on individuals within a given society. Take idolatry, for example. In America today, and throughout the world as consumer culture spreads, the idolatry of money is pervasive. Temples are built to this god, elaborate shopping malls and luxurious dwellings that glorify wealth and extravagance. Corporations design clever jingles that are deliberately geared toward getting people to consume, then play them again and again on television and radio until these mantras sink deep into our unconscious minds. People pay to be walking advertisements, to wear T-shirts, jackets, and shoes with corporate logos. Our young imprint themselves with the mark of corporate idols, enjoying the status that comes from wearing clothes that bear the symbol of popular brand names.

When Mammon becomes a god, the sin of greed becomes a virtue. People are valued according to how much money they have, or by how much they contribute to the economy as investors, workers, or consumers. Plants, animals, and land are reduced to "resources" and "property" whose value is measured by their ability to generate profits. When these idolatrous views become institutionalized as the basis for public policy, people are victimized and the natural world is exploited. In this climate, people's self-image and understanding of their place in the world is likely to be affected by how much money they have.

In a radio interview,[5] a teenager told what it was like to be homeless from the time he was seven until he was ten years old. His family once had a nice home, where his friends often came to spend the night. When they lost their home, he and his family lived in their car, in shelters, and on the streets. The boy still went to school and had the same friends, but he didn't want to admit to them that he was homeless. The sense of shame about his family situation was even worse for him than was the actual experience of being homeless, so he made up elaborate lies to explain to his friends why that they could no longer visit him. He convinced them that his mother was seriously ill and dying. While this child suffered the hardship of homelessness, his overriding experience was a sense of shame. The message he received from society was, "It is shameful to be poor."

In a society that serves the god of Mammon, people's sense of morality can be distorted. Their loyalty to God can be divided and their spiritual understanding can be confused. The wealthy become role models. The poor may become scapegoats. As William Stringfellow said, "The idolatry of money means that the moral worth of a person is judged in terms of the amount of money possessed or controlled. . . . Where money is an idol, to be poor is a sin."[6]

But poverty is not necessarily evidence of sin, laziness, or even bad luck. Wealth is not necessarily evidence of virtue or prudence. In a country like the United States where there is extreme inequity, both wealth and poverty may be the fruit of unjust social policies. On a worldwide scale, where rich and powerful nations dominate the global economic system and set the terms of finance and trade for poorer, weaker nations, those who benefit may not simply be enjoying the rewards of sound financial policies. On the contrary, as Walter Wink points out, "Those of us who now enjoy affluence and freedom as well as power are predisposed to believe that benign forces shape our destiny. But to the extent that our blessings are incidental by-products of our citizenship in nations that currently enjoy dominion status over others, our well-being may be more a result of flagrant injustice than divine providence."[7]

Sin resides not only in the human heart, but also in the "Powers," that is, in societies, institutions, ideologies, and systems that influence, shape, inform, and act upon human beings. Moral weaknesses and deliberately sinful choices made by individuals are not enough to account for the extent of evil in our world today.

We must also consider the apathy, moral blindness, and enslavement of human beings that is engendered by the Powers. This, too, can be called "sin," but it is largely unrecognized, unacknowledged, or accepted as inevitable. To acknowledge the influence of the Powers over human beings does not excuse individual actions, nor does it take away the moral accountability of the individual before God. Rather, it increases it by adding another dimension: the responsibility of the individual in relationship to the Powers.

THE POWERS DEFINED

> **For our struggle is not against blood and flesh, but against the rulers, against the authorities, against the cosmic powers of this present darkness, against the spiritual forces of evil in the heavenly places.**
>
> —Eph. 6:12

The concept of the Powers comes from the New Testament idea of the "powers and principalities," which is "a generic category referring to the determining forces of physical, psychic, and social existence."[8]

Biblical names for these forces include: "principalities, powers, virtues, thrones, authorities, dominions, demons, princes, strongholds, lords, angels, gods, elements, spirits (Luke 8:29-33; Gal. 4:3; Eph. 2:1, 6:10-13; Col. 1:15-16, 2:10-23)."[9]

According to William Stringfellow, the "powers and principalities" referred to in the Bible are not vague, amorphous forces, but actual institutions, structures, and systems. They include "all authorities, corporations, institutions, traditions, processes, structures, bureaucracies, ideologies, systems, sciences, . . . all images, all movements, all causes, all corporations, . . . all methods and routines, all conglomerates, all races, all nations, all idols. . . . The principalities and powers are legion."[10]

The concept of the Powers goes beyond institutional, systemic, and social forces. The Powers include inner psychic and spiritual forces, including archetypes, the gods, angels, and demons of myth. They include the forces of nature, the outer, physical, as well as the inner dimensions of the natural world—the "elemental spirits," the forces of nature and the very depths of matter. As Walter Wink says, "All of social reality falls under the category of the Powers, and a good slice of physical and psychic reality as well."[11]

This book, however, focuses primarily on the institutional Powers, their effects on the world, and their effects on human beings. Particular emphasis is given to "the Powers that be," that is, the dominant institutions of our age.

THE INNER DIMENSION OF THE POWERS

> These powers usually consist of an outer manifestation and an inner spirituality or interiority. Power must become incarnate, institutionalized, or systemic in order to be effective.
> —Walter Wink[12]

The external aspects of the institutional Powers are obvious: their by-laws, written policies, resources, structures, actions, and physical effects. But institutions, structures, and systems also have an inner dimension, an "interiority" or "spirituality" that can be discerned as well.

When you walk into a McDonald's, it has a certain "feel" to it. The same is true of your place of work, your local library, your church, or the Pentagon or White House—each has its own culture or milieu. You could call this the spirit of the place. Each institution has a within that includes its core values, ideology, and ethos, both written and unwritten. Institutional Powers exhibit not only external, physical attributes such as buildings, symbols, or resources, but internal or spiritual manifestations as well.

Where do these institutional Powers come from? What are their origins? Human beings are social animals, like many other animals: birds gather in flocks, lions in prides, fish in schools. Humans are created to live in community. We evolved within families, clans, and tribes. Throughout human history we have arranged ourselves in various expanded social groupings: villages, cities, nation-states, global institutions. We have developed systems of thought: creation stories, ethics, ways of thinking about the world through religions, myths, and philosophies. We have found ways to organize human societies, creating various roles and divisions of labor, developing different ways to trade within and among groups, creating currencies and ways to buy and sell. The purpose of these organized patterns of culture and systems of thought is to nurture our species and provide for our needs. The vocation of the Powers is to nurture life.

So how do the Powers go awry? People create institutions for a variety of reasons: to nurture life and serve the common good, to advance their own self-interested goals, sometimes to accomplish both. People create institutions to promote agendas that may either help or harm human beings or the earth. They invest their energy and resources in these institutions, serve them, become loyal to them, and promote and defend them. In this way, institutions gain power and authority over human beings. When an institution invested with authority assumes this degree of importance in people's lives, the survival and growth of the institution itself may become paramount. This tendency is always present, regardless of the initial purpose for which an institution was created.

What many people do not realize is that institutions are not simply groups of individuals working together. Invested by human beings with authority, institutions tend to take on a life of their own, to develop their own personality, goals, ethos, culture, milieu. As an institution becomes larger, wealthier, and more powerful, individual human beings within the institution have relatively less control over what it does. Those who rise to positions of authority within the institution generally do so because they support and further its overall goals.

In other words, an institution is more than the sum of the human beings who make it up. It is an actor, a protagonist, an agent, interacting for better or for worse with human beings, with other institutions, and with the nonhuman parts of creation. It is a Power. In a very real sense, through the people who make it up, it takes on a life of its own.

In theological terms, one could say that the Powers are primarily concerned with their own survival and growth, even at the expense of mortal human beings. An institution demands loyalty from those who identify themselves as part of the institution, that is, those who have vested themselves in the institution and have an interest in furthering its goals. In Stringfellow's words:

> The principalities preempt God by their demands for obeisance, service, and glorification from human beings (Rev. 13:1-6). . . . The principality, insinuating itself in the place of God, deceives humans into thinking and acting as if the moral worth or justification of human beings is defined and determined by commitment or surrender— literally, sacrifice, —of human life to the survival interest, grandeur, and vanity of the principality.[13]

When this happens, people end up serving the institution, instead of the institution serving life. People are dehumanized in the process of furthering institutional goals. They may even be reduced to behaving as cogs in the institutional machine, without conscience or choice, serving as slaves or acolytes of the institution. As Stringfellow put it: "Corporations and nations and other demonic powers restrict, control, and consume human life in order to sustain and extend and prosper their own survival."[14] This is evil, says Stringfellow, even "demonic." It is a form of idolatry, in which the institution takes the place of God in people's lives.

In order to be at ease in such a situation, we need to turn off our powers of discernment, critical thinking, and moral agency, that is, our ability to freely choose to do what is good and right. We need to turn a blind eye to any harm done by the institution, or to any disconnection between our personal morality and the morality of the institution. We have to go into denial, become defensive, support the institution's decisions, and act accordingly. In other words, we have to become less than fully responsible and discerning human beings, in order to carry along the goals of the institution without objection. This means rationalizing and justifying our participation, that is, lying to ourselves.

Sometimes these systems, structures, and institutions take over and destroy rather than nurture life. When people serve institutional goals rather than living as full and free human beings, they are in grave spiritual danger. The Powers can become false gods, idols that demand loyalty, obedience, sacrifice, and even praise. People may die or even kill for them, without even realizing the Powers' inner, psychic effects or their effects on the outer world.

Instead of being faithful to their true vocation of nurturing life, the Powers attempt to survive, extend their authority, and reign supreme. Stringfellow attributes this dynamic to the "fallenness" of the Powers.

THE FALLENNESS OF THE POWERS

> The Powers continue to fulfill one half of their function. They
> still undergird human life and society and preserve them from
> chaos. But by holding the whole together, they hold it away
> from God, not close to Him. They are "the rulers of this age"
> (1 Cor. 2:6). In their desire to rule they are in enmity toward
> the Lord of glory, who can suffer them only as instruments,
> not as lords.
>
> —Hendrik Berkhof[15]

The doctrine of the fall is a theological attempt to reconcile the belief in a loving God and an original "good" creation with the reality of evil and suffering in the world. It is based on the ancient story in Genesis 3 about the sinful disobedience and expulsion of Adam and Eve from the Garden of Eden.

When this ancient tale is taken literally, all evil, suffering, and death results from the "original sin" of these first two human beings. Elements of this story have been used to justify male domination of women and human domination of the natural world.

If we believe in an evolving universe, however, we know that suffering and death are not simply the consequences of human sin. Death is part of the cycle of life, and suffering is part of life as we know it in a physical universe. In other words, what has been called natural evil, that is, mortality, is not evil at all, but part of the ongoing cycle of life.

But the concept of the fall, taken as a cultural and spiritual myth,[16] can provide us with theological language with which to discuss the problem of moral evil and sin in the world. It is a way of describing the human experience of the seemingly incongruous situation in which we find ourselves: in relationship with a loving God yet aware of radical evil in the world.

Indigenous people lived, and millions still do, in tribes with various forms of social organization. Many were nonhierarchical and respectful of the natural world. This demonstrates that hierarchy, violence, and exploitation are not integral to human association. Native peoples have much to show us about how to live creatively, cooperatively, and sustainably in the future. This is not to say that native societies are perfect or idyllic or that evil is not a problem in such cultures, simply that human communities can be more or less peaceful, just, and sustainable. They can carry out their intended purpose: to nurture and serve life.

The nurturing, positive qualities of human associations can also be observed in many institutions, such as some churches or other nonprofits that serve the homeless, support the families of prisoners, educate, advocate, or provide other needed services. Such organizations, however imperfectly, serve and foster life. The amazing growth in the numbers and strength of nonprofit organizations around the world has created a global network of groups working for a better world, providing positive models of human organization that can help guide us into the future.

None of these institutions are perfect. Some are hierarchical. Fraud and corruption can break out in any organization. Disagreements and personality conflicts can develop. Mob mentality can take over. This is part of what is meant by the idea of the fallenness of the Powers.

Furthermore, in any organization, the survival needs of the organization can usurp the original purpose for which it was created. Institutional demands can assume more importance and use up more resources than the service the institution was meant to provide. In this case, it, too, shows its "demonic" aspect, to the extent that it demands the subjugation of human beings to its own institutional goals. This in itself is dehumanizing. All institutional Powers are prone to this occurrence.

Stringfellow's claim that the Powers are "fallen" is a descriptive statement, not a historical one.[17] It acknowledges that although institutions and systems have a role in serving life, their purposes are often perverted. This idea is a way to describe the negative effects of the Powers without blaming them on God.

SPIRITUAL EFFECTS OF THE POWERS: A PARALYZED CONSCIENCE

> There are persons who have become so entrapped in tradition, or, often, mere routine, who are so fascinated by institutional machinations, who are so much in bondage to the cause of preserving the principality oblivious to the consequences and costs either for other human beings or themselves that they have been thwarted in their moral development.
> —William Stringfellow[18]

The negative external effects of the Powers at work in the world today are not too difficult to see: environmental destruction, growing inequity, violence, and so on. But the internal effects are what prevent most people from effectively engaging the Powers. These internal effects are apathy and moral deadness, what Stringfellow calls "a paralyzed conscience"[19] or "moral decadence."[20] This condition is pervasive in America today. Many people are enslaved or enthralled by the Powers, or are beholden to them. This dehumanizing bondage of body, mind, and spirit enables the Powers to have their way with individual human beings, and have their way in the world.

Stringfellow is relentless in his criticism of "the American institutional and ideological ethos," which, he says, "incubates a profound apathy toward human life . . . ." He speaks of the "silent majority" of people in the United States who are "morally retarded," "deprived of moral insight," suffering from "moral impoverishment," "stupefied as human beings, and thus relieved of moral sanity." He speaks of "the cruel and somber daily existence of the multitudes of automatons of lower status and lesser privilege" and of people in places of power and authority who have become "immobilized as human beings by their habitual obeisance to institutions or other principalities as idols." He goes further:

> There are those who actually define their humanity as non-human or subhuman loyalty and diligence to the interests and appetites of the principalities. There are many who are dumb and complacent in their captivity by institutions, traditions, and similar powers. There are persons who have become automatons. There are humans who know of no alternative to an existence in vassalage to the principalities. There are people who are programmed and propagandized, conditioned and conformed, intimidated and manipulated, fabricated and consigned to role-playing. There are human beings who are demonically possessed.[21]

Stringfellow's analysis is harsh. It does seem, though, that many people in the United States are comfortable with or resigned to the current state of affairs. The Bible describes this condition as "hardness of heart." The Powers capture the conscience:

> You will indeed listen, but never understand,
> and you will indeed look, but never perceive.
> For this people's heart has grown dull,
> and their ears are hard of hearing,
> and they have shut their eyes;
> so that they might not look with their eyes,
> and listen with their ears,
> and understand with their heart and turn—
> and I would heal them. (Matt. 13:14b-15)

There are also many soft-hearted people who are genuinely concerned and want change, but feel that nothing they do will have any effect on the anonymous economic, political, and technological forces that seem to be in control. People feel powerless to stop them, and so retreat from engagement with these Powers into the personal sphere. But retreat, too, amounts to consent and participation in the direction the Powers are leading, which is in the direction of global death.

At some level we all know that if we do not take responsibility, our children or grandchildren will have to deal with the consequences of our inaction. For instance, at some level everyone must know that society's addiction to fossil fuels is unsustainable. But people feel powerless to stop, hopeless about significantly changing what seems to be the inevitable course of events.

The demons of anxiety, apathy, denial, despair, rage, helplessness, and hopelessness are pervasive in our culture. They are the other side of the colorful media images of seemingly endless choices of products and entertainment opportunities. People try to lock out the reality that threatens the future, and the Powers are quite willing to help. In fact, that is what they require of human beings: to become less than fully human and to leave the Powers in control.

According to Stringfellow, the challenge is to maintain our humanity, even in the midst of the dehumanization that is going on all around. The primary ethical question is, How can we live humanly in the midst of the fall? "Any viable ethic . . . is both individual and social. It must deal with human decision and action in relation to the other creatures, notably the principalities and powers in the very midst of the conflict, distortion, alienation, disorientation, chaos, decadence of the Fall."[22]

How can we live humanly, enmeshed as we are in a global system that is creating misery, destroying life, and threatening the future? In times when social sin and institutional evil are pervasive, the only way to maintain our humanity is to resist.[23]

Resistance can take many forms. Resistance grounded in faith begins with spiritual struggle. In the words of James Douglass: "In solitude, in the depth of aloneness, lie the resources for resistance to injustice. Resistance arises first from a perception of suffering and from the assumption of one's own responsibility to seek the transformation of a murderous system into a human society. . . . In the age of genocide, to be human is to resist."[24]

BABYLON, THE BEAST, AND THE DRAGON: ARCHETYPES OF THE POWERS

> The crimes of the greatest military and economic empire in history make the Apocalypse an even more living prophecy in our day than it was to the embattled Christians of the first century.
> —James Douglass[25]

The apocalyptic images in the book of Revelation seem frighteningly real in this age of global crisis. The vision of disasters and woes poured out on the earth remind us of the grave dangers we face, from collapsing ecosystems, pollution of our air and waters, collapsing economies leading to widespread famine, or nuclear holocaust.

Fundamentalist Christian groups choose certain passages in Revelation as evidence that the "last days" are upon us. This idea scares people into submitting to certain doctrines, including the belief that the Bible must be taken literally. This deterministic form of Christianity exacerbates the very problem that is threatening our souls and the earth itself. It rejects the human abilities of discernment and thought, and promotes passive acceptance of the status quo, stealing energy that could be used to address problems and create solutions in this world by focusing attention on the afterlife, that is, by glorifying death. Hence, such belief systems support the Powers and their rush toward global destruction.

The book of Revelation contains ideas that can be helpful if looked at in a different way. The author of Revelation was not writing about today's events, but about the spiritual and political struggle of the time in which it was written. The catastrophic events described in the book were meant to describe events of that time theologically as well as politically, giving the persecuted Christian community a context for their faithfulness and spiritual motivation for resistance.

But the apocalyptic language and imagery in Revelation describe events that are, in a sense, always happening. This, too, is a form of myth, with both political and spiritual content. As myth, its images and stories can serve as metaphors to help interpret current reality. Revelation provides an analysis of the material and spiritual reality of the powerful institutional forces that work against life, represented by the images of Babylon, the Beast, and the Dragon. It presents a call to Christians to resist the domination of empire, even at the cost of persecution and even to the point of death.

In the book of Revelation, the archetypal demonic Power is represented by Babylon, the nation that had defeated Israel and taken the Jewish people into captivity. But Revelation was written over five hundred years after these events took place, using Babylon as a symbol of the Roman Empire, the nation that was dominating Israel and persecuting Christians in the author's day. At that time, it would have been dangerous to write anything overtly critical of Rome. Apocalyptic literature was a form of political writing that made sense to those to whom it was addressed, similar to political cartoons of today. Early Christians knew that "Babylon" was Rome.

The visions in the book of Revelation reveal the spirit of the Roman Empire to be Babylon, the archetype of a fallen nation, a nation full of idolatry, greed, exploitation, and violence. The Beast was simply another metaphor for Rome, and the various heads of the

Beast represented the Roman emperors who came and went, as the nation continued on. With amazing insight, the visions also reveal the satanic power, symbolized by the Dragon, which dominated Babylon, Rome, and every other evil and idolatrous institution and system that has come to power throughout the ages.

In biblical terms, the Beast is the personification of a political entity—the Roman Empire. It is an institution, a Power. People worship it as an idol and are enslaved by it. It is motivated by an insatiable appetite for its own survival and the expansion of power. This evil institution directly opposes the goodness of God. It opposes life. It generates fear, demands obedience, and leaves destruction and misery in its wake, wreaking havoc on the earth.

A System of Global Domination

My plea [to Americans] is for freedom from this awful naïveté and for healing from this moral flaw. My hope, therefore, as a human being, begins in the truth that America is Babylon.
—William Stringfellow[26]

In *An Ethic for Christians and Other Aliens in a Strange Land*, Stringfellow overlays these metaphors from the book of Revelation onto the world situation in the mid-twentieth century. He draws parallels between the devouring appetite and the destructive power of ancient Rome, portrayed as Babylon and the Beast, and contemporary America.

Walter Wink, too, sees the demonic at work in the United States. He believes that Martin Luther King, Jr.'s declaration in 1967 that "the United States is the greatest purveyor of violence in the world" is truer now than when it was uttered:

But we do not feel possessed. . . . We go about our lives largely oblivious to the demon, kissing our children before school, patting the dog, being polite to the bus driver. We are sane, civilized, perhaps a bit too given to violence and sadism on TV, but by common national consent still the most genial people on the face of the globe. We do not see that the demonic has been installed at the heart of national policy. The nation (administration, Congress, armed forces, CIA) carries out for us the dirty work required to maintain American political and economic dominance in the world. Most of us would rather not know the bloody tale of deeds performed on our behalf. We are content to be beneficiaries . . . [27]

But Wink goes beyond America in his analysis of the Powers. He speaks of the whole grid of interlocking worldly authorities and systems that he calls the "Domination System,"[28] an overarching system that includes the dominant political, economic, social, and religious institutions of any given age. The Domination System, the interlocking network of institutional Powers that seeks to control human life, is a manifestation of the satanic system represented in Revelation by the Dragon, which has been playing itself out in countless ways throughout human history.

When William Stringfellow wrote *An Ethic for Christians* in the 1960s, he considered nations to be the preeminent Powers, with greater relative power than other institutions. Since that time, transnational corporations have expanded their reach, accumulated ever-greater wealth, and consolidated their control. Their influence over governments and global institutions lead many to claim that we are living in a time "when corporations rule the world,"[29] as David Korten's book by that title suggests.

The point is arguable. Corporations are still in an uneasy tension with governments and global bureaucracies. We will look at these complex relationships in coming chapters. But the power of corporations relative to these other institutions is growing quickly. Corporate wealth and power are being consolidated, and corporate rights are being institutionalized. We are quickly moving toward a form of globalization dominated by huge transnational corporations that promote their agenda at every level of human society.

The most powerful and obvious manifestation of the Domination System in this early part of the twenty-first century is the global network of political, economic, and military institutions that make up the system of corporate globalization, designed by the United States and imposed upon other nations, dominated by corporations, and enforced by the most powerful weapons the world has ever seen. Another word for it is empire.

A GLOBAL SYSTEM RUN AMOK

> Behind the spreading terror of nuclear and ecological catastrophe is a pervasive sense that there is no one in control. The demonic has become the everyday policy of national leaders trapped in the momentum of a spirituality they can neither name nor discern, but which constrains them, against the best interests of humanity, toward rationalized suicide.
>
> —Walter Wink[30]

Though the United States still dominates world events in many ways through economic pressure and military force, corporations are growing in power relative to governments, including the United States. U.S. policies support the system of corporate globalization, since it is seen to further U.S. interests, but the United States does not control this global empire, nor does any other nation. And although human beings consent to it and participate in it, human beings do not directly control it either.

The system that is overseeing the destruction of the earth has a life of its own and functions largely on automatic pilot. Even those people who make the rules and set its course are acting within the framework set by the system itself. In this system, like the emperors of ancient Rome, presidents, CEOs, and heads of global institutions have a degree of power, but in reality, they are replaceable. The system goes on. In order to rise to power within the system, they have to support the dominant ideology and generally accepted practices of the system as a whole, probably without even knowing that they serve a system that is idolatrous, in rebellion, and working at cross-purposes with God. They are rewarded by the system, but they are still its acolytes, servants, or slaves. Only rarely does a person who serves in a high position of authority within the system have the moral insight and courage to break out of the dominant paradigm and challenge the foundations of the system as a whole.

Even those of us who benefit from the system in small ways and simply go about our daily lives contribute to the problem. Until we recognize the underlaying flaws of the system of which we are a part, we are blind to its milieu and to its effects on our lives.

No one is a true beneficiary of this system of corporate globalization, for its goal is its own expansion and survival. As it acts for this purpose, through human beings, it opposes life itself. This Beast, figuratively speaking, is running amok. It is on a rampage of destruction, devouring the earth. Its work is "the undoing of creation."[31] It has the power of life and death over people, and uses economic as well as military power to enforce its will. It is responsible for growing injustice and oppression. It is the ultimate manifestation of the idolatry of Mammon, the god of money. The degree of death and destruction caused by this global system as a whole can only be attributed to evil—ultimate evil, which the biblical authors identify as demonic, even satanic.

This is not to claim that the personified "Satan" is an actual entity. Rather, according to Wink,

> if Satan has any reality at all, it is . . . as a profound experience of numinous, uncanny power in the psychic and

historic lives of real people. Satan is the real interiority of a society that idolatrously pursues its own enhancement as the highest good. Satan is the spirituality of an epoch, the peculiar constellation of alienation, greed, inhumanity, oppression, and entropy that characterizes a specific period of history as a consequence of human decisions to tolerate and even further such a state of affairs.[32]

In the following chapters we will take a closer look at this global empire, at the institutions that make up this system of corporate globalization, at how the system is designed, at the underlying ideology that supports it, and at the institutional momentum that is propelling us toward a hell on earth. These topics are painful. As the awful truth of our current situation dawns on us, it becomes clear why many would rather stay in denial. But we can't afford that luxury; time is too short. Besides, the path of denial leads to darkness and spiritual death. It also leads us further along the path of complicity to evil and destruction. For unless we recognize the extent to which the Powers control human life and the direction they are taking us, we will fail to see how extreme is the crisis we face, and we will fail to understand the depth of our need for divine aid.

Furthermore, the future has not yet been determined. The structures of the global economy are not absolute, and the direction it is moving is not inevitable. It continues only with the willing conformity and active compliance of the masses of people who support it, either knowingly or unknowingly. Without this support, it cannot survive.

There is yet hope for the earth if enough of us reclaim our identity and our authority as children of God, refuse to go along, and choose another path. As people around the world join together to resist global domination and to develop life-giving alternatives, hope becomes more real, creative change becomes possible, and in the process we learn to live as fully human beings.

CHAPTER NINE
A Modern Parable:
The Beast of Corporate Globalization

Resistance is not futile.

—Banner seen at WTO protest

Star Trek, the popular science-fiction television series, has been running off and on for over thirty years, through several incarnations. In a recent series, *Star Trek: Voyager*, the greatest alien threat to the heroic crew of the *Voyager* space ship is the Borg, a "Collective" made up of living beings that have been captured from various planets throughout the universe. Borg "drones" do not have a sense of individuality, but share in a collective consciousness.

The Borg travel through the universe colonizing cultures, incorporating what is valuable and distinctive about different species to enrich their Collective. They incorporate the knowledge and abilities of other species telepathically, taking advantage of their weaknesses in order to assimilate them, the Borg's power growing ever stronger.

Technology is all-important to the Borg, who despise anything "flawed, weak, human." They "improve" the species they conquer by implanting devises into their bodies that will enhance their utility and keep them technologically connected to the Collective, under constant surveillance and thought control.

When the Borg move in to conquer a planet, they announce, "Your culture will be adapted to service ours" and "We will add your distinctiveness to our own." As the nightmarish, robotlike drones approach their intended victims, they counteract potential opposition by announcing, "Resistance is futile. You must comply." This is their theme and their ongoing refrain. They count on the power of suggestion to take away the will to resist, so that other species will simply surrender in the face of the Borg's overwhelming psychic, physical, and technological power.

The Borg even have an ideology with which they justify their incredibly evil form of empire building, based on a bizarre concept of "seeking perfection" through the unlimited expansion and growth of their culture. They consider themselves to be on a quest for perfection since they are assimilating all the wonderful and diverse qualities of species throughout the universe into themselves. Through this process of assimilation, they claim to be bringing other species closer to perfection as well. They see the whole colonization process as a way of evolving toward perfection, to a sort of "higher mind." Of course, the drones don't question this logic. They simply serve the interests of the Collective, no questions asked.

Like the Beast in the book of Revelation, the Borg can serve as an up-to-date myth or metaphor as we talk about corporate globalization. I am not using this image to refer to any particular institution, but to the culture and network of institutions that make up the system of global free-market capitalism as a whole. Following chapters will include an overview of the global economy and the specific institutions that make it up. For now, I am simply using the Borg as a metaphor to illustrate the overall system of corporate globalization and the worldly Powers that promote it, the individuals who support it, and the bizarre ideology that attempts to justify even the most harmful aspects of the globalization process.

COLONIZING THE PLANET, ASSIMILATING THE EARTH

> In amazement the whole earth followed the beast..., saying,
> Who is like the beast, and who can fight against it?
> (Rev. 13:3b-4)

The current global economic system is a monster, a "Beast" more scary and dangerous than any science-fiction story. The Beast of corporate globalization grows ever bigger, incorporating more and more of the earth's surface and assimilating more and more of its creatures. It drinks in pristine rivers and lakes, excreting toxic effluents into aquifers and oceans and onto the surface of the earth. It inhales clean, fresh air, exhaling poisonous fumes. It eats up fertile land, leaving deserts behind. It consumes majestic old-growth forests, spewing out clear cuts. It colonizes the earth.

Wealthy corporations, along with many governments and global institutions, support this Beast and conceive of its goals as their own. Complex webs of competing and complementary interests maintain a tenuous stability in this global economic system and hold these various institutions together. No individual human being or group of human beings is in charge of this system. It is rather like the Borg, with people acting together in a collective way to support the overall goal of global capitalism: to expand indefinitely, incorporating cultures and natural species throughout the world into one integrated market economy that encompasses the whole earth.

Commercial spokespersons and government figureheads, generals and CEOs serve this Beast, carrying its goals and ideology forward. Investors eagerly feed it money, betting on large returns. Individuals are conditioned and adapted to serve it as compliant workers and eager consumers in order to increase corporate profits and further overall economic growth. The Beast of corporate globalization has no use for people who are destitute, the unemployed, or others who do not fit into the market economy, so it renders them invisible and expendable. It puts economic growth and corporate profits first, demands the obedience of human beings, and employs police and military power to enforce its will.

Most people who have economic or political power portray the process of corporate globalization in a positive light, appealing to the dominant economic ideology that undergirds this system with logic that is similar to that of the Borg. They argue that trade liberalization, endless economic growth, and integration of the global economy will lead to peace and prosperity (the quest for perfection), and furthermore, that it is inevitable ("Resistance is futile!"). They justify the process of cultural assimilation by appealing to the superior value of Western-style industrial development, which, so the argument goes, leaves cultures better off than they were before (bringing them closer to perfection).

With this kind of development, of course, corporations lead the way. Media networks owned by huge conglomerates transmit satellite images of Western sitcoms and advertisements around the world, marketing not just products but a superior way of life. Mega-corporations such as Nike and Wal-Mart roam the world to find places to set up sweatshops where there are weak labor and environmental laws and where they can take over the businesses and markets of local artisans and small-business owners. Amid charges of "bio-piracy," pharmaceutical corporations search remote jungles for unique species of plants and animals, then try to coax secrets of healing from indigenous people so that they can patent the knowledge. Military and paramilitary forces protect Western interests such as oil drilling or rain-forest development projects from indigenous or other subsistence communities who have lived on their lands for generations. In even the poorest countries, fast-food restaurants like Burger King and McDonald's serve burgers and fries to wealthy customers who are protected by armed guards as famished children roam the streets outside.

Corporate globalization assimilates cultures and people into one huge global marketplace. Some people benefit. Many have moved from subsistence living to wage jobs and new opportunities. But this process of assimilation extinguishes both cultural and biological diversity, as transnational corporations dominate agriculture and trade, and as they exploit the wealth of nature, pollute the earth, destroy communities, and put farmers, artisans, and small-business people out of work. Subsistence farms with diverse crops are lost. Corporate-run farms take their place, growing monoculture crops that require extensive use of pesticides and chemical fertilizers. Patented, costly, genetically modified seeds that must be purchased each year replace varied seed stocks that have been developed and saved for generations. Colorful community marketplaces where neighbors buy, sell, and barter give way to shopping malls. Traditional forms of work give way to sweatshops. Species are lost to what Vandana Shiva calls "maldevelopment," as the earth is paved over for strip malls, walled housing complexes, and parking lots. Indigenous cultures are extinguished. Even human genes are patented and put up for sale. People around the world who have depended upon the natural world for their subsistence become dependent upon the global economy, immersed in the values portrayed by Western commercial media, plugged into jobs in corporations, dependent upon low wages to purchase essentials—all from corporations. Those who cannot make it in the global market economy are left behind.

And yet, all this is done as if it is in the best interest of all concerned. The U.S. government and the rulemaking institutions of the global economy, such as the World Bank, International Monetary Fund, and World Trade Organization, promote this style of development and sing its praises, in spite of resistance from citizens' groups around the world. The standard economic ideology so dominates discussions of economics that other views are usually dismissed or ignored altogether. Public officials, economists, corporate executives, and media representatives rarely question the generally accepted view of economic development and world trade. The underlying ideology that supports corporate globalization is pervasive; it is a given. This entrenched worldview dictates economic policies and limits creative alternatives. It functions as a collective mind-set that expresses the "spirit," that is, the inner dimension, of the network of Powers that make up the Beast of corporate globalization.

This ideology includes an unquestioning loyalty to the value of technology. Computers, though they do enhance individual access to information and grassroots organizing efforts, bring far more benefits to corporations and governments as ever-expanding tools of surveillance, money transfer, and the waging of war. Television, controlled by corporations, pervades households in the United States and around the world, delivering the official line on current affairs, promoting a commercialized version of American culture, and delivering the corporate message that purchasing commercial products brings happiness. Nuclear and other military technologies continue to advance, making possible increasingly sophisticated weapons of mass destruction.

Genetic engineering and nanotechnology are progressing in ways that threaten to change the course of life on earth, moving us away from all that is "flawed, weak, human." Yet public discussions rarely focus on whether particular technologies should or should not be developed. Those decisions are primarily left to corporations.

Although some individuals, groups, and institutions benefit in the short term from corporate-led globalization, its long-term and overall effects are harmful, and its immediate effects are devastating to many vulnerable people, including children and the poor. The system of corporate globalization is the latest manifestation of the Domination System. It is a new form of imperialism; like ancient Babylon and imperial Rome, it seeks to dominate the whole world. Together with the institutional Powers that support it, this monolithic system seeks to colonize the earth and to assimilate people, cultures, and other species into an integrated, homogenous whole, modeled upon Western corporate culture. Its goal is its own survival, which depends upon its increasing profits and expanding power. It is evil, it is demonic, and right now it has the upper hand.

In the long term, however, this system itself, as powerful and absolute as it may seem, is unsustainable. It is based on the faulty premise of human dominance over the natural world, supported by the seemingly inevitable advance of technology. But as the earth's natural bounty is depleted and as its ecosystems fail, this idolatrous system, too, is destined to collapse. God is the only absolute, and if we lose sight of that reality and live beyond the natural limits God has set for us as created beings, we do so to our peril.

Like the Borg, the interlocking network of political, economic, social, and military institutions, which together make up the global capitalist system that seeks to dominate the earth, functions as a Collective that tends to dehumanize and disempower human beings. It is a monster, a "Beast" in the biblical sense, and though it is not sentient except through us, it acts in a coordinated way to sustain itself and to expand its power. People serve it, benefit from it, or are victimized by it, but individual human beings do not control or direct it. In other words, the system is driven by its own imperatives.

RESISTANCE IS NOT FUTILE

The Powers are limited by the very presence of men who will no longer let themselves be enslaved, led astray, and intimidated, against whom the program of the Powers, that is, their effort to separate men from God, suffers shipwreck.
—Hendrik Berkhof[1]

Like the Borg in *Star Trek*, as the dominant system assimilates more and more people and places, its constant message is that such assimilation is inevitable, that "resistance is futile." And yet our only hope is in resistance, since this system, overall, is working at cross-purposes with God. It is engaged in "undoing creation" and consolidating the reign of death. In such a situation, the only moral stance is one of resistance, for compliance means bondage and complicity. Resistance, on the other hand, means freedom and hope for both personal and social transformation.

To illustrate this hope, let us return for a moment to the spaceship *Voyager*. One crew member is a former Borg. She was born human, but the Borg killed her parents and assimilated her into the Collective at an early age. The valiant *Voyager* crew later helped free her from the Collective. She retains the name given to her by the Borg: "Seven of Nine." It took Seven a tremendous initial effort to regain her inner freedom and individuality. Several episodes have focused on her ongoing struggle to resist the Borg's continuing efforts to reclaim her. As they try to reassimilate her, the words "resistance is futile" resound in her mind, almost overpowering her.

In one episode, Seven is helping another drone who has managed to break free from the Collective. As the Borg pursue the drone, who is still connected through technological implants, both he and Seven hear their "billions of voices speaking as one," saying, "Resistance is futile. You must comply."

"We must resist that voice," says Seven. "The *Voyager* will be destroyed if we don't." In the end, knowing that the Borg will pursue him throughout the universe, the drone sacrifices his life rather than continuing to endanger the spaceship crew. He is a Christlike figure resisting the temptation to give in to the influence of evil, even though it costs him his life.

This myth of resistance to overwhelming psychic, ideological, technological, and military pressure to comply echoes the challenge in the book of Revelation and the examples of the martyrs and the calls of the prophets through the ages. It also recalls William Stringfellow's appeal to live as fully human beings, in resistance to the dehumanizing influences of the Powers. And so we are challenged to form supportive communities and to act as people who have been set free from the power of death, seeking to see, hear, and understand what is at stake for ourselves, for future generations, and for the whole community of life.

CHAPTER TEN
Economic Insanity:
An Overview of the Global Economy

> This is a new strategy for accumulating capital, which is called the strategy of globalization. . . . This strategy—and its blind pursuit—is a sort of fundamentalism of the religion of the market. . . . Free-market fundamentalism has become the fundamentalism of Talibans of the religion of the myth of infinite growth.
>
> —Franz Hinkelammert[1]

Sitting in a coffee shop one day in downtown Santa Cruz, I tested my economic literacy by reading several articles in the "Business Day" section of the *New York Times*. A headline caught my eye: "Snow Urges Consumerism on China Trip." According to the article, U.S. Treasury Secretary John W. Snow was touring China to promote "financial modernization," urging the country "to take lessons from the United States on how to spend more, borrow more and save less."[2]

It seems that the Chinese are saving too much—50 percent, while U.S. savings have slipped to less than zero. China has thriving markets and an economic growth rate of 9 percent per year, far above that of the United States. But Snow was trying to convince China that it needs to save less, and to consume and borrow more.

Snow's task was a hard sell, "awkward," according to the article. In Mulan, a village in the Sichuan province, Snow "wandered through a thriving farmers' market," where he said, "Good credit facilitation and consumer finance is going to help consumers buy more things." At a traditional rural credit cooperative, he urged them to use more "objective judgments of risks and opportunities" when making loans because "capital is getting into the hands of those who cannot make the best use of it."

Snow was promoting "financial products" such as loans, stocks, and credit cards to be provided, of course, by U.S. banks and other financial firms. According to the article, "Administration officials are also backing efforts by Wall Street firms to let American companies own a controlling stake in financial firms in China."

The U.S. government needs to close its trade deficit with China. It needs markets for U.S. products, and so it continues to push. This kind of economic pressure and proselytizing by U.S. government officials is a common practice in countries around the world. But as we have seen, overconsumption is already devastating the planet. The earth cannot afford U.S. consumption patterns to be expanded to the rest of the world. And yet, our leaders can see no other path than to promote policies that lead to global death. Who is in control of this system? And what choices do our "leaders" really have?

THE MANIC LOGIC OF GLOBAL CAPITALISM

> **I wish we could slow this train down, I told Adeeb, but there's no one at the controls.**
>
> —Thomas Friedman[3]

Thomas Friedman describes the global economic system as a fast-moving train with no one at the controls. He and many other proponents of the current form of globalization are aware of its dangers and drawbacks, but see its growing momentum as inevitable.

This perspective is understandable. Not only individuals are seemingly helpless in the vast, complex, interconnected global economy. As economist Lester Thurow points out: "National governments are losing their ability to control their own economies, since financial wealth can easily be held outside the jurisdiction of one's own government."[4] Likewise, corporations and financial institutions must adapt themselves to the rapidly changing global landscape and take advantage of the economic opportunities of the moment or lose out to their competitors. "There's no one at the controls."

In his book, *One World, Ready or Not: The Manic Logic of Global Capitalism,* William Greider uses the metaphor of a gigantic machine to illustrate the "free-running economic system that is reordering the world," that is, "modern capitalism, driven by the imperatives of global industrial revolution".[5] He says, "Imagine a wondrous new machine, strong and supple, a machine that reaps as it destroys. As it goes, the machine throws off enormous mows of wealth and bounty, while it leaves behind great furrows of wreckage. Now imagine that there are skilled hands on board, but no one is at the wheel. . . . It is sustained by its own forward motion, guided mainly by its own appetites. And it is accelerating."[6]

Greider seems to agree with Friedman when he says, "no one is at the wheel." He says, "No one can be said to control the energies of unfettered capital, not important governments or financiers, not dictators or democrats."[7] At the same time, he points out that "there are skilled hands on board." Although the global economic system tends to perpetuate itself and to create its own dynamics, it does require human participation at every level, including the highest levels, where decisions are made to continue the present course, to restrict or increase momentum, or less likely, to change direction or turn around.

Usually the decision makers are "true believers," so thoroughly invested in the system, immersed in its ideology, and aware of its imperatives that they can't see or act outside the box. In this sense, the global economic system is out of human control. As with other institutional Powers, it has its own tendencies and momentum (metaphorically one could say its own goals—that is, to survive, expand its reach, and extend its power). But these goals can only be realized with the consent and participation of human beings.

At the most basic level, people participate simply by going along with things as they are, by taking the path of least resistance, by complying with a system that they feel powerless to change. The myth that the direction things are moving is inevitable increases their sense of powerlessness. It seems like anonymous forces are at work, that no one is in control, so people don't know where to start, where to apply pressure to bring change.

But the forces that propel us along the current course are not anonymous at all. They are embodied (incarnate) in very concrete and specific institutions and representative human beings, that is, in the Powers. As Anthony Giddens points out in his book *Runaway World*, the economic forces at work in the world today are "not of nature, but shaped by technology and by decisions of governments to liberalize and deregulate national economies."[8] In other words, the direction we are headed is neither accidental nor inevitable—it is by design.

In working with churches on renewal, Ezra Earl Jones, former general secretary of the General Board of Discipleship the United Methodist Church, promoted the following idea: "The system is designed for the results it is getting. If you want different results, you will have to redesign the system."[9] Neither churches nor any other institutions get to be the way they are by accident. They are paying off in some way for somebody.

This becomes obvious when we look at the system of institutions that make up the global economy, and at who creates the rules, who benefits, and who pays the price. If we follow the money, we will see that the system is designed for the results it is getting. The architects, rule makers, and enforcers of the global economy are reaping the benefits of what they have designed.

Those who make the rules of the global economy do so for a particular purpose: to keep the money flowing to international banks and corporations, to keep the interest payments coming in and stock prices going up so that the system as a whole does not collapse. The rules are not designed to provide a just distribution of the world's goods, but to protect and multiply wealth. They are not designed to preserve the earth, but to turn its gifts, such as forests and water, into money. They are not designed to improve the lives of the majority of human beings, but to bring financial benefits to the few. The machine of the global economy is not simply out of control. It is not malfunctioning. It is functioning according to its own rules, and continually expanding those rules and making new ones. As William Greider points out, there is a "manic logic" to global capitalism. The system is not just out of control. It is insane.

Nevertheless, global capitalism does have an ideology that supports and justifies it. Most who have risen to power within this system have adopted its ideology and goals as their own. They serve as its high priests or acolytes, preaching its idolatrous doctrines of salvation through unrestricted free trade and endless economic growth, demanding conformity to its principles, excluding those who cannot or will not fit in, persecuting those who resist. In many ways, the ideology that supports corporate globalization is more than a set of economic principles or guidelines. It functions more like a religion.

Market Fundamentalism: The Religion of Mammon

The Market is becoming more like the Yahweh of the Old Testament—not just one superior deity contending with others but the Supreme Deity, the only true God, whose reign must now be universally accepted and who allows for no rivals.

—Harvey Cox[10]

Theologian Harvey Cox began reading the business section of the newspaper after a friend suggested that this was where he would find out what was going on in the real world. To his surprise, Cox found the language of economics quite familiar. He writes of a comprehensive "business theology" based on a belief in the market as God: "Behind descriptions of market reforms, monetary policy, and the convolutions of the Dow, I gradually made out the pieces of a grand narrative about the inner meaning of human history, why things had gone wrong, and how to put them right. Theologians call these myths of origin, legends of the fall, and doctrines of sin and redemption . . ."[11]

Jesus warned, "You cannot serve God and mammon" (Matt. 6:24), but the ideology of corporate globalization would have us ignore that counsel. The foundation of this ideology is the love of money, "a root of all kinds of evil" (1 Tim. 6:10). It knows nothing of the sanctity of life or the call to faithful and just living, but takes a purely utilitarian view. It supports a user-based approach to life by promoting an ideology that expresses the inner dimension, or "spirit," of the complex web of institutions that make up the global economic system. The dominant ideology that undergirds this system has been called "Market Fundamentalism."[12] Because it functions as a secular religion, I will use capitalized words to describe it in terms similar to how we describe other religions. Market Fundamentalism has its own economic orthodoxy that, for the most part, is unquestioningly accepted. It is an idolatrous religion, because it makes a god out of the Market. It puts money above all else. This religion has its own high priests, those economic advisors, corporate executives, and government officials who make the rules and oversee the functioning of the economic system as a whole. It has its own saints, people who have attained the success that the system promises: millionaires and billionaires, CEOs and media moguls, sports idols and movie stars, people who make it all seem possible, people upon whom we can pin our hopes. It has its own symbols, corporate logos such as the Golden Arches and the Nike swoosh that can be seen everywhere. This religion prepares children as candidates for confirmation through corporate links to schools and universities and the privatization of public schools. The religion of Mammon has its own sacraments: you have to be baptized with at least some of the money upon which the religion is built in order to partake of the "means of grace," the fast foods or caviar, depending upon what level of success you have attained. This religion encourages the use of its rituals, such as investing in the stock market and shopping, whether you have a lot of money or only a little to invest or spend. (The manic aspect of consumer culture is especially apparent before Christmas, when it contrasts so markedly with the somber purples that symbolize the message of repentance during Advent, creating a strange and discordant synchronizing of religions.) This religion has its own preachers, whose message is carried by commercials that promote its sacraments and rituals, by news programs that carry its official ideology, and by sitcoms and other programs that are steeped in its milieu.

To understand the strange logic of this secular religion, we have to understand its doctrines: its object of faith, foundational values, goals, and hopes. The secular religion that supports corporate globalization is based upon these basic "articles of faith" of economic theory:

- the sanctity of the Market
- the value of self-interest
- the goal of generating wealth
- the vision of limitless economic growth

The object of faith, the god or idol at the apex of this belief system, is the Market, whose "Invisible Hand" supposedly allows the greatest good to flow to the greatest number of people through the Universal Law of Supply and Demand. Governments are supposed to have faith in this higher power and interfere with it as little as possible. In order for the Market to do its mysterious work (its wonders to perform), it must be set free from government interference. (Governments interfere with the free Market by making laws that regulate banks and corporations, provide public services, establish a social safety net, and protect the commons.) For this reason, free market enthusiasts push privatization, deregulation, and cuts in social services. The essence of free-trade agreements is to spread this religion of unregulated free-market capitalism around the world.

The Right Reverend Frederick H. Borsch, former bishop of the Episcopal Diocese of Los Angeles, writes satirically about faith in the Market in an article entitled "Pry Loose the Cold, Hard Fingers of the Market's 'Invisible Hand'": "Capitalism . . . has proved to be universally successful. Indeed, almost all government is evil to the extent that it does not keep hands off the hand. Markets based on self-interest, and that take into account and even sanction natural human greed, are the only way to sort out economies and people. Blind faith in an invisible hand becomes a form of piety. . . . All praise to the hand."[13]

If the object of faith in unrestrained free market global capitalism is the Market, the primary value upon which it is built is self-interest. From this foundational value (so the logic goes) comes the well-being of the whole community. Individuals and businesses who act in their own self-interest, seek to "maximize their utility" and compete with each other, contribute to the well-being of the whole economy and all its various parts. Companies that are allowed to act freely in their own self-interest, in competition with each other, are motivated to make high-quality goods to meet the demand for such goods. In turn, consumers acting in their own self-interest buy the best goods, stimulating further competition and, thus, improved quality. Successfully competitive companies provide jobs for people and provide wages that allow workers to purchase goods, which helps to keep the whole system going.

The Market works best, however, when people (and corporations) act rationally according to the values of this system—that is, when they act in their own self-interest. In this way, natural human competitiveness is harnessed for the greater good, allowing the Market to produce goods and offer services efficiently, for the benefit of all concerned. Self-interest is the engine that drives the whole system and keeps it going.

Adam Smith developed his basic theory of capitalism over two hundred years ago in vastly different circumstances, and qualified his theory by saying it would only work if capital remained local and if private-property ownership was widespread. Neither of these conditions is true today, but capitalism's faith in the Market and the value of self-interest still remain.

The primary goal of capitalism is to generate wealth, that is, capital. Capital is not simply money earned as wages, but profit, money made over and above the costs of doing business. Capital also refers to the means of production, that is, the factories, tools, and other equipment used for manufacturing. The idea is that profit can be invested and the means of production can be employed to generate more capital, in an ongoing cycle of economic growth.

The vision that springs from these ideas is of a world growing ever richer and more technologically advanced. People everywhere will gain access to the "good life" that is available in the United States. Advances in technology will allow us to clean up the environment and end world hunger. Poor countries will develop along Western lines, with fast-food restaurants, computers, televisions, and cars. And, its advocates say, countries linked economically will have the incentive not to go to war with each other. Globalization will create a truly global village of material abundance, understanding, and peace.

According to this vision, in a globally integrated capitalist system, with each country gaining a comparative advantage in a particular area by contributing the best of what it has to offer, with increasing efficiency and technological advancement, with ongoing development and decreasing trade barriers, the global economy will continue to expand, and its benefits will be shared with all the people of the world. This utopian vision is based on belief in the possibility and necessity of limitless economic growth. If the economic pie continues to get bigger, no one will have to take a smaller piece, and there will be more pie to go around. This is a central premise of capitalist doctrine, for without growth, wealth cannot be generated. There is no capitalism without economic growth.

Clarity about these basics can help us to understand how the global economic system works and why it works in the way it does. And since almost all government and business leaders accept this economic ideology, it becomes clear why they support the policies they do.

For example, government policies often favor big business—but why? Besides the obvious influence of corporate money in politics, government leaders generally believe that supporting big business is good and necessary for society as a whole. After all, corporations have lots of capital, so giving them incentives to invest it stimulates the economy and helps the economy to grow. From this perspective, it also makes sense for corporate leaders to have input into decisions made by government and global institutions in areas that affect them. Corporations may have more expertise in these areas than lawmakers, with studies and data to back them up, and can assist government officials in creating conditions that are favorable for growth. It makes sense for the government to give corporations subsidies and to cut their taxes and interest rates, because such moves free up money that can be reinvested to create yet more wealth, leading to more jobs and products and development and economic growth.

Corporate policies, no matter how heartless, can also be justified from the perspective of this underlying economic ideology. When corporations restructure, they often cut jobs and show record profits in the same year, but this doesn't seem so bad if we believe that when corporations act in their own self-interest to generate profits and raise the value of their stocks, they are doing exactly what they are supposed to do according to the basic values, goals, and beliefs of the system. (Besides, this is what they are required to do by law.) Returning to these basic tenets can help explain most aspects of the global economy from the point of view of the current economic orthodoxy.

You will rarely hear alternative views in the mainstream press, except when, rarely, the message of protesters breaks through the sensationalized reports about the growing protests taking place at economic summits around the world. Usually, though, these dominant economic concepts are simply taken for granted. They are part of the milieu in which we live. When we hear them, they seem to make logical sense unless we are grounded in something deeper and more real: in the earth, in the love of God that is showered upon us through the creation; in a sense of the sanctity of life; in the bonds of love that we have for each other and the interdependence that we share with all creation; in the teachings, life, death, and resurrection of Jesus, who showed us who God is and what human life can be when lived in faithfulness to God; in the vision of peace on earth and goodwill to all creation; in the gift of discernment that enables us to appreciate true wealth, which has nothing to do with money; in the freedom to live as fully human beings. From this vantage point, we can look at reality with eyes that see through the economic dogma that colors everything, with ears that hear through the "doublespeak" and "overtalk" that muffles the truth, with hearts that understand both the faulty assumptions and the grave implications of where this unjust and idolatrous global system is taking us.

We will now look more closely at how this system works, and at how completely it depends upon the ideology/religion that justifies it.

Together, this system and ideology are pushing the world toward corporate-dominated globalization, toward the ever-greater generation of wealth, and toward the ecological destruction and human misery that accompany it. If we keep in mind the basic teachings of the economic ideology that supports corporate globalization, we can follow the thread of these beliefs as we seek to understand the big picture of the global economy and the rationale behind it. As you will see, it is built upon a foundation that is faulty, and the system as a whole is idolatrous, unjust, and unsustainable.

THE GOLDEN STRAITJACKET: THE RULES OF THE GLOBAL ECONOMY

> The Golden Straitjacket is the defining political-economic garment of this globalization era. The Cold War had the Mao suit, the Nehru jacket, the Russian fur. Globalization has only the Golden Straitjacket. If your country has not been fitted for one, it will be soon.
>
> —Thomas Friedman[14]

The global economic system is made up of a network of institutions: governments, corporations, banks, regional and global trade agreements, and global institutions. These Powers relate to each other in a complex web of mutual cooperation and competition in ways that keep the overall system going.

Progress toward the vision of global economic and cultural integration, that is, assimilation, requires governments to allow the market to decide how money flows around the world It requires governments to stop interfering with market forces. For this reason, ironically, a global "free market" requires rules—lots of rules. These rules are based on faith in the Invisible Hand of the Market; they require governments to "keep their hands off the hand" so that human beings and corporations acting in their own self-interest will be able to compete with each other, thus generating profits and stimulating economic growth.

Thomas Friedman has coined a term for the system of "golden rules" that countries must follow: "The Golden Straitjacket." The rules that are imposed on governments require them to:

- gear their economies toward export
- offer incentives to entice corporations to invest
- privatize public services, utilities, and other industries
- deregulate private utilities and other industries

- cut spending on social programs
- eliminate currency controls
- eliminate all barriers to free trade

In short, the rules press governments to remove any laws that might interfere with the free movement of corporations, the free flow of goods, and especially the free flow of capital.

Who gets countries to put on the Golden Straitjacket? The rule-making institutions of the global economy, such as the IMF, World Bank, and WTO.

Poor countries have been wearing the Golden Straitjacket for years. The World Bank loans money to poor nations for development projects, usually large, expensive industrial development projects that help the World Bank meet its lending targets. When countries find themselves in economic crisis and have trouble paying the interest on their debt, the World Bank and the IMF step in to give them new loans or to guarantee loans from private banks so they can refinance their debt and infuse additional money into their economies. These lending institutions make these loans available only on the condition that these countries enact the structural adjustment policies that they dictate. That is, these countries must put on the Golden Straitjacket. Poor countries are told that the rules will enable them to develop along Western lines and help their economies grow.

We will return to this topic in a later chapter to explore the actual effects of these policies on various countries. For now, let us just acknowledge that the Golden Straitjacket does not always benefit the people in the countries that put it on. In one country, it may be too tight in the belly; in another, it may need a little padding in the shoulders, but as Thomas Friedman also points out, this Golden Straitjacket is "one size fits all."[15] It may not fit right, but a country has to wear it. It is "the only model on the rack this historical season."[16]

The WTO, NAFTA, and other free trade agreements enforce similar rules among their member nations. These institutional Powers create and enforce complex systems of rules that regulate international trade and investment by restricting the authority of governments in order to grease the wheels of free trade and investment, integrate the economies of member nations, and (supposedly) create a level playing field so that all member nations, rich and poor alike, can have equal opportunity to benefit. Such agreements require governments to eliminate quotas that limit imports, protective tariffs that make imports more expensive, and all other nontariff barriers that might limit the free flow of goods and capital across borders. In this way, foreign companies have the same access and opportunity to invest, produce, and sell goods and services in a country as domestic companies do.

The WTO gets countries to put on the Golden Straitjacket through dispute tribunals, where the government of one member nation can challenge the laws of another by claiming that certain laws are nontariff barriers to free trade. These trade barriers may include environmental or labor laws, consumer-safety standards, or human-rights laws. If a defendant country loses its case it must agree to change its offending law or pay a voluntary settlement fee; otherwise the WTO will approve tariffs to be imposed on its products. The official position of the U.S. government is that it will change its offending laws in order to comply.

NAFTA has an enforcement mechanism that is even more rigorous than that of the WTO. Through NAFTA a corporation can directly sue a government for lost profits, that is, for profits that the corporation might have earned if the government had not had its offending laws.

WTO and NAFTA tribunals have usually ruled in favor of plaintiff governments and corporations and against defendant governments, forcing governments to change their laws or pay to keep their laws in place. We will look at specific trade disputes in later chapters.

The WTO and regional free-trade agreements give governments strong incentives to "keep hands off the hand."[17] Although wealthy nations seek to impose such rules inequitably, that is the supposed goal of free-trade agreements: to remove government interference and to give the market free reign across borders around the world. The elimination of government restrictions on foreign corporations is the essence of what free trade or trade liberalization is all about. It gives freedom to corporations to move production, goods, and capital in and out of countries at will. It extends the Invisible Hand of the Market across borders, so that corporations (seeking their own self-interest) can compete with each other around the world.

Note that the Golden Straitjacket is for governments to put on. The rules of the global economy are for governments to follow, not corporations; they give rights to corporations without corresponding responsibilities. And although corporations benefit from these rules, they do not even sign onto trade agreements—these are for governments to sign and follow. As you can see, free trade is not free at all, but highly protectionist. It protects large corporations from laws created by government.

Since corporations have great influence over these rulemaking institutions, it is no surprise that the rules benefit them. Still, for those who accept the articles of faith, all this makes perfect sense, since they believe that self-interested corporations competing with each other to seek maximum profits keep the global economy growing. So this global extension of the power of corporations to get governments "off their backs" is a logical next step.

The rules of the global economy are not imposed on countries in a uniform way, nor are they in effect everywhere. But comprehensive new trade agreements are being negotiated, such as the proposed Middle East Free Trade Area (MEFTA), and the General Agreement on Trade in Services (GATS) in the WTO. If passed, these agreements will restrict the freedom of governments and expand the rights of corporations even further, moving us toward the consolidation of corporate rule.

A CASINO ECONOMY

> Momentum trading, trend-following currency speculators, overleveraged hedge funds, and corporate managements obsessed with daily fluctuations in share quotations are unlikely to produce the optimal distribution of scarce resources in the global economy.
>
> —Edward Chancellor[18]

The stock market, like other markets, supposedly functions through the Invisible Hand, which is supposed to provide goods efficiently through the law of supply and demand. But ironically, through the stock market, money is no longer primarily a means through which people exchange goods and services; money has become an end in itself. For the most part, the stock market is not engaged in trading anything tangible, such as goods and services, but in the trading of money. The majority of these financial transactions are not related to anything concrete, but are simply electronic blips that show up somewhere on a computer screen. What has been called a paper economy is increasingly becoming an electronic economy, with little connection to the real, physical economy of human beings and the earth.

As a matter of fact, the global economy as a whole functions largely without reference to the physical economy. World trade amounts to around $3 trillion a year, while world financial transactions amount to over $100 trillion a year. In other words, less than 5 percent of global financial transactions are related to the actual trade of goods. In a book called *Economic Insanity: How Growth-Driven Capitalism is Devouring the American Dream*, author Roger Terry states: "Both the world economy and the American economy are growing more and more distant from the real world in which people eat, sleep, live, work, die, and consume. The mitotic propagation of money has totally overwhelmed the direct, beneficial type of transactions in which people buy and sell products to better their lives."[19]

Thomas Friedman calls the millions of people who invest in the stock market the "Electronic Herd," since there is something of a herd mentality to the way the whole system functions. Fickle investors transfer huge sums with the click of a mouse, depending on how the economic wind is blowing, pouring money into and out of companies or countries at will, sometimes causing a stampede.[20]

The global economy has been called a "Casino Economy," because in a sense the stock market functions as an elaborate system for placing bets on whether the value of particular stocks will rise. If stock in a particular company is popular, many people buy it, and its value goes up. When a stock begins to seem less desirable, people start selling it off, and its value goes down.

In the currency markets, investors (or rather, speculators) bet on the value of your country's currency, and depending on how they bet, the value of your currency goes up or down, and with it, the attractiveness of investments in your country overall. In the late 1990s there was a stampede out of the Asian countries that left most of them devastated. Could the same thing happen to the U.S. dollar? Yes. Our massive trade deficit, our huge and growing debt, a weakening dollar, together with foreign-policy blunders or other unknown factors, could make speculators nervous and trigger a stock market crash and a fall in the value of the dollar, with huge repercussions for the global economy as a whole. A best-selling book in Europe, *After the Empire: The Breakdown of the American Order*, predicts: "The most likely scenario is a stock market crash larger than any we have experienced thus far that will be followed by the meltdown of the dollar—a one-two punch that would put an end to any further delusions of 'empire' when it comes to the U.S. economy."[21]

A "run" on stocks is like a run on banks—panic destabilizes the whole system and could lead to its collapse. In his book *Panic Rules*, Robin Hahnel has identified two rules of behavior that guide investors in the stock market: "Rule #1 is the rule all participants want all other participants to follow: DON'T PANIC. Rule #2 is the rule each participant must be careful to follow: PANIC FIRST."[22] If others panic, they will withdraw their money and drag the value of your stocks down. But if others are going to panic, it is best for you to panic first and get your money out quickly. These rules negate each other, and highlight the inherent contradictions of an economic system built upon financial speculation.

The threat of a meltdown of the global economy is a serious concern. Many famous financiers and economists have warned of the dangers of "hot money" and "gypsy capital". Paul Volcker, former chairman of the Federal Reserve board of trustees, has suggested a World Financial Authority or a World Central Bank that would help stabilize the global economy.[23] Citizen activists insist that any new multilateral finance, development, or trade institution should function under a reformed United Nations.

A GLOBAL SYSTEM BUILT UPON DEBT

> The person who has hope for the future saves in the present and invests for the time ahead. The person who has no hope and no desire for the future enjoys the present and piles up debts, which have to be paid by his children, or by somebody else, at some later point. A society's hope and its hopelessness can be read very clearly from its investment and its debts.
>
> —Jürgen Moltmann[24]

This whole global system is built upon debt. Individuals as well as businesses and governments deposit their money in banks, which are legally required to hold only a small percentage of those funds in reserve. Banks then lend out many times the amount of money actually deposited to individuals, businesses, and governments, who deposit their money in banks and start the process all over again.

Debt funds economic growth by introducing new money, and hopefully, productivity, into what would otherwise be a closed system. This can work well in some cases. For instance, student loans can enable students to develop their skills and increase their earning ability. Mortgages can enable a family to improve their quality of life by buying a home, which might be impossible if they had to pay cash. On one level, corporations function in the same way.

Corporations borrow money to fund growth in productivity. In order to make a profit, corporations must bring in more money than they pay out for production. Taking out loans and selling initial stock offerings are ways to introduce more money into the system, and thus squeeze out more profits. Rising corporate profits translate into a growing economy, which according to economic orthodoxy is a healthy economy.

The buying and selling of debt has become big business. Debt is publicly traded on the stock market. Banks and other financial firms compete to lure businesses and individuals to take out bank loans and credit cards, sometimes engaging in "predatory lending" that can trap the most economically vulnerable in a vicious cycle of debt. Nevertheless, this continues the seemingly limitless process of economic growth, endlessly building on debt.

This reliance on debt to keep the economy growing helps explain why the IMF and World Bank continue giving new loans to heavily indebted nations. According to standard economic ideology, infusions of capital will stimulate economic growth, especially if these countries also put on the Golden Straitjacket in order to free up enough capital to service their debts and keep the cycle going. In this way, it is supposed, stable, growing national economies will contribute to the growth of the global economy as a whole. Even when poor countries flounder, the system as a whole can be seen as successful as long as the money keeps flowing to the transnational banks and corporations that the global economic system is designed to serve.

It is not only poor nations that are staggering under the burden of debt—so are developed nations, including the United States. The United States is the "consumer of last resort," supporting the global economic system by importing far more than it exports, thus creating a trade deficit that compromises U.S. economic strength. By borrowing money to fund our way of life, we have become the largest debtor nation in the world. We are mortgaging the future. As Jürgen Moltmann says, "we are laying an appalling burden of debt on our children and making life hard for them. This is 'no-future' politics."[25]

In *Blowback: The Costs and Consequences of Amercian Empire*, Chalmers Johnson says: "The United States went on a consumption binge and provided virtually all growth in demand for the excess output of the world. Can American 'shop till we drop' be sustained indefinitely? No one knows."[26]

CORPORATE GLOBALIZATION: MADE IN THE U.S.A.

America is blamed for this because, in so many ways, global-ization is us—or is at least perceived that way by a lot of the world . . . The Golden Straitjacket was made in America and Great Britain. The Electronic Herd is led by American Wall Street bulls, and the most powerful agent pressuring other countries to open their markets for free trade and free invest-ment is Uncle Sam, and America's global armed forces keep these markets and sea lanes open for this era of globalization, just as the British navy did for the era of globalization in the nineteenth century.

—Thomas Friedman[27]

As the originator and primary model of a free-market capitalist system, the United States exports corporate culture around the world. Thomas Friedman, as always, says it in picturesque terms: "Today, globalization wears Mickey Mouse ears, eats Big Macs, drinks Coke or Pepsi and it does its computing on an IBM PC, using Windows 98, with an Intel Pentium II processor and a network link from Cisco Systems. . . . In most societies people cannot distinguish anymore between American power, American exports, American cultural assaults, American cultural exports and plain vanilla globalization. They are all now wrapped into one."[28]

With our patterns of consumption, the United States has also become the prime market for the exports of other countries around the world. With only 5 percent of the world's population, we consume 40 percent of its resources. This has led to a huge and growing trade deficit, but it has also propped up the global economy by providing demand for the world's excess output of consumer goods.[29]

In addition to being the primary model for global capitalism and the consumer of last resort, the United States is also its primary promoter. The U.S. government strongly influences the rules of the global economy through the IMF, World Bank, and WTO in order to smooth the way for the free movement of U.S.-based corporations across borders. In addition, the United States offers incentives, such as high-tech military equipment and training, to nations that open their doors to U.S.-based corporations. It also offers disincentives, both economic and military, using force when necessary to protect what it considers its vital interests throughout the world. These vital interests are often economic interests, that is, the investments of U.S. transnational corporations.

The United States also employs its massive military/security/surveillance network in order to create stability so that corporate globalization can proceed. This can be seen in its international relations, in its relations with allied nations, even some that oppress their own people, and in its dealings with its own citizens who challenge or threaten the status quo. As the primary model and promoter of economic globalization, the United States backs up economic globalization through the threat and use of force. According to Friedman, "McDonald's cannot flourish without McDonnell Douglas, the designer of the U. S. Air Force F15. And the hidden fist that keeps the world safe for Silicon Valley's technologies to flourish is called the U. S. Army, Air Force, Navy, and Marine Corps. And these fighting forces and institutions are paid for by American taxpayer dollars."[30]

In his book, *Runaway World*, Anthony Giddens asks, "How much is the system designed and managed in order to benefit the USA, the preeminent state?"[31] As we have seen, the global economic system is not simply out of control but runs according to carefully crafted rules designed by transnational corporations, promoted by the U.S. government, institutionalized by powerful global institutions, and enforced by the U.S. military. Today's global economy is truly "made in the U.S.A." It may be harming U.S. workers, whose jobs are being exported and whose overall living standards are going down, but it is benefiting those for whom the system is designed: a relatively few wealthy individuals, corporations, and the politicians who are supported by them.

We can better grasp the situation if we follow the money. Of course, that is hard to do in a global economy, with over $1.5 trillion in fund transfers taking place every day. Still, it is pretty clear what is happening when ExxonMobil boasts of the highest yearly profits a corporation has ever seen[32] while families are paying over $3 per gallon of gas at the pump. It is easy to see what is taking place when Halliburton, with its connections to vice-president Dick Cheney, makes billions on no-bid contracts to rebuild a newly privatized Iraq, as the U.S. government spends billions in tax dollars and sacrificed lives to destroy Iraq's infrastructure and throw it into chaos and civil war. A wealthy and powerful few benefit from corporate profits while millions of others pay the price.

But even those individuals who seem to be in positions of power and who are apparently benefiting from this dehumanizing system may also be its victims. These "rulers" and "authorities" (presidents, elected representatives, military commanders, CEOs) are Powers by virtue of their position. Although society has invested them with status and position, they often function primarily as figureheads within the system, carrying its overall agenda forward. Stringfellow believed that such people were among society's most pitiable victims: "It is more accurate, more truthful, to perceive the President as a victim and captive of the principalities and powers . . ."[33] So while political cartoons, editorials, and bumper stickers that blame particular presidents or CEOs or other political or corporate leaders may release tension and provide a focus for political action, the problem is not just with an inept, "morally bereft," or evil leader but with the system that brought such a person to power. For that, we are all responsible. Those who function as leaders within the system may be well positioned to change the system if they are so inclined. But those who stand in resistance are less invested in the system and may be more likely to take radical action that such change requires.

A SYSTEM SPINNING OUT OF CONTROL

> The world financial system has become exquisitely vulnerable to technological breakdown, the high-risk consequences of short-term speculation, and freelance decision making. If

anything goes wrong in this fragile relationship, which is increasingly likely in the context of a wired-up economy based on free trade . . . we are quickly threatened by a rapid domino effect among the world's interdependent stock markets. Global economic collapse is possible.

—Richard Barnet and John Cavanaugh[34]

The ongoing growth of the global economy is necessary for the success of the global free-market capitalist system. And yet, this growth can only be accomplished by building on debt, generating ever greater amounts of capital, promoting Western-style development, converting more of the earth's natural wealth into commodities for sale, creating more markets by turning people around the world into consumers, opening other sectors of society to the highest corporate bidders, and getting rid of any barriers that hinder the free flow of capital around the world.

The scope of this process of economic globalization is expanding, encompassing ever-more people and nations. The speed of the process is accelerating. It is dizzying. There seems to be no way out, and proponents of this process argue that there is no alternative, that it is inevitable. We simply must keep the global economy going, and growing. It seems that we are stuck, trapped in an endless, ballooning cycle that is spinning out of control.

The global economic system is, however, designed to generate wealth, and it is doing just that. It may seem that environmental destruction and growing inequity are just by-products of this goal, but that is not the case. The system is designed to extract money from the earth and from human society, to turn as much as possible into commodities in order to generate profits. It is designed to exploit the earth's resources and human labor. The system is designed for the results it is getting, and it is paying off handsomely for those for whom the system is designed.

But these benefits are only temporary. In the long run, the whole system is unsustainable, for the accumulation of wealth at the top depends upon the exploitation and repression of people at the bottom and upon the unlimited extraction of limited natural wealth. The current course will only lead us further along the road towards the hell of environmental devastation, social chaos, and growing human misery.

When presented by the High Priests of Mammon, the functioning of the global economy seems to make sense, in a highly rational and even mathematical way. It seems exciting and visionary in its promise of bringing prosperity and peace to the entire world. Some globalization proponents paint a utopian picture in almost religious terms. In their book, *A Future Perfect: The Challenge and Hidden Promise of Globalization*, John Micklethwait and Adrian Wooldridge point in the direction of a "future perfect" opened up to us by "the hidden promise of globalization." They argue that

> Globalization is helping to give birth to an economy that is closer to the classic theoretical model of capitalism, under which rational individuals pursue their interests in the light of perfect information, relatively free from government and geographical obstacles. It is also helping to create a society that is closer to the model that liberal political theorists once imagined, in which power lies increasingly in the hands of individuals rather than governments, and in which people are free, within reasonable bounds, to pursue the good life wherever they find it.[35]

The vision of hope for the world's future that these authors present is secular, but their enthusiasm has an almost religious fervor, which is not unusual for globalization proponents. As an epigraph to the book, they quote Lord Tennyson's poem, Locksley Hall:

> For I dipt into the future, far as human eye can see,
> Saw the Vision of the world, and all the wonder that would be;
> Saw the heavens fill with commerce, argosies of magic sails,
> Pilots of the purple twilight, dropping down with costly bales . .
> Till the war-drum throbb'd no longer, and the battle-flags were furl'd
> In the Parliament of man, the Federation of the world.[36]

This hoped-for future, however, does not represent God's triumph over the Powers, or hope for God's future, but the triumph of the dominant Powers over world affairs. Hope does not depend upon the dubious promises of Market Fundamentalism. It does not depend upon technology, innovation, wealth-creation, or corporate success. A hopeful future for human beings and the earth will require, rather, a revolutionary shift in values and worldview, a deep commitment to change, and the active presence of the Spirit of God.

CRITIQUING THE IDEOLOGICAL FOUNDATIONS OF MARKET FUNDAMENTALISM

No business in the world can long survive on its capital reserves. Every businessperson understands this, yet many

ignore the fact that this same principle applies equally to energy and the environment.

—Paul Hawken[37]

As we have seen, there are many reasons to be concerned about corporate globalization. It is important to look critically at the underlying justification for this economic system, that is, at the basic articles of faith upon which the whole ideology is built. Of course, these ideas have some validity. The market mechanism is an efficient way of providing goods and services in some contexts, for instance, in the grocery store. No one denies that self-interest can motivate human beings or that competition can create incentives. Under the present system, businesses survive by making a profit, and under the right circumstances economic growth can enable people to meet their basic human needs.

But these ideas have been institutionalized as gospel to support a system that is neither sane nor realistic. Economic principles are often presented and taught as if they were natural laws, like the law of gravity, which they are not. If we elevate these ideas into an ideology, we will be tempted to use them as a template around which to shape our view of reality. This then will become our paradigm; we will be unable to see beyond it. We need to be clear that faith in the Market, the value of self-interest, the goal of profit, and belief in the illusion of limitless growth are not the ideological building blocks we need to build a better world. Let us look at each of these ideas in turn.

1. As we have seen, in Market Fundamentalism the Market is always right because it is guided by a Higher Power, an "Invisible Hand" that brings harmony and well-being to all through the universal law of supply and demand.

We have acknowledged that the Market has its place. But we can see from observation that it does not bring benefits to everyone, only to those who can afford them. Those who have no money, the Invisible Hand leaves behind.

The problem is, the Market doesn't deal with needs, only with "wants," with demand. It measures only what people can afford to buy. Whole parts of life are left out of the Market economy: the value of the environment, the well-being of children, subsistence gardening, unpaid work of any kind, the work of most of the world's women. It cannot be applied universally to all sectors of society. In addition, the rule makers of the global economy themselves manipulate the Market, creating advantages for large corporations and wealthy countries at the expense of small businesses and poor countries.

Furthermore, the Market cannot deliver on the ludicrous promises of Market Fundamentalism. The idea of the sanctity of the Market is idolatrous. It puts the Market in the place of God, as if has ultimate value, which it does not. The Market is not omnipotent, omniscient, or infallible. It is not a worthy object of faith in which to place our confidence and hope.

2. According to this ideology, if everyone acts in their own economic self-interest, competing with each other, it will lead to the well-being of the whole and all its various parts. Besides, it is just human nature to act in a self-interested way—that is the "rational" way to be.

This idea of rationality is divorced from the heart; compassion and love of other are absent. Selfishness cannot be justified simply by saying that it is human nature to act in a self-interested and competitive way. Although some people are primarily self-seeking, many are motivated to cooperate with others and to give of themselves unselfishly. Many native societies and many other human societies throughout history have been organized around values of cooperation and caring, which demonstrates that acting solely in one's own self-interest is not basic to human nature. To say that self-interest is the primary motivation of human beings is a belittling view of human nature and degrades the image of God within us.

Furthermore, self-interested action does not always serve the good of all. Action motivated solely by self-interest is not a "good" at all. In most religions, selfishness, self-centeredness, and preoccupation with one's own self-interest above the good of others are considered either delusion or sin. Self-interest as a primary value is the exact opposite of the teachings of all the major world religions, which promote compassion, selflessness, service to others, cooperation, and concern for the common good.

3. The primary goal of this secular religion is to generate profits and to accumulate wealth. It turns greed and love of money into virtues, contrary to Jesus' warnings that one can not serve both God and money. This is simply another version of the worship of the Golden Calf. Golden Calf or Golden Arches: to worship or serve either is idolatrous.

4. Finally, the ideology that supports corporate globalization requires the belief that limitless economic growth is both possible and desirable, and will lead to a higher standard of living for all, rich and poor alike. But as we have seen, that claim is false. The wealth is not shared equitably. Indeed, any claim that economic growth brings benefits to everyone can easily be put to rest by taking a look at the

actual effects: a growing gap between the rich and the poor throughout the world. Never has such wealth been created, yet never has there been such inequity.

Current accounting methods do no tell the whole story. They do not distinguish between economic activities that are helpful and those that are harmful to society or the earth. For instance, Gross Domestic Product (GDP) and Gross National Product (GNP) count all economic activity as positive, including the costs of natural disasters, environmental pollution, and war. David Korton points out that using GDP as a measure of economic or social health "makes no more sense than taking the rapid expansion of one's personal girth as an indicator of improved personal health."[38]

Many scholars, including Nobel Prize laureates in economics, are calling for alternative accounting methods. A Genuine Progress Indicator (GPI) would include factors such as resource depletion, pollution, and nonmarket transactions, and would make positive adjustments for gains to society or the environment and negative adjustments for harm caused.[39] "Full cost accounting" would bring externalized costs, those costs paid by society, into the budgets and operating costs of corporations and would in turn be reflected in the prices of their goods. "Natural resources accounting" would reflect costs of depleting resources as capital losses, instead of gains. "Steady state economics" would measure progress not in terms of material or economic growth, but in terms of health, education, employment, and other social indicators.[40] Those who promote such alternative accounting methods reject the view that economic growth is the sole measure of a society's well-being.

Furthermore, we live on a finite planet with limited resources—the economy can't grow indefinitely! Kenneth Lux points out: "We live on a finite planet. If human beings are defined as being made up of infinite wants, and the task of an economic system is to fulfill that infinity, then such a system will go on endlessly churning out goods in an attempt to reach what is from the beginning an impossible goal. When the infinite production of goods meets up with a finite planet there is bound to be a collision."[41]

Yet this idea drives the current insanity. The Beast of corporate globalization continues to grow bigger and bigger, at a faster and faster rate: using up resources, spewing out toxins, pressing countries to gear their economies toward export, giving corporations ever-more rights while taking away the rights of governments to regulate them, privatizing and deregulating government services so corporations can make ever greater profits—all this to keep the global economic system going and growing. Where will it end?

We can see where we are headed—we are plunging headlong toward a living hell, a hell of human misery on a degraded and desolate earth. And according to standard economic theory, there is no logical place to stop. The ideology/religion that supports corporate globalization is the current version of what the Bible calls the "wisdom of this age" (1 Cor. 2:6). It is a rationalized pseudo-logic divorced from the heart and even from common sense. The global economic system is based on faulty and idolatrous assumptions that have led us to the pinnacle of economic insanity, far removed from any sense of being grounded in the natural world, far from the values of faith. It has brought human beings and all life to the edge of a dangerous precipice, to the verge of global catastrophe.

The articles of faith are the building blocks, set one upon another, glued with the mortar of belief into what seems to be a superstructure that holds up the global economic system. But in reality, it is only a facade, destined to crumble. It is not ultimate. For the only power that is ultimate is the power that undergirds creation and draws us forward in creative, compassionate action—God's loving, persuasive power that is made perfect in weakness (2 Cor. 12:9), the power of nonviolence, the power of the cross.

THE CURSE OF THE GOLDEN TOUCH

> **We can only preach the manifold wisdom of God to Mammon if our life displays that we are joyfully freed from its clutches.**
>
> —Hendrik Berkhof [42]

As we have seen, the so-called logic of this economic ideology is divorced from the heart and even from plain common sense. If we believe in this view, we have made the same mistake as Midas, who wished for the golden touch. He wanted everything he touched to turn to gold, and when he got his wish, for a time it made him happy.

But gold, money, wealth, and profit are not of ultimate value, and if we make them so, we lose what is dearest to us. Through glorifying profit and economic growth and by making them the foundational values around which we organize our lives and global society, we have succumbed to the religion of Mammon, which turns the natural world and workers into commodities, which are then used to generate yet more capital. It commodifies the very things that we hold most dear.

Midas, when he saw that his little daughter had been turned into gold, realized that the golden touch was not a blessing, but a curse. When the curse was removed he was grateful and joyous, able to appreciate the living, breathing, joy of his life—his daughter—and all the other precious things that he had so taken for granted.

In spite of the material wealth it generates for some, the global economic system is spiritually and morally bankrupt. It is idolatrous, unjust, and unsustainable. But as we have seen, none of this is happening by accident. None of this is inevitable. Human beings are involved in the institutions that make the rules of the global economy, certain human beings benefit from them, and human beings must be involved in their transformation.

The Powers that are behind the accelerating destruction of the earth and the growing gap between the rich and poor are not just abstract forces floating around in the air, but are concrete, physical institutions that are served by living, breathing human beings. It is to these institutions that we now turn.

CHAPTER ELEVEN
Of, By, and For the Corporations: A System of Corporate Rule

> Before NAFTA we thought corporations could only buy Southern governments. Now we see they also buy Northern Governments.
>
> —Ignacio Peon Escalante[1]

In August 2000 I traveled to Los Angeles, where the Democratic National Convention was being held. On the evening before the convention, I gathered with other demonstrators outside an amusement park on the Santa Monica Pier, where one of many social events for convention delegates was being held. This event was sponsored by Kraft Foods, a subsidiary of tobacco giant Phillip Morris, which church groups and others were boycotting because of its practice of marketing tobacco to youth in poor nations.[2] It had also recently been in the news for marketing Taco Bell taco shells that were contaminated by their genetically modified Starlink© corn.

As convention delegates were leaving the amusement park, we could see that they were carrying boxes of Kraft Macaroni and Cheese emblazoned with the words "Democrats 2000." In the banter between delegates and demonstrators, some delegates were generous enough to give some of the familiar orange and blue boxes to demonstrators as souvenirs. My friend Maggie was delighted to end up with one. As we examined the box, which contained donkey-shaped macaroni, we read the small print, and were amazed to see these words, paraphrasing the words of the late President Kennedy: "Ask not what Kraft Macaroni and Cheese can do for you, ask what you can do for Kraft Macaroni and Cheese."

The irony was not wasted on those of us who were demonstrating on the pier outside the bright lights of the amusement park; after all, we were there to protest the corporate takeover of the democratic process in the United States. Protests had also focused on this theme three weeks earlier at the Republican National Convention in

Philadelphia, where (we found out later) Republican delegates were given boxes of elephant-shaped Kraft Macaroni and Cheese emblazoned with the words "Republicans 2000." Phillip Morris sponsored both Democratic and Republican party events and made contributions to both parties, as did other major corporations. This assured them of access to the halls of power regardless of which candidate was elected.

In this chapter, we will look more closely at transnational corporations, the primary actors in the global economy, and at human participation in these entities. In many ways, this challenges our ability to understand and take action for change, for the scale, scope, power, and complexity of today's global corporations is enough to boggle the mind.

Many people are concerned about the growing power of corporations. In the United States, the government grants civil rights to corporations. But since they are not human, they have an advantage over actual human beings. Corporations can accumulate wealth and political power far beyond that of any flesh-and-blood human being.

Furthermore, corporations use their vast wealth to extend further their power over human beings and their governments through campaign contributions, lobbying, and the commercial media. The growing political influence of corporations presents a very real threat to our democracy and to governments around the world.

Transnational corporations heavily influence not only governments, but also global economic, development, and trade institutions such as the IMF, the World Bank, the WTO, and regional trade agreements, which enforce rules limiting national sovereignty and promoting global economic hegemony based on the values of U.S.-style unrestrained free-market capitalism. These rules pressure governments to create a favorable climate for corporate investment, even at the expense of humanity and the earth.

The term *corporate globalization* seeks to express the ubiquitous influence of corporations over governments, global institutions, human beings, and life itself. As we have seen in the first section of this book, the overall effects of this corporate dominance are devastating. Democracy is undermined. Traditional cultures are thrown into chaos. Police and military forces protect and extend corporate interests. Human lives and whole ecosystems are destroyed.

In the emerging global marketplace, we are being programmed to put the needs of corporations above the needs of human beings. In other worlds, "Ask not what Kraft Macaroni and Cheese can do for you, ask what you can do for Kraft Macaroni and Cheese."

CORPORATIONS 'R' US

> The genius of the corporation as a business form, and the reason for its remarkable rise over the last three centuries, was—and is—its capacity to combine the capital, and thus the economic power, of unlimited numbers of people.
>
> —Joel Bakan[3]

Words from Abraham Lincoln's Gettysburg Address have been used to define democracy as "government of the people, by the people, for the people." But because corporations in the United States now have more power to influence our government than people do, it could be said that we now have a government of, by, and for the corporations. That is, ours is a system of corporate rule.

Corporations did not always have so much power. How did it get to be this way?

When the United States was founded, only white males with property could vote. In this way, moneyed interests already had the upper hand. Still, the new government strictly limited the rights and functions of corporations. The colonists had learned all they wanted to know about abuses of corporate power from the British corporations that had controlled trade in the American colonies. The Boston Tea Party was an example of popular resistance to unjust actions by the East India Tea Company, which had been chartered by the king.

In the new nation, corporations were chartered to serve the public good. They could only engage in the specific activities for which they had been chartered; if the purpose of a certain corporation was to make and market horseshoes, that was all it could do. It could not lobby the government, for instance, or acquire another corporation. After twenty or thirty years, the corporation was automatically disincorporated. In order for it to continue doing business, its representatives had to make the case officially that the corporation had served the common good. Directors were held personally responsible for any harm the corporation caused.

Over the years, corporations gradually gained more power. In 1886, without giving any rationale for doing so, the Supreme Court extended the Fourteenth Amendment, which had given African Americans equal rights, to give corporations the status of "persons" under the law. This legal fiction of granting personhood to corporations resulted in a gradual expansion of their rights, privilege, and power.

Over the years as the legal rights and power of corporations grew, the relative power of human beings shrank. Today, large corporations harness vast wealth, influence public opinion by purchasing time through the media, and buy government influence through campaign contributions that are, in effect, political bribes. Since they are not mortal, corporations have no natural lifespan as humans do, which would limit them by physical death. They can span generations, accumulating wealth and power. They are not spatially limited; their operations can span the globe. Corporations can make the most of subsidies and tax loopholes of various countries with the click of a mouse. When they cause harm, laws protect them from legal consequences that real human beings would face. Paid advertisements are considered forms of free speech, even when corporations give false information about their products. This gives them tremendous public influence, since they can afford more free speech than can real human beings—and such speech is tax-deductible! In all these ways, corporations now have more political power than do living, breathing human beings.

The major role of government is to protect the common good. This includes chartering corporations that will serve the public, regulating them so that they do not cause harm, and restricting them from engaging in activities that go against the public interest. Governments create regulations that govern corporations; these include labor, environmental, public-safety, and consumer-safety laws. In the United States, most of the existing laws that regulate corporate behavior were enacted through the democratic process, usually through union activities and grassroots organizing.

In recent years, however, corporations have successfully pressured governments to ignore or undo many such regulations. During the 1980s and 1990s, the U.S. government deregulated the airlines, the savings and loan associations, and many other industries, while ignoring or providing minimal enforcement of many existing laws. The Reagan administration sent a clear message to industry that it would not support organized labor when it fired the air-traffic controllers during their strike in 1980. The lax enforcement of existing labor and environmental laws has continued to the present.

During this same period, while many of the laws regulating corporate behavior have been weakened or removed, corporate privileges have increased. Changes in the tax laws have led to tremendous corporate tax cuts as well as subsidies and rebates for corporations, while taxes on the working poor have increased overall and social services have been cut. In the new century, tax policies continue this pattern of growing inequity.

Corporations donate huge sums of money to elect candidates and to influence politicians who support their agenda, which is to make a profit and attract stockholders. They pay lobbyists to promote specific legislation in Congress for their benefit; sometimes they write the legislation themselves. Grassroots groups and nonprofit agencies spend countless volunteer hours raising money, lobbying Congress, and organizing referendums and initiatives, only to be outspent many times over by moneyed interests who can afford to fund think tanks, buy advertisements, hire full-time lobbyists, and pay industry scientists to do studies that support their interests.

Meanwhile, legislators, succumbing to pressure from the corporations that support them, present legislation on various issues favoring cost-benefit and risk-benefit analysis, which reduce the value of human life and the natural world to a set of financial calculations. Under the banner of getting rid of "big government," the Golden Straitjacket is put on here in the United States, complete with cuts in services that benefit the public and the poor.

The "revolving door" between the government and corporate world is an example of how entrenched government representatives and corporate executives have become in a system that benefits both groups. People from the corporate world are often given appointments to government positions. Upon leaving these positions, these same people often go on to earn huge salaries as high-level executives in major corporations. Trade officials, who help guide national and global economic and trade policies, generally come from the world of big business as well. Their shared interests, values, and worldview lead to policies that benefit corporations at the expense of public welfare and the natural world.

Corporations are increasingly being set free from government regulation to pursue their one and only goal—the generation of wealth. U.S. law explicitly rejects the idea that corporations have ethical obligations other than obeying the law and providing the best financial returns for their investors. They are generally prohibited from placing the larger good of workers, communities, or the environment above the financial interests of their shareholders. Under U.S. tutelage, supported by the rule-making institutions of the global economy, governments are bequeathing to corporations the power to challenge regulations of every kind.

This is not to say that the problem is simply, or even primarily, with corporations. The problem is with the system of corporate globalization as a whole, made of up interconnected linkages of mega-corporations, powerful nations, the U.S. military and its allies, and global beaurocracies. These are all powers and principalities, each with their own goals, rules, and values that serve to enhance their survival and expansion. To the extent that they serve each other's purposes they work together, but conflicts among the Powers abound.

Today, huge corporations are amassing greater and greater wealth and are increasing their cultural and political influence. They are growing in power relative to individual human beings, governments, and global institutions. They influence and in some ways drive the whole system of global free-market capitalism, using their vast wealth and power to manipulate public opinion as well as national and global policies. In this way, these lifeless entities generate support for policies that benefit them.

"THEY BREATHE PROFITS; THEY EAT THE INTEREST ON MONEY"

> The bank is something else than men. It happens that every man in a bank hates what the bank does, and yet the bank does it. The bank is something more than men, I tell you. It's the monster. Men made it, but they can't control it.
>
> —John Steinbeck, *The Grapes of Wrath*[4]

The dictionary definition of a corporation is "a body formed and authorized by law to act as a single person although constituted by one or more persons and legally endowed with various rights and duties including the capacity of succession."[5] It has powers and rights that the individuals within it do not have, and those same individuals are legally shielded to some degree from personal responsibility for its debts or for whatever harm it might cause. But the fact that a corporation is authorized to act as a "person" under the law creates a troubling dynamic, given the (profit-seeking) purpose of corporations and their growing power.

Still, it helps for our purposes here to personify them. By so doing, we can better describe the relationship of human beings to these "principalities," that is, these institutional Powers.

A corporation is a legal fiction, a fictitious person, but not a fantasy. It has a life—in perpetuity no less (by virtue of its "capacity of succession") granted by the law, though it is not alive. It is a major protagonist on the stage of world events, though not a human one. It has motivation and a purpose—to survive and expand through growing profits—but no moral agency, no ability to choose right over wrong, no conscience but the bottom line. As Joel Bakan says in *The Corporation: The Pathological Pursuit of Profit and Power*: "[The corporation] remains . . . a legally designated 'person' designed to valorize self-interest and invalidate moral concern. Most people would find its 'personality' abhorrent, even psychopathic, in a human being, yet curiously we accept it in society's most powerful institution."[6]

John Steinbeck's classic novel *The Grapes of Wrath* contains a remarkable passage that portrays human idolatry and servitude in relation to the Powers. In this case, Steinbeck takes on the economic "rulers," the banks and corporations that profited from misery during the Great Depression, and shows how human beings relinquish their freedom in service to such Powers.

And all of them were caught in something larger than themselves. Some of them hated the mathematics that drove them, and some were afraid, and some worshiped the mathematics because it provided a refuge from thought and from feeling. If a banker or finance company owned the land, the owner man said, the Bank—or the Company—needs–wants–insists–must have—as though the Bank or the Company were a monster, with thought and feeling, which had ensnared them. These last would take no responsibility for the banks or the companies because they were men and slaves, while the banks were machines and masters all at the same time.[7]

Steinbeck employs the metaphors of the "machine" and "monster" to demonstrate how human beings tend to relinquish their own personal responsibility in relation to institutions, become enslaved by them, and participate in their harmful actions in the world. The machine metaphor is an apt one for banks or other for-profit corporations because after being invented and set in motion, a machine runs on its own. Human input is generally limited to making technological improvements, repairing or replacing parts, or helping the machine do whatever it is designed to do, on the assembly line, for example. In a similar way, once a corporation is chartered and established, humans at every level are replaceable, like the mechanical cogs in a machine. Their ability to control it is constrained by both inner, institutional realities and by outside pressures that drive the corporation and the people within it to put profits first.

Even CEOs rise to their positions because they accept and promote the corporation's primary goal, that is, to make a profit and raise the value of its stocks so that it can survive and grow. Corporate CEOs serve as figureheads, giving a human face to the corporation. Whatever socially or environmentally responsible policies a manager might like to enact can only be enacted if they will bring financial profit to the stockholders. The law prohibits him or her from enacting such policies unless they will affect the bottom line in a positive way.

Although individuals within a corporation may be ethical, the corporation, like a machine, is impersonal; it does not have a conscience.

Its only "conscience" is the bottom line. It is designed to bring profits to stockholders, regardless of the social or environmental costs.

In pursuit of profits, a corporation must minimize its expenses, so it seeks to "externalize" them, that is, to shift as many costs as possible over to society at large, so that they don't affect the bottom line. If a corporation creates a product that causes cancer, or pollutes the air and water, or creates a hazard for consumers, it seeks to avoid paying for medical bills or cleanup or damages by promoting deregulation and risk-benefit or cost-benefit analysis or by threatening to relocate to another community or country. Joel Bakan calls the corporation an "externalizing machine:" "The corporation . . . is deliberately programmed, indeed legally compelled, to externalize costs without regard for the harm it may cause to people, communities, and the natural environment. Every cost it can unload onto someone else is a benefit to itself, a direct route to profit. . . . The corporation, like the psychopathic personality it resembles, is programmed to exploit others for profit. That is its only legitimate mandate."[8]

There are some socially responsible corporations that have built their businesses by marketing to socially concerned shoppers who are willing to pay for alternative products that cause less harm or that benefit society. These corporations, including Ben and Jerry's, Working Assets, and Newman's Own, model a healthy corporate ethos. Other corporations seek to mitigate harmful effects and to improve their public relations through writing ethical standards into their bylaws. But because the global economic system is itself flawed, high standards can place socially and environmentally responsible companies at a competitive disadvantage. Furthermore, some corporations are duplicitous in their attempts to appear environmentally and socially responsible. They contribute to various environmental or social programs or projects with the right hand while lobbying against environmental regulations or social programs with the left.

The primary guiding principle of corporations is the bottom line. Their survival depends upon it. In Steinbeck's words: "They breathe profits: they eat the interest on money."[9] If their books do not show profit, their stockholders will pull out, top management officials will be fired, or they will be taken over by a company that "utilizes its assets" in ways that generate higher profits. This is not a problem that can easily be solved by socially concerned corporate executives, workers, or stockholders. It is a systemic problem. Joel Bakan says, "Nothing in its legal makeup limits what [the corporation] can do to others in pursuit of its selfish ends, and it is compelled to cause harm when the benefits of doing so outweigh the costs. Only pragmatic concern for its own interests and the laws of the land constrain the corporation's predatory instincts, and often that is not enough to keep it from destroying lives, damaging communities, and endangering the planet as a whole."[10]

Even when a corporation breaks the law, it can incorporate the costs of lawyers and fines as a normal part of doing business. Except in specific circumstances, people within the corporation are not legally liable for harm done. In this, too, the corporation is different, and less controllable, than human beings.

Steinbeck's "monster" image portrays something of the *spiritual* effects of corporations and how they capture human beings in their service. In this dehumanizing process, people may justify harm by appealing to corporate imperatives, that is, what the monster that has ensnared them "needs, wants, must have" (that is, profits). In such a situation, people are serving the institution instead of the institution serving life.

Of course, individuals may have personal goals that intersect with the goals of the corporation. CEOs receive high salaries, bonuses, status, and stock in the corporations they manage. Stockholders receive the economic value of their stock, workers receive a job and a wage. Consumers receive whatever products or services the corporation offers—for a price. All these people are rewarded for consenting to the corporation's values and goals and for serving its needs.

But people are often blind to their own contribution to the corporation's overall effects in the world. Most people within a large corporation—for instance, workers—do not participate in its decision-making processes. Most stockholders only pay attention to the economic value of the corporation's stocks. Most workers, even when unionized, focus primarily on jobs, wages, and benefits. Most customers focus on the product or services they purchase. Members of the board of directors can write ethical standards into the corporation's bylaws if they can justify such standards in terms of profit, but their main focus is on the corporation's "fiduciary responsibility" to its stockholders, which is their primary responsibility under the law. Upper level managers and CEOs usually put the goal of generating short-term profits above all else, for if a corporation does not show a profit, these executives are out of a job. In Steinbeck's words, "The bank has to have profits all the time. It can't wait. It'll die."[11]

The corporation may engage in practices that most of the people who serve it don't even know about. Workers, consumers, and lower-level managers may not know how the company treats workers in other countries or whether it follows environmental laws at home or abroad. They may have no idea of the social or environmental costs of doing business, since such costs are externalized and do not show up on corporate ledgers but are borne by society as a whole.

Even directors and upper level managers generally focus primarily on the corporation's finances and may not have a clear overview of what the corporation does. Those who do know and who participate in the decision-making process may be fully identified with the corporation's goals and go along willingly in its service. Or they may go along sadly, reluctantly, like the bank representatives in *The Grapes of Wrath*. "We have to do it. We don't like to do it. But the monster's sick. . . ."[12]

When human beings are in these kinds of relationships with a huge corporation, the corporation can cause immense harm, far more than could be caused by individual human beings. Individuals have been "caught in something larger than themselves." This fosters a collective mindset. As Stringfellow observed, "People are relieved of their individuality, along with their sense of judgment and choice."[13] Knowingly or unknowingly, those who serve a corporation without questioning its effects in the world adopt the corporation's collective ideology and values. Willingly or unwillingly, they work to serve its purpose and extend its power. They are complicit in what the corporation does. They "take no responsibility for the banks or the companies because they [are] men and slaves, while the banks [are] machines and masters all at the same time."

With this kind of human support, a corporation can shape an environment in which it can thrive. This may include firing workers or moving factories or supply chains to countries where there is cheap labor and lax environmental, consumer-safety, and human-rights laws. It may also include pressing governments and global institutions to make laws and regulations that protect a corporation's interests and further its goals, that is, to increase its profits and stock values. In Steinbeck's words, "When the monster stops growing, it dies. It can't stay one size."[14]

Virtual Corporations: The Global Assembly Line

> Our corporations have built a global production system that is so complex, and geared so tightly and leveraged so finely, that a breakdown anywhere increasingly means a breakdown everywhere.
>
> —Barry Lynn[15]

The same values, technologies, policies, and bureaucratic processes that make globalization possible enable the world's largest corporations not only to compete as players on the market's global playing field, but to shape it. Their global reach enables them to undercut lesser economic Powers and create their own networks of supply and demand, thus creating a global assembly line.

As corporations have gone global they have vastly expanded their power and extended their access to resources, supplies, and labor from around the world. They can now take advantage of tax laws by playing off one country against another, moving components from one country to be assembled in another, with the final product emerging from yet another. By moving their (virtual) headquarters to the Cayman Islands or another tax shelter, they can avoid paying taxes that smaller local companies must pay.

In this process, the nature of corporations themselves has changed. Most transnational corporations are no longer vertically integrated companies with their own in-house offices and manufacturing plants. Instead, they are organized horizontally. They span the globe, using outside suppliers in various countries to provide everything from data entry to customer service to information processing to the manufacture and delivery of goods, creating a global assembly line, a network that services various corporations and extends around the world. This new structure enables large corporations to keep a lean inventory, ready for just-in-time production, with less capital locked up, thus making it easier for them to upgrade or move their operations. They can shift their center of gravity from day to day.

This horizontal structure, needless to say, also drives down the cost of labor. No longer are workers able to count on a job that gives them wage increases, health-care benefits, and the security of a pension in exchange for their hard work and loyalty. The outsourcing of factories, offices, and supply chains has greatly increased the power of corporate management in relation to labor. In the United States, this power shift results in labor unions making concessions that would have been unthinkable a few decades ago. Globally, as we have seen, it pits workers in wealthy countries against workers in poor countries, setting up a race to the bottom that drives down wages around the world.

Instead of providing factories to manufacture goods from start to finish, corporations increasingly buy, move, assemble, and deliver goods that are made by others. In other words, they oversee and track the manufacturing process using outside suppliers. Some large corporations even outsource this tracking function to corporations that handle logistics, such as Federal Express, which specializes in organizing products and components that flow through the supply chain. This new corporate structure shifts both the costs and the risks of operations to the suppliers. Companies that supply goods and services to these virtual corporations compete with each other for their place in the global assembly line, driving down costs and exacerbating the race to the bottom in these areas as well.

Sometimes just one or two companies supply something that is needed by many corporations, or even by governments. For instance, in the 2003–2004 flu season there was a global shortage of flu vaccine because one of the two leading companies that produced it shut down.[16] Global outsourcing of production to a limited number of suppliers creates risk for corporations, governments, and for the global system as a whole.

This global assembly line also shifts power away from manufacturers, even virtual manufacturers, to transnational retailers. Since the big retailers are at the top of the global chain, they can pit suppliers against suppliers, thus controlling their costs. These transnational giants don't just compete in the global marketplace—in a sense, they are the market. As the largest retailer in the world, Wal-Mart "does not participate in the market so much as use its power to micromanage the market, carefully coordinating the actions of thousands of firms from a position above the market."[17]

Transnational corporations can exert a great deal of power in setting the terms of their relationships with their workers, suppliers, communities, and even countries. These corporations, although they control more assets than do many countries, nevertheless are lightweight in the physical sense. Although they virtually span the globe, they don't have bodies; they do most of their business in cyberspace. And because there exists a global assembly line, they can move operations easily and cheaply.

Relatively speaking, that is. Compared to the old, "vertically integrated" corporations of the past, they can travel light and fast. These free-flying entities can touch down in communities or countries just long enough to out-compete local artisans, small farmers, and local businesses, and to create complete dependency. They assimilate people and resources, then lift off or threaten to lift off to another locale. Corporations are now "offshoring the offshorers."[18] Data-entry jobs that were outsourced from the United States to India are now being moved to Bulgaria, Romania, Cambodia, and Laos, where wages are even lower.[19] As mentioned earlier, maquiladoras, the factories opened in Mexico by U.S. corporations seeking cheaper labor and weaker environmental laws, are now moving their operations to China.[20]

The monster is sick. It can't stay one size.

These global monsters are voracious. They even feed off each other, through what has been called "vulture capitalism." Where forests are intact, for instance, they show up on corporate ledgers as "underperforming assets," ripe for a hostile takeover. Only when the forest has been liquidated does it show up as economic growth that contributes to the Gross Domestic Product (GDP). Some corporations specialize in taking over "unproductive" corporations and "restructuring" them, which often means "downsizing," laying off workers, closing factories, moving operations, and sometimes dismantling the corporations and selling off their assets as spare parts.

Ironically, as busy as corporations are in recreating the world in their image and restructuring governments to suit themselves, they are not really acting in their own institutional self-interest at all. In the long run, the current system is unsustainable, even for corporations. Their job is to multiply money and to extract wealth. They "breathe profits, they eat the interest on money." But corporations are not real; they are legal fictions. They are virtual, even in this sense. They are accumulations of property, of capital. Corporations act not on their own behalf but on behalf of their stockholders, the absentee landlords, the owners of this capital. Managers are increasingly being rewarded by stock options, so that they are personally more invested in the rising value of the company's stock than in the actual profits, which come from productive activity, or the long-term health of the company.

The price of each share of stock should reflect the actual value of the company, that is, the company's profits or promise of future profits. But the gauge of a company's profitability can be manipulated, and there is often a gap between the price of a company's stock and its profits. When stock prices rise far above profits in an individual corporation or in the stock market overall, it may indicate a speculative bubble caused by "irrational exuberance,"[21] an unstable situation that can lead to a crash.

Corporations continually pursue growing short-term profits and rising stock values that, as we have seen, can come at great social and environmental cost to life as a whole. Nevertheless, the global economy is geared toward greasing the wheels of these powerful profit-making engines and setting them free from government control in order to stimulate so-called progress measured as economic growth.

A Doom Machine?

How do we deal with a world where the Electronic Herd gets to vote in all kinds of countries every day, but those countries don't get to vote on the herd's behavior in such a direct and immediate manner?

—Thomas Friedman[22]

As corporations gain more power in relation to governments, they are remaking governments in their own image. Thomas Friedman says this is not so bad, that it can actually be seen as form of democracy: "Joining the global economy and plugging into the Electronic Herd is the equivalent of taking your country public. It is the equivalent of turning your country into a public company, only the shareholders are no longer just your own citizens. They are the members of the Electronic Herd, wherever they might be. And, as I noted earlier, they don't just vote once every four years. They vote every hour, every day, through their mutual funds, their pension funds, their brokers and, more and more, from their own basements via the Internet."[23]

But "one dollar, one vote" through the stock market does not a democracy make. This is speculation, not representation. It has nothing to do with democracy, that is, with weighing issues, taking responsibility, and making decisions to further the common good. This may be plutocracy—that is, rule by the wealthy—or corporatocracy—rule by corporations—but it is not democracy. It is a form of global corporate rule.

In the next chapter, we will look at the rulemaking institutions of the global economy, and show how they, too, foster corporate well-being over the well-being of human beings, their communities and governments, and the earth itself. We will also look at how the United States dominates the institutions and structures of the global economy. As we have seen, global free-market capitalism originates in, proceeds from, and is dominated by the United States. But what exactly does this mean if transnational corporate "monsters" have hijacked the U.S. political process and faceless stockholders from around the world control the U.S. economy? No wonder people feel powerless and things seem out of human control.

The dilemma that we face is not simply that corporations are growing in power over human beings, but that we human beings and the governments that represent us are relinquishing more and more of our power and responsibility in relation to corporations. We are being caught in something larger than ourselves. We are acting as if these transnational giants are monsters that have ensnared us, as if we are slaves and not free human beings capable of decision and action.

Global corporations not only dominate decision making at the highest levels, they are working to create systems that allow them to fill every gap left by human indecision and inaction, leaving us feeling even more powerless and less able to affect change. As Stephen Kobrin says, the more that the economy is globalized, "the more individual citizens start to feel that the locus of economic control and political decision making on economic matters is shifting from the local level, where it can be controlled, to the global level, where no one is in charge and no one is minding the store. When all politics is local, your vote matters. But when the power shifts to these transnational spheres, there are no elections and there is no one to vote for."[24]

As powerful corporations influence governments and global institutions, human beings have less say over the direction these Powers are taking us. As undemocratic global institutions such as the IMF, World Bank, and WTO enable corporations to restrict governments in setting social and environmental standards, individuals and communities have less input into their destinies. As anonymous stockholders make decisions based on financial considerations, human values and choices fail to have an effect on where these decisions lead. The resulting loss of human input into the economic, social, and political institutions that drive world events is "demonic" and leads toward global catastrophe.

Corporations are unrelenting in their pursuit of money and power. As we have seen, this motivation is basic to their institutional make-up. It is built in, for it is the only way a corporation can survive and expand, which is the goal of all the Powers. But because corporations have no conscience but the bottom line, and because they are undemocratic to the core, their domination of human culture, governments, and global institutions is damaging and dangerous. As corporate consultant Robert Monks points out: "The difficulty with the corporate entity is that it has a dynamic that doesn't take into account the concerns of flesh-and-blood human people who form the world in which it exists . . . in our search for wealth and for prosperity, we created a thing that's going to destroy us . . . a doom machine."[25]

IF IT DOESN'T BREATHE, IT DOESN'T DESERVE FREE SPEECH

Lacking the sort of physical, organic reality that characterizes human existence, this entity, this concept, this collection of paperwork called a corporation is not capable of feelings such as shame or remorse. Instead, corporations behave according to their own unique system of standards, rules, forms, and objectives, enshrined in state charters and confirmed through our legal structures.

—Jerry Mander[26]

Much of the power that corporations wield over human societies comes from our giving them the legal status of persons under the law. A corporation is not really a person, but accumulated property: capital, money, wealth. Just as slavery was the legal fiction that persons can be property, corporate personhood is the legal fiction that property can be persons. As Joel Bakan says, "The corporation is not an independent 'person' with its own rights, needs, and desires that regulators must respect. It is a state-created tool for advancing social and economic policy."[27]

Corporations, like all institutions, are created to serve life, not dominate it. But that is not possible under our current laws, which favor the rights of corporations above human and all other life. As corporations grow in wealth and power, they require more oversight, not less. There are many ways that human beings could limit corporate power.

Because corporations are chartered in particular locales, they could be required to abide by the laws of the government where they are incorporated, no matter where they do business. Some have suggested that corporate charters in the United States take place at the federal level so that states are not competing with each other in a race to the bottom to provide the best terms. Charters should be revoked if a corporation does not serve the public good.

As stated above, corporate costs of doing business should be internalized, so that both costs and prices include environmental and social costs. Right–to-know laws could require annual public corporate reports and audits of the overall effects of a corporation on their many stakeholders, including workers, consumers, communities, and the environment. "Bad Boy" laws could be passed at any government level to prevent corporations that repeatedly violate laws from doing business in their jurisdiction. Some locales have instituted such laws.

Limited liability could be lessened or eliminated, leaving both managers and investors vulnerable to being held liable for harm caused by the corporation. This would greatly change both individual and corporate financial decision-making and could help protect people and the earth.

Corporate tax laws could be reformed and tax havens abolished. Various corporate tax deductions could be eliminated, including the deduction for corporate advertising. Corporations could be prohibited from engaging in political lobbying and from giving contributions to candidates. Corporate personhood, and the privileges that go with it, could be eliminated, leaving civil-rights laws to protect natural persons, not corporations.

New, more democratic global trade and development institutions could be created under the auspices of the United Nations. Such institutions would provide oversight and rules for corporations to follow, based on just and sustainable principles, and would replace current bureaucracies and trade agreements that enable corporations to police governments.

I have heard it said, "If it doesn't breathe, it doesn't deserve free speech." I agree. And if its only conscience is the bottom line, it doesn't deserve to determine the quality of life for future generations. It has been suggested that a simple six-word amendment to the U.S. Constitution would go a long way toward bringing change: "A corporation is not a person."

CHAPTER TWELVE
The Unholy Trinity:
The IMF, World Bank, and WTO

> Whether intended or not, the policies so successfully
> advanced by the Breton Woods institutions have inexorably
> empowered the super rich to lay claim to the world's wealth
> at the expense of other people, other species, and the viabili-
> ty of the planet's ecosystem.
>
> —David C. Korton[1]

In April 2000 the annual World Bank and International
Monetary Fund (IMF) meetings took place on the Monday and
Tuesday of Holy Week. I went to Washington, D.C., where the meetings were to take place, to give a presentation about these institutions
at a conference and to participate in demonstrations and other actions
of public witness.

One day I went to an "Economic Stations of the Cross" event
focusing on Jubilee 2000. When I arrived at the steps of the U.S.
Capitol for the beginning of the walk, I joined a group of about
three hundred people, many of whom were pastors, priests, and
members of various religious orders, wearing robes, collars, or
stoles. Each person held a white wooden cross with the name of a
country written from top to bottom and the amount of debt it owes
written on the crossbar. The amounts were staggering. Because a
teenage Salvadoran refugee named Julio had lived with us for two
years and because of the country's name ("The Savior"), I chose to
carry the cross representing the debt burden of El Salvador:
$4,782,000,000.[2]

A young man stopped by, telling me that he had just recently
become a Christian. After listening to the speakers talk about the
world's debt crisis and the Jubilee 2000 Campaign, he decided that he
wanted to carry the large cross that would lead the procession. He
allowed others to alternate in helping him, but this willing Simon of
Cyrene carried the significant weight of this cross the whole way.

We sang as we walked, including a song someone made up to the
tune of "Wade in the Water." The verses were relevant to the present
situation and ended with the refrain:

Come to the World Bank,
Come to the World Bank, children,
Come to the World Bank,
The Spirit's gonna trouble the World Bank.

Our procession took us to the White House, Department of Treasury, Department of Commerce, the IMF building, and other centers of power; we stopped at each place for a reading and a prayer. Finally, at the World Bank headquarters, we attempted to deliver a letter to then World Bank president James Wolfensohn. The building was surrounded by barricades, and our path was blocked by several rows of police dressed in riot gear. Since we could proceed no further, most of us sat down to sing and to wait. Finally, a World Bank representative came out and received our letter, which called for the complete cancellation of the debt of the world's poorest nations.

The group that organized the protest was the Religious Working Group on the IMF and World Bank, a group of people representing religious denominations, institutions, and organizations who regularly meet and act "to address the causes of the debt that is crushing the world's poor." Their actions include witness, outreach, and political advocacy. Their statements of principles includes the following: "Social sin is present where there are growing economic disparities, increasing concentrations of economic power, and accelerating environmental abuse. . . . The biblical witness mandates just and equitable commercial relationships, selfless help to those in need and the cancellation of oppressive debts that keep people locked in poverty."[3]

The World Bank, IMF, and WTO are the rule makers of the global economy. They claim that the rules they impose raise living standards and improve the lives of people around the world. But the realities on the ground conflict with these claims. In spite of their rhetoric, the practical purpose of these ruling institutions seems to be their own institutional survival and expansion. There are other dominant Powers with this same purpose that see their interests as aligned with the interests of the IMF, World Bank, and WTO—namely, wealthy governments, especially the United States, and transnational corporations. Although, as Stringfellow noted, "the demonic powers do exist chaotically, apparently thriving in confusion, rivalry, and complexity,"[4] these dominant institutions support each others' existence and further each others' goals.

As with many other institutions, the origins of the IMF, World Bank, and WTO were steeped in idealistic fervor. Their initial founders called together world leaders at the end of World War II to a meeting in Breton Woods, New Hampshire, for the purpose of creating new global institutions that would prevent another depression or world war by fostering peace through prosperity. The World Bank would provide loans to help rebuild Europe, the IMF would stabilize world currencies and provide short-term loans, and a new trade organization would facilitate global trade. This trade organization later became the General Agreement on Tariffs and Trade (GATT), precursor of the WTO.

As it turned out, Europe was rebuilt with the help of the U.S. Marshall Plan and declined loans from the World Bank, which then turned to developing nations to market its loans. The IMF became one of the most destabilizing economic forces in history, causing "IMF food riots" to erupt in poor nations after imposing stringent austerity measures and creating conditions for wildly fluctuating capital markets by forcing countries without stable financial systems to eliminate capital controls. And the GATT became the World Trade Organization, which, as I will demonstrate, raised trade above the value of workers, communities, and the earth itself. Similar to all institutions, as these institutions developed they took on a life of their own.

At Breton Woods, U.S. Treasury Secretary Henry Morgenthau gave an impassioned opening speech that set the tone for this gathering of heads of industry, heads of state, and economists. The speech provides a glimpse into the underlying hope-filled philosophy that inspired the creation of these institutions. He spoke of "the creation of a dynamic world economy in which the peoples of every nation will be able to realize their potentialities in peace and enjoy increasingly the fruits of material progress on an earth infinitely blessed with natural riches. . . . Prosperity has no fixed limits. It is not a finite substance to be diminished by division."[5]

Although we have seen in the last half-century that the great wealth generated by the Western model of industrialized development is distributed unequally and does not necessarily improve the lives of the poor, these institutions continue to proclaim this idealistic vision to justify their policies and existence. And although we now know that the earth is not *infinitely* blessed with natural riches, these institutions continue to promote the same ideology and to engage in practices that deplete the earth's bounty at an ever-accelerating rate.

Institutional pressures and this entrenched ideology make it almost impossible for these institutions to change course. Furthermore, they were not created through a democratic process, but emerged out of a milieu that was dominated by a wealthy elite, whose interests they continue to serve to this day. For this reason, many of their critics are calling for them to be abolished and for new, more democratic institutions, to take their place.

Some consider the IMF, World Bank, and WTO to be tools of Western colonial powers. At the end of World War II, with most of Europe shattered, the United States was the only Western nation that could help the world rebound from the devastation of war. For this reason, it took on a leadership role that continues to this day. Western nations, especially the United States, dominate these institutions. Both the IMF and World Bank are based in Washington, D.C. According to custom, the World Bank president is always American, while the IMF managing director is always European.[6]

The IMF and World Bank are funded by member nations, but at different levels—wealthy nations pay more, poor nations pay less, based on the size of their economies. Decisions are based on the principle of one dollar, one vote, so the wealthy nations have far more say than do poor nations in what IMF and World Bank policies will be.[7] Clearly, the United States has more influence within these institutions than any other nation; moreover, it is the only nation with veto power.

The General Agreement on Tariffs and Trade (GATT) regulated tariffs and quotas for forty years until the Reagan Revolution in the early 1980s. At this time the Uruguay Round of trade negotiations was initiated, which gradually expanded GATT's authority and transformed it in 1995 into the World Trade Organization, an institution based in Geneva that has far-reaching powers and an enforcement mechanism far stronger than that of any other international agreement or treaty. This process of transformation was "pushed largely by U.S.-based global corporations and their allies in the U.S. government."[8] An analysis by the International Forum on Globalization concludes: "In sum, it has been Washington's changing perception of the needs of its economic interest groups that has shaped and reshaped the international trading regime. It was not global necessity that gave birth to the WTO in 1995 but rather the U.S. government's assessment that the interests of its corporations were no longer served by a loose and flexible GATT."[9] As we will see, many proposals to further expand trade liberalization and extend the authority of the WTO continue to originate in the United States.

Developing nations signed on to the WTO because they were reassured that its multilateral rules and enforcement mechanisms would "level the playing field" among member nations on trade matters. But as the WTO began implementing its mandate, poorer nations discovered to their dismay that there were still great imbalances among trading partners. Poor countries were no match for the United States and other wealthy nations, which could enforce trade rules to their advantage by spending millions to bring a case to the WTO.

In chapter 9, we looked at Thomas Friedman's concept of the Golden Straitjacket, the one-size-fits-all pattern of rules that the IMF, World Bank, and WTO impose on every country. As stated earlier, these basic rules require governments to remove barriers to the free movement of corporations, the free movement of goods, and the free flow of capital. But in actuality, the rules of the global economy are imposed unequally, and the playing field continues to be far from level, since the wealthy nations use their considerable leverage to skew the game to their own advantage. Besides, "It really doesn't matter how level the playing field is," says Njoke Njoroge Njehu of the U.S. Network for Economic Justice, "If it is a basketball court and you're on it with Michael Jordon, it's not going to make much of a difference."[10]

THE WORLD BANK AND IMF: DEBT HAS A CHILD'S FACE

Must we starve our children to pay our debts?
—Julius Nyerere, former president of Tanzania[11]

In his book *When Corporations Rule the World*, David Korten gives us a glimpse of the disconnect between the rhetoric and the actual policies of the IMF and World Bank. At one week-long IMF/World Bank meeting, then World Bank President Barber Conable spoke to the assembly about their responsibility to the poor, saying, "Our institution is mighty in resources and in experience, but its labors will count for nothing if it cannot look at our world through the eyes of the most underprivileged, if we cannot share their hopes and their fears." Korton notes, however, that the meeting itself cost a total of $10 million, including a single formal dinner that cost $200 per person.[12] As Korton points out, if the delegates had made an effort to look at their world through the eyes of the most underprivileged, they "might well have lost their appetites." Not far from where this meeting was taking place, in Selma, Alabama, Raymond Wheeler of CBS did an interview with a poor child:

"Do you eat breakfast before school?"
"Sometimes, sir. Sometimes I have peas."
"And when you get to school, do you eat?"
"No, sir."
"Isn't there any food there?"
"Yes, sir."
"Why don't you have it?"
"I don't have the 35 cents."

"What do you do while the other children eat lunch?"
"I just sits there on the side" (his voice breaking).
"How do you feel when you see the other children eating?"
"I feel ashamed." (crying).[13]

Ashamed. In a world where the rich are getting richer and the poor are getting poorer, this little boy felt ashamed. But it is not the children who should feel ashamed. As stated in the 1989 UNICEF report, *"The State of the World's Children"*, "Allowing world economic problems to be taken out on the growing minds and bodies of young children is the antithesis of all civilized behavior. Nothing can justify it. And it shames and diminishes us all."[14]

As we will see, though their rhetoric says otherwise, the IMF and World Bank are institutional vehicles for the continuation of a system that impoverishes people and destroys the earth. What powers these vehicles? Transnational corporations and banks, the primary engines of the global economy, supported by powerful governments whose interests they supposedly serve. What is their goal? Their own institutional survival and consolidation of their power, which require them to participate as players on the world scene as part of the network of Powers that make up today's Domination System.

Again, I am not simply speaking of the human beings involved in these institutions. As Stringfellow pointed out, a distinctive feature of people who serve in high places is that they are "not exceptionally immoral; they are, on the contrary, quite ordinarily moral."[15] Many of them may not be aware of the overall direction and effects of the Powers that they serve.

The World Bank began promoting loans to developing nations as a way for them to modernize, build infrastructure, and stimulate economic growth. The Bank had lending targets, so it usually focused on large and expensive projects such as power plants, large dams, agribusiness operations, or tropical forest "development." Such projects often create massive environmental damage, rarely help the neediest people, and can displace whole communities of subsistence farmers and indigenous peoples. The World Bank continues to loan money for such projects to this day.

Because loans were loosely administered and often poorly managed, money was often lost through bribes, theft, and mismanagement. Because the Bank's primary lending criteria was financial, it often loaned money indiscriminately to corrupt regimes and dictatorships that siphoned money off the top, took it out of the country, or spent it on weapons. The IMF and World Bank treat these loans as the sole responsibility of the borrowing nations, but nations in the

South and debt campaigners claim that those who loaned money irresponsibly should also be held accountable.

In addition to World Bank loans, governments and private banks also loaned money to developing nations. Throughout the Cold War both the United States and Soviet Union provided loans to countries they perceived as being friendly or geopolitically important. In the early 1970s, oil-producing countries earned billions from a quadrupling of oil prices. Flush with dollars invested from these earnings, Western banks needed places to invest. Believing that sovereign governments would not default, they got into the business of pushing loans to developing nations, sometimes without normal banking precautions. For their part, developing nations were desperate for loans for development and for keeping up with rising oil prices. The IMF supported this arrangement. For a while, the money flowed.[16]

In the late 1970s, oil prices rose again. Interest rates on these loans also rose sharply, triggered by rising U.S. interest rates. At the same time, prices for commodities like bananas, coffee, cotton, cocoa, and other products that were exported by developing nations fell dramatically.[17] Suddenly, everything changed. In the global recession that followed, developing nations could not service their debt.

What had begun as a problem of debt between private banks and developing nations became a problem for the global economic system as a whole. The governments of wealthy nations were concerned that if developing nations defaulted on their loans, it could undermine confidence in major banks and trigger a global crisis. The IMF and the World Bank stepped in and began refinancing these loans.[18] In other words, bilateral loans and private loans became debt owed to the IMF and World Bank, institutions that were funded by the tax dollars of member nations.

These loans, however, came with conditions that were intended to enable countries on the verge of default to earn the foreign currency needed to pay them back. Countries were required to accept a package of austerity measures, a set of conditions that were outlined in IMF and World Bank Structural Adjustment Programs (SAPS). These conditions varied from country to country, but typically required countries to open up their economies to foreign corporations, reduce wages, focus on exports, devalue their currencies, eliminate food subsidies, institute fees for health and education, sell off public utilities and services, and reduce social expenditures. The purpose of these policies was to get countries to spend less, export more, and open up their economies to foreign corporations. A country would have to take this bitter "medicine," it was said, to bring it into economic health. It would have to "tighten its belt" for its long-term well-being.

But what does it mean to tighten your belt in a nation where people watch their children starve? It is this logic and these demands that have put such a burden on poor countries, especially on the poorest of the poor within the countries, who never benefited from these loans in the first place. Once poor countries become ensnared in the bonds of debt, it often becomes a vicious cycle, with loans being refinanced again and again, always with new conditions added to further "reform" the economy.[19]

Both UNICEF and the United Nations Economic Commission for Africa claim that the World Bank and IMF bear substantial responsibility for dramatically worsening the plight of the poor in Africa and throughout the developing world, with an overall lowering of health, nutritional, and educational levels for tens of millions of children. Since 1980 sub-Saharan Africa has undergone more than eight thousand debt renegotiations, and its total debts have nearly tripled.[20] It now pays almost $15 billion a year in debt service, almost the exact amount that experts say could reverse the AIDS crisis in Africa.[21] According to the All Africa Council of Churches: "Every child in Africa is born with a financial burden which a lifetime's work cannot repay. The debt is a new form of slavery as vicious as the slave trade."[22]

In the 1990s activists around the world formed the Jubilee 2000 Campaign, a faith-based movement calling for cancellation of the debt of the world's poorest nations, which continues as the Jubilee Campaign today. In 1996, bowing to public pressure, the IMF and World Bank introduced the Heavily Indebted Poor Countries Initiative (HIPC), in which creditors would join together to cancel the debt of the poorest nations. Some countries have experienced improved conditions with debt relief under HIPC. Tanzania, for instance, although still carrying a heavy debt burden, has been able to improve education, water provision, rural roads, and health care, including care for those with HIV/AIDS.[23]

Sadly, though, although HIPC has delivered over $48 billion in debt cancellation, not one country has achieved "debt sustainability."[24] The initiative was too limited and, not surprisingly, too myopic to actually lift the targeted countries out of poverty. Debt campaigners criticized HIPC for its "harmful economic conditions," which for some African and other nations included water privatization with "full cost recovery." Most of the countries that have received some debt relief under HIPC still pay more on debt than on health care. Several HIPC countries are paying as much or more in debt service as they were before they joined the initiative.[25]

In 2000, the Clinton administration responded to incessant pressure from activists by canceling bilateral debt owed by the poorest nations to the United States. In June 2005, G-8 leaders announced a plan to immediately cancel 100 percent of the multilateral debt, that is, debt owed to the IMF, World Bank, and African Development Fund, by eighteen poor nations. Jubilee USA Network immediately expressed strong concerns that such cancellation must not be accompanied by harmful conditions and that the debt of the many other poor and indebted nations also be cancelled.[26]

According to Noreena Hertz, "The promised Jubilee never took place." The debt now owed by the world's poorest nations amounts to $458 billion.[27] The total debt owed by developing nations amounts to an astounding $2.5 trillion. Every month, poor countries pay the banks, financial institutions, and governments of the developed world over $31.3 billion, that is, almost $1 billion each day.[28] The principle of many of these debts has been paid many times over, but compound interest keeps them growing as nations sacrifice the health, education, and even the lives of their people to service these debts. According to UNICEF, the actual effect of this debt crisis falls largely on children:

Debt has a child's face. Debt's burden falls most heavily on the minds and bodies of children, killing some, and stunting others so that they will never fully develop. It leaves children without immunization against fatal, but easily preventable, diseases. It condemns them to a life without education or— if they go to school—to classrooms without roofs, desks, chairs, blackboards, books, even pencils. And it orphans them, as hundreds of thousands of mothers die in childbirth each year, die as a result of inadequacies in health care and other services that poverty perpetuates.[29]

In her book *The Debt Threat*, Hertz shows vividly how the debt crisis not only impoverishes people, destroys the environment, and creates widespread misery, but also threatens us all. With stunning vision and insight, she rivals Jared Diamond in painting the picture of a world facing almost unimaginable horrors, and shows how the massive debt borne by poor nations makes this future ever more likely:

And in this ever globalizing world of ours what is "theirs" fast becomes "ours," their sickness becomes our sicknesses, their despair our despair, their damage our damage; their dysfunctionality, the dysfunctionality of us all. We will never be able to build walls high enough to keep angry beggar armies out. No amount of "shock" or "awe" will be sufficient to dispel the ever growing hordes of the disgruntled and disenfranchised. Paper surgical masks will be unable to protect us from the spread of diseases that respect no borders. No number of herbicide-spraying sorties will stop poor, dispossessed farmers from growing drugs. Our environment will be irrevocably damaged by decisions taken by others many thousands of miles away. Our economies threatened, by the game of chicken that Wall Street and the leaders of the developing world so often play.[30]

Fortunately, Hertz also addresses the major problems with debt cancellation and makes concrete suggestions for resolving them. She points in the direction of global transformation and healing, which I will discuss in the final section of this book.

THE WORLD TRADE ORGANIZATION: A CORPORATE BILL OF RIGHTS

We are writing the constitution of a single global economy.
—Former WTO Director-General Renato Ruggiero[31]

Let us now turn to the World Trade Organization, the third "person," or rather, "personality," of this Unholy Trinity of global rule-making institutions. Transnational corporations have been active from the beginning in promoting and attempting to extend the scope and authority of the WTO. And this is no wonder, since the WTO restricts the power of governments to regulate corporations or to interfere in their profit-making purpose.[32] The WTO has been called "a corporate Bill of Rights."[33]

It is impossible to talk about the formation of the WTO without also talking about the North American Free Trade Agreement (NAFTA), since their foundations were being laid at the same time. NAFTA went into effect on January 1, 1994, and the WTO on January 1, 1995. The same organizations that lobbied for the passage of NAFTA lobbied for the creation of the WTO. These included individual corporations, but corporations also pooled their resources to promote their interests by forming corporate coalitions such as USA NAFTA, made up of more than two thousand member corporations and business coalitions, Alliance for GATT Now, a coalition that claimed more than two hundred thousand businesses, and America Leads on Trade, which worked to promote fast-track trade-negotiating authority. Corporations also lobbied, and continue to lobby, through established associations such as the Business Roundtable, U.S. Council for International Business, U.S. Chamber of Commerce, and the National Foreign Trade Council.[34] Labor unions, environmental organizations, and human-rights and consumer-safety groups all worked to defeat these agreements, but political leaders, Republicans and Democrats alike, bought (or were bought) into the dominant free-market ideology and sold out to corporate power. Though similar in intent, there are important differences between NAFTA and the WTO. NAFTA is a regional free-trade agreement between Canada, the United States, and Mexico, while the WTO is a global establishment, based in Geneva, that sets policies and adjudicates trade disputes among the 150 member nations around the world. We will look at regional trade agreements like NAFTA later in this chapter. For now, we will focus on the WTO.

The WTO's predecessor, the General Agreement on Tariffs and Trade (GATT), moved beyond simple regulation of tariffs and quotas in the mid-1980s, when it began considering cases that dealt with nontariff barriers to trade, which included labor, environmental, human rights, and consumer-safety laws that could have a negative impact on trade. GATT had a dispute-resolution process, but member nations often ignored its rulings because it had no serious enforcement power.

That changed radically after the formation of the WTO, which can enforce its decisions. Through the WTO, any member nation can challenge a law of any other member nation as being a nontariff barrier to trade. When a case is brought to the WTO, a tribunal of three trade bureaucrats hears arguments and makes its ruling behind closed doors. There are no requirements for these trade "experts" to have knowledge of environmental, labor, or human-rights issues. Those who serve on tribunals generally have past or present ties to corporations, and there are no conflict of interest restrictions. Documents, hearings, briefs, and records of proceedings are confidential; only the decision is announced. Only national governments can participate in these cases, even if state or local laws are being challenged. Countries that lose such disputes have three choices: they can voluntarily change the law, agree to pay fines, or face permanent tariffs imposed on their products.

The first WTO trade dispute was brought by Venezuela and Brazil, at the behest of its oil companies, challenging the U.S. Clean Air Act, which they claimed discriminated against foreign oil producers. The United States had enacted the law in 1990 to reduce air pollution caused by vehicle emissions, since studies showed that such emissions contribute to asthma and other respiratory problems and weaken the body's immune system. Although domestic oil companies originally lobbied against the law, when faced by the WTO challenge six years later they claimed that they had spent $37 billion to implement the law. The U.S. Environmental Protection Agency (EPA) claimed that weakening the law would have adverse environmental impacts. Nevertheless, the WTO tribunal ruled against the United States, stating that "WTO members were free to set their own environmental objectives, but they were bound to implement those objectives only through measures consistent with [WTO's] provisions."[35] The United States amended its Clean Air Act to comply.[36] The ruling generated a flurry of WTO activity, as several countries brought successful suits against various U.S. public-health and environmental laws.[37]

WTO critics charge that such rulings and such concessions are a violation of national sovereignty. Sovereignty is not something that the United States (or any nation) gives up lightly. To enter into treaties with other nations requires a two-thirds vote of the U.S. Senate. Even then, compliance is enforced voluntarily by each participating country. Participation in the WTO, a trade agreement, required a simple majority vote in both houses. It was passed in a lame-duck session of Congress in December 1994, just a month before it went into effect. Yet it has the power to force the change of democratically enacted domestic laws, which goes far beyond the power of any treaty.

Why would a nation, especially the most powerful nation on earth, relinquish its sovereignty by sacrificing a domestic law that was enacted through the democratic process? The only way it makes sense is in the context of corporate globalization.

Most trade disputes are brought to the WTO by governments on behalf of their corporations. As we have seen, corporations lobby hard to get these trade agreements passed. They also contribute financially to government leaders who support them. These same corporations then use the WTO and other free-trade venues to attempt to shape the global marketplace to their advantage. Although transnational corporations engage in fierce competition, they are united in their support of trade agreements that restrict government interference in their ability to make profits. And in fact, the laws that are challenged at the WTO by governments on behalf of corporations are often the same laws that domestic corporations fight at home.

The United States depends upon its corporations to help establish and maintain economic and geopolitical dominance in regions that it considers vital to its interests. In short, the U.S. government sees its well-being as wrapped up with the well-being of its corporations. As Charlie Wilson, chairman of General Motors in 1955, said in Senate hearings, "What's good for General Motors is good for the rest of America."[38] We are obviously not talking about the well-being of the people here. We are talking about the Powers.

Although the United States does not always win trade disputes, it has the lawyers and the money, supported by powerful corporations, not only to put up a good fight, but to intimidate less-privileged nations into changing their laws simply by threatening WTO action. An example is Guatemala.

In 1983 Guatemala passed a law based on World Health Organization (WHO) standards to encourage breast feeding and to alert new mothers to the risk of using baby formula or baby food as a breast-milk substitute. In order to make the information accessible to illiterate women, the law prohibited labels that depicted healthy babies on infant-formula and baby-food packaging. Infant mortality rates dropped significantly, and the United Nations Children's Fund (UNICEF) held up the law as a model of success.

According to UNICEF, over 1.5 million infants die each year because mothers in poor countries substitute infant formula for breast milk. This leads to malnutrition when babies become dependent on formula and women cannot afford to buy it, and to death from diarrhea when formula is mixed with polluted water. Nevertheless, Gerber, which features the pudgy "Gerber baby" on its products and whose motto is "Babies are our business," issued a threat to Guatemala that it would enlist the U.S. government in a challenge to the labeling law at the WTO. In response the government of Guatemala changed its law to exempt imports from its stringent labeling restrictions.[39]

It is not just poor nations, however, that change their laws under threat of WTO action. The United States removed a provision in its Marine Mammal Protection Act (MMPA) after Mexico threatened to challenge it at the WTO. In 1988, a "dolphin-safe tuna" amendment to the MMPA was passed to protect dolphins from being trapped in tuna "purse seine" nets after a massive grassroots effort that included millions of children writing to Congress to "save the dolphins." Rather than face the public's outrage at a WTO ruling to overturn the popular law, the Clinton administration, over a period of years, quietly weakened the provision, while allowing the "dolphin-safe" label to stand.[40]

Massachusetts had a preferential purchasing law that penalized companies that did business with Burma's military dictatorship, which employs slave labor. The policy had been called for by Burmese human rights activists, was passed through grassroots citizen action, and was modeled after similar laws targeting business in South Africa under apartheid. The EU and Japan challenged this law in the WTO. The dispute was put on hold when a U.S. corporate front group called Engage*USA challenged the law in U.S. courts. The U.S. Supreme Court finally ruled that the Massachusetts law restricting purchases from Burma was illegal.[41] A similar law focusing on Nigeria's military dictatorship was on the verge of passing in Maryland but lost by one vote after U.S. State Department staff lobbied against it on the basis that it would violate the rules of the WTO.[42] In this way, the threat of WTO action has a chilling effect on the creation of new laws. Njoke Njoroge Njehu of the Network for Global Economic Justice said, "If not for laws like this against businesses in South Africa, we would still be under Apartheid."[43] Today such laws are illegal according to the WTO.

In a ruling favorable to the United States, the WTO ruled against the European Union's ban on beef containing residues of artificial hormones because the EU could not prove that hormone residues harm human health, even though evidence proves that the actual hormones do. The WTO approved $116.8 million per year in sanctions after the EU refused to change its law.[44]

Countries have threatened WTO action or have brought disputes against other countries challenging their environmental, labor, consumer safety, and even human rights laws. Such cases include domestic laws that would require the labeling of GMO foods, local or national laws that "discriminate" against foreign transnational corporations by giving preferences to local small businesses, laws that ban toxic chemicals from domestic production or use. We have mentioned several cases. Others include challenges to: an EU ban on steel jaw leg traps, a Danish law to protect children by banning lead in certain compounds, an Australian quarantine on imported raw salmon, an EU law regulating plastic softeners in teething rings and other toys, a Thai law that would allow traditional healers to register traditional medicines with the government in order to prevent "biopiracy," the EU's preferential treatment of banana producers from former colonies in the Caribbean, a U.S. law requiring fumigation of wooden boxes carrying imports from China and Hong Kong, designed to prevent infestations by Asian longhorned beetles, and South Africa's Medicines Law, which promotes competitive pricing of pharmaceuticals.

The WTO, while claiming to promote free trade, actually is a highly regulated system of trade and investment based on a seven-hundred-page document with rules for governments to follow. It is actually "a global system of enforceable rules . . . where corporations have all the rights, governments have all the obligations and democracy is left behind in the dust."[45]

As Debi Barker and Jerry Mander state in their book, *Invisible Government*, "The single, clearest, most direct result of economic globalization to date is a massive global transfer of economic and political power away from national governments and into the hands of global corporations and the trade bureaucracies they helped create. This transfer of power is producing dire consequences for the environment, human rights, social welfare, agriculture, food safety, workers rights, national sovereignty, and democracy itself." [46]

Not all provisions in free-trade agreements restrict government regulations, only those that interfere with corporate profits. The WTO requires governments to establish and enforce laws that deal with intellectual property. These rules favor corporate rights over the rights of indigenous communities to the traditional plants they have used as medicine, and over the needs of HIV/AIDS patients and people from developing nations for cheap, generic drugs. Strong intellectual-property laws give a large advantage to people in industrialized nations, particularly the United States. Such provisions extend the power and increase the wealth of global corporations and their national allies, and place protection of corporate property rights above protection of human rights.

NAFTA rules are based on many of the same principles and mechanisms as those of the WTO, but in some areas they go even further. For example, NAFTA's Chapter 11 enables corporations to challenge governments directly. In this way, corporations can bypass the troublesome step of having to convince their home government to file cases on their behalf.

United Parcel Service (UPS), based in the United States, brought a NAFTA case against the government of Canada. Because Canada's mail service is partially privatized and partially provided by the Canadian government, UPS claims that Canada is providing an unfair subsidy that interferes with free trade and cuts in on UPS's potential profits. This case has been pending for years, with long, time-consuming, and expensive legal briefs being filed continuously by both sides.

Who has the money to continue these sorts of lawsuits? Corporations. If UPS loses this case, the only thing really lost is the (tax-deductible) cost of pursuing this dispute If UPS wins, it will be entitled to damages for estimated lost profits—past, present, and future. Who will pick up the tab? Canadian taxpayers.

An important exemption to WTO, NAFTA, and other free-trade agreements is the national security exemption. Discussion of this topic leads up to the last two chapters in this section, where I will discuss the police and military enforcement mechanisms of corporate globalization. For as we have seen, growing poverty, rising inequity, and ecological degradation lead to massive dislocation, social upheaval, and chaos, both within and among countries. The Powers that be must deal with these unpleasant but inevitable results of global free-market capitalism somehow. The national security exemption is a brilliant method that allows corporations to profit from tax dollars that subsidize government purchases of police and military hardware, the construction of prisons, the hiring of public or private "security" forces, and weapons for use at home and abroad, including foreign military sales. Since every government can decide for itself what constitutes national security, this exemption can be interpreted broadly, as in the case of Iraq, where the United States claimed a "national security exemption" in offering no-bid contracts to U.S. corporations in the rebuilding of Iraq's infrastructure, which U.S. weapons had destroyed.

You would think that governments and multilateral institutions such as the IMF, World Bank, and WTO would be moving in a more constructive direction, but many people both within and outside of these institutions believe that the current course is already set and is inevitable. Why, for instance, is the United States government not using its vast financial resources to create a better life for the majority of its people and for people around the world? Why does it support policies that trap people and nations in generations of debt? Why does it allow domestic laws that protect people and the environment to be overturned?

Clearly, the United States and other nations see their interests as tied to corporate interests. As corporate power increases, however, the power of governments decreases, until governments, the lucky ones, end up riding on corporate coattails. But corporations, once they are truly globalized, have no loyalty at all, except to the bottom line. They are not even loyal to their "home" governments. They can change nationalities at will.

Though the rhetoric of the IMF and World Bank has been about development and raising the standard of living, the actual effects of these multilateral bureaucracies has been to integrate poor nations into a world economy dominated by global corporations and powerful nations. They have used structural adjustment policies (SAPS) to "pry open" the economies of developing nations, creating complete dependency.

How can global corporations further pry open the U.S. economy and the economies of other industrialized nations? How can they finish what they started during the Reagan Revolution in the 1980s? How can they bypass the messiness of the democratic process altogether while gutting regulatory agencies and eliminating troublesome laws that interfere with corporate profits? How can they perpetuate the "smoke and mirrors" illusion that nation-states have power, while eliminating the very laws that governments use to protect the rights and well-being of their people? How can they privatize the potentially lucrative public-services sector, including publicly funded hospitals, schools, libraries, prisons, utilities, water services, and social services, and offer these and all other services up for sale? How can they ensure that wealthy, industrialized nations will ultimately be as dependent upon the global system that they dominate as are poor and indebted nations? How can they bring structural adjustment policies home? How can global corporations extend their power and consolidate their dominance over people, their governments, and the earth itself? The answer: by creating trade agreements and global bureaucracies that convince governments to do this for them, institutions like NAFTA and the WTO, which essentially take the matter out of government hands.

Why should local governments, states, or national governments be restricted in their ability to set standards for the common good of their people? As we consider principles that can provide a basis for a more hopeful future, the principle of *subsidiarity* must be mentioned here. Subsidiarity reverses the present top-down approach to governance that is exhibited by global bureaucracies like the IMF, World Bank, and WTO, which dictate and restrict what governments can or cannot do. The principle of subsidiarity is based on the idea that participatory democracy is more easily expressed at the local level, where people can directly affect governing institutions. With subsidiarity the primary locus of decision making would be local, with communities networking regionally, nationally, and even globally in a "bottom-up" approach. Decision making would move up to the next level of government only when necessary to meet social and ecological goals that cannot be met at a local or regional level, or when human rights are being violated.

The principle of *food safety and food security* is another basic principle for a future where people will be able to sustain themselves and their families. Local, regional, state, and national governments must have the right to protect local production and the safety of the food supply. Global bureaucracies must not interfere with the rights of governments to limit food imports, set and enforce safety standards, or restrict the sale of foods based on the precautionary principle.

The *right to a means of livelihood* is another necessary principle. Governments, trade agreements, and global institutions must honor the right of independent trade unions to organize and must restrict child labor and forced labor. People have a right to a job with dignity and those who are unemployed, underemployed, or who work in the non-money economy have the right to sustenance. Policies that force subsistence dwellers and small farmers off the land must be reversed.

The IMF, World Bank, and WTO have lost all legitimacy and have caused more poverty, inequity, and environmental damage than they have prevented. For this reason, many citizens groups are calling for substantial systemic change. All further trade liberalization and economic restructuring through these existing institutions should be immediately halted. They should be decommissioned and replaced with new democratically accountable trade, development, and finance institutions that function under the authority of a reformed United Nations. Such institutions must ensure the rights of federal, state, and local governments to enact and enforce laws that protect the common good, and should create a bottom line for participating nations that would protect human rights and the environment, and should also require full disclosure of corporate standards and behavior. Nations that refuse to abide by just and sustainable standards would not be allowed to participate.

All "odious," unjust, and unpayable debt of poor nations must be forgiven. Noreena Hertz in *The Debt Threat* puts forth a comprehensive plan for ending the debt crisis through a system of National Regeneration Trusts that channel debt savings towards meeting human needs. Such trusts would include democratic oversight by civil society.

We still have two chapters to go before we continue this hopeful discussion of alternatives, before we consider how we can find our way out of this interlocking network of institutional Powers that would squeeze the life out of us all and of all that we hold precious in the world. It may feel like a maze, like a complex web that we will never find our way through, but that is not the case. Once we have seen what is at the heart of this global system our lives will never be the same. Simply put, we can resist corporate domination and buy out of the system. We can take a new direction. We can heed the warning: "Don't buy corporate rule."

CHAPTER THIRTEEN
No More Mr. Nice Guy:
The Corporate Security State

> The way of the crucified God seeks God in earth's humanity,
> which has been abandoned, rejected, and despised, the people
> who know life amid their struggle.
>
> —Mark Lewis Taylor[1]

On a rainy day in Washington, D.C. in April 2000, I was arrested while participating in a peaceful protest. A U.S. marshal threatened me as he escorted me into jail, saying, "We can do whatever we want to you. There are no TV cameras in here."

This threat did not take place in a vacuum. I am a middle-class white woman with connections to other people of privilege. I had consented to arrest during an organized protest. If anything bad happened to me, my friends, family, colleagues, and even my bishop would have helped me out. Every day much worse threats are made and carried out against poor people and people of color who are locked up against their will for years at a time. All I suffered during this arrest was verbal abuse, hunger, thirst, and a night in wet clothes on a cold concrete floor.

It has been said that the gates to hell are only locked from the inside. In other words, God doesn't create hell—we create our own hells and lock ourselves inside. But this is not altogether true, for what we do affects other people, and the systems and institutions we support have effects that we may never see. If we don't find out what's going on inside our jails and prisons, we may never see this hell that the Powers are creating, for the gates to this hell are shut from the outside—not even the media is allowed inside, and those of us who live on the outside hold the key.

The nature of today's global empire is revealed most clearly in the system's police and military enforcement mechanisms. Economic globalization is often presented as benign, as simply a matter of trade, development, international cooperation, and financial flows. In reality, as we have seen, violence pervades the global system at every level. The appeal of the ideology that promotes consumption as desirable and assimilation into the global economy as beneficial is not enough to keep the system of corporate globalization going. Global bureaucracies can impose economic sanctions, and governments can institute free market policies, but the system also requires police and military force. The Powers use fear as a means of control by making clear that those who cannot or will not play by the system's rules are expendable. Such people serve as scapegoats and examples to others. Cooperation of the majority is gained by appealing to self-interest and by threatening exclusion, stigma, physical coercion, abuse, torture, even death. The IMF, World Bank, and WTO foster this process, pressuring countries to cut or privatize government services and weaken restrictions on corporate activities while granting national security exemptions and encouraging governments to provide security, if necessary through force. The greater the gap between rich and poor, the more repressive the government must be to maintain order against those who expose the system's injustice, interfere with its success, or challenge the status quo.

This relationship between repression and corporate dominance is most apparent in many poor, indebted countries where police, mercenaries, and military forces protect foreign corporate operations by subduing impoverished people, while killing or otherwise making an example of those who resist. For instance, Ken Saro Wiwa and eight other indigenous Ogoni activists were hanged in Nigeria in 1995 for leading a nonviolent campaign against Royal Dutch Shell, whose oil operations were destroying Ogoni land.[2]

Since the United States is the primary model, promoter, and exporter of free-market capitalism, this chapter will focus on the U.S. approach to the enforcement mechanisms of the global system. Enforcement of corporate globalization is primarily the job of the United States, the purveyor of the world's global corporate empire. As Thomas Friedman says, "Without America on duty, there would be no America online."[3]

In this chapter we will explore domestic enforcement mechanisms, which are provided primarily by the U.S. criminal-justice system. The next chapter will take on the subject of U.S. foreign policy and the military/industrial complex. In both of these systems, death is the ultimate sanction.

CONTRADICTIONS OF CAPITALISM

The way of the cross in Lockdown America, then, is a way across a terrain that is a locus of empire. It is a terrain where people—deemed surplus, junk, or dynamite—are sacrificed to maintain a public order in the United States and increasingly to sustain the U.S.-led global imperium.
—Mark Lewis Taylor[4]

In the late 1990s, budget cuts in Greensboro, North Carolina, led to the decommissioning of its library's bus-sized "bookmobile." Within months, the police department bought the bookmobile for its elite twenty-three-member Special Response Team and converted it into a mobile command-and-control center.[5]

The transformation of a bookmobile into a SWAT Team command center symbolizes the economic shift that has taken place in the United States since the early 1980s. As the nation's wealth has been siphoned off from the poor, working, and middle classes and has accumulated at the top, government's benevolent functions, which serve the common good and provide a social safety net, are being replaced by repressive functions, which contain and punish those who are dispossessed and who threaten the established order.

In recent decades, as economic inequality increased, the number of people in U.S. jails and prisons grew to over 2.2 million, eight times as many as in 1975.[6] The United States, which contains just 4 percent of the world's population, now makes up 25 percent of the world's prison population. The "land of the free" incarcerates a higher percentage of its people than any other country.[7] Two-thirds are sentenced for nonviolent offenses.[8] More than 70 percent of prisoners are people of color.[9] Whites are incarcerated at the rate of 393 per 100,000, Latinos at the rate of 957 per 100,000, and blacks at the rate of 2,531 per 100,000.[10] The fastest-growing prison population is women. Most women are incarcerated for nonviolent offenses; three-quarters of them have dependent children.[11]

In his book *Lockdown America*, Christian Parenti points out an inherent contradiction of capitalism[12] that pressures governments to choose between policies that promote equity and policies of social repression. In order for capitalism to work, wealth must be accumulated and economies must grow. Unemployment is an integral part of this system. The system is designed to create unemployment so that there will be enough competition for jobs to keep wages down and make it more difficult for labor to organize. But unemployment leads to poverty, and visible poverty is bad for business. So poverty both helps and hurts business. This is where the contradiction lies.

The very presence of those whom criminologist Steven Spitzer called "social junk" or "junk people," people like the homeless, prostitutes, or drug addicts, threatens business. At the same time, the presence of what Spitzer called "social dynamite" or "dynamite people," those who are angry at the system or who could organize, such as unemployed youth, threaten the capitalist system itself.[13]

Capitalist societies have dealt with these surplus populations in a variety of ways. From the time of the New Deal on, the United

States provided social services as a humane way of dealing with the problem, with government programs such as student grants, unemployment insurance, minimum-wage laws, Medicaid, Aid to Families with Dependent Children, Head Start, and summer jobs for youth. Such programs provide a safety net that ensures that no one in the country is left destitute and provide opportunities through which individuals can better themselves. Most developed countries in Europe and elsewhere still have "mixed" economies that provide universal health care, maternity and paternity leave, and various other services that redistribute income and support the general population.

But in the United States, beginning with the Reagan years, corporate interests assumed center stage. Since that time, corporate taxes have been reduced and corporate subsidies have increased, while social services have been cut. Inequity has grown tremendously. The middle class has been squeezed. Manufacturing jobs that paid a living wage have been eliminated as businesses move their plants overseas to take advantage of cheap labor. Poverty has increased. Homelessness has soared. Mental hospitals and county hospitals have closed. This elimination of social services leaves surplus populations to their own devices.

During this same time the issue of law enforcement became increasingly politicized. Politicians from both major parties have tried to outdo each other in appearing tough on crime. Instead of providing services that could alleviate conditions that underlie crimes of poverty and despair, U.S. policy makers have passed increasingly harsh and punitive laws. Police forces around the country have been militarized and are using police tactics, such as sweeps, that terrorize whole neighborhoods, especially neighborhoods of color. Courts are enforcing mandatory minimum sentences and "three strikes" laws that consign even youthful and nonviolent offenders to years, and sometimes life, behind bars. Executions have been revived. Overcrowded jails and prisons have cut rehabilitation programs and have become places of misery, warehouses of human flesh. Many families say that their loved ones are far worse coming out of prison than when they went in. This presents a danger to society as a whole.

Thus, U.S. policy makers are currently dealing with surplus populations through paramilitary policing, longer and harsher sentences, and a prison-building spree. This approach keeps junk people away from the public eye and prevents dynamite people from organizing, while the media follows the official line, convincing a fearful public that such policies are necessary to protect them. But what exactly are the mechanisms behind this frenzy of incarceration? What is driving the crackdown? Whom do such policies benefit? And how do these policies fit into the system of corporate globalization as a whole?

THE CORPORATE CONNECTION

> From a management point of view, a prison is like a hotel or motel: You want to fill every bed, every night. If you don't have enough guests, you do whatever you can to get them, including supporting campaigns for mandatory minimums and longer sentences.
>
> —Si Kahn and Elizabeth Minnich[14]

Prisons have become an important part of the U.S. economy. "Corrections" (a euphemism) is now a $50 billion industry,[15] employing 523,000 full-time employees—more than any Fortune 500 company.[16]

The shift in national priorities from social programs to prison construction and incarceration has spelled profits for corporations. Indeed, corporations have had a hand in bringing these changes about. Corporations lobby for corporate tax cuts, which result in cutbacks in social programs and lead to social unrest. Corporate outsourcing of jobs, too, creates more unemployment and with it more desperation and crime.

Corporations are adept at using the U.S. justice system, which is biased against the poor and people of color. Corporate money buys lawyers.

Corporate money also buys laws. Corporations that profit from the prison-industry lobby for tough–on–crime legislation, make campaign contributions to those politicians who support it, draft and promote such legislation, and help shape public opinion through the media. This includes corporations that run private prisons.

In 1983 there were no private prisons in the United States; today there are over 120,000.[17] The two largest private prison operators in the nation are Corrections Corporations of America (CCA)[18] and GEO (formerly Wackenhut),[19] global corporations with lucrative lobbying operations and prisons on several continents. CCA's detention facilities turned a $95 million profit in 2005.[20] GEO stock soared 68 percent in the same year.[21]

During the 2002 and 2004 election cycles, private prison companies, directors, executives, and lobbyists gave $3.3 million to candidates and state political parties in forty-four states.[22] There is a revolving door between the public and private sector, that is, among former corrections administrators, PAC lobbyists, consultants to private prison companies, and state officials, which further corrupts the political process. For this reason, the U.S. criminal-justice system has been called the "prison/industrial" complex.[23] Others have called it the "corporate security state."[24]

In addition to private prisons, many other corporations profit from the prison industry: construction firms, corporations that provide technology for surveillance and restraint, MCI and other phone companies (which charge exorbitant prices for collect calls from prisoners), food service (2.2 million prisoners need 6.6 million meals per day), for-profit health-care providers, and many others. American Express, General Electric, and other companies help finance prison construction, while Wall Street brokerage firms sell prison-construction bonds.[25] Many corporations use prison labor, which pays just a few cents an hour, to keep costs down:

> Nordstrom department stores sell jeans that are marketed as "Prison Blues," as well as t-shirts and jackets made in Oregon prisons. The advertising slogan for these clothes is "made on the inside to be worn on the outside." Maryland prisoners inspect bottles and jars used for Revlon and Pierre Cardin, and schools throughout the world buy graduation caps and gowns made by South Carolina prisoners. . . . Prisoners do data entry for Chevron, make telephone reservations for TWA, raise hogs, shovel manure, make circuit boards, limousines, waterbeds, and lingerie for Victoria's Secret—all at a fraction of the cost of "free labor."[26]

The point I am making here is that crime is not the only thing that stimulates the growth of prisons. There are many financial incentives for locking people up: to provide jobs, to provide income to poor communities, to sell commodities, to turn a profit, to keep a lid on social tensions in a time of extreme inequity, and to protect the survival of the free-market capitalist system as a whole. Incarceration solves the problem of surplus populations that are generated by capitalism in a way that keeps profits up and wages down.

GULAG AMERICA

> Within the U.S. superpower, there is, increasingly, a subjugation of its citizenry to forces of transnational empire, and thus that citizenry comes under the control of state-sanctioned prisons, death penalties, and paramilitary policing. As U.S. military force and aerial bombardment back the process of economic globalization, so the power to jail and execute grows in the United States.
>
> —Mark Lewis Taylor[27]

Since September 11, 2001, the government has taken many actions in the name of national security that continue to build up the corporate security state. The Patriot Act has reduced civil liberties by creating a broad new crime of "domestic terrorism" that permits the government to conduct warrantless searches and seizures, engage in domestic surveillance, strip citizens and noncitizens of some constitutional protections, and engage in several violations of the First and Fourth Amendments.[28] The Bush administration has gone far beyond even these provisions and has engaged in widespread domestic surveillance, to the point of spying on nonprofits and entering peace groups into a "terror suspect" database. Control is the watchword. Control at any cost.[29]

The government arrested hundreds of immigrants after the September 11 attacks without due process, categorized them as terror suspects or enemy combatants, and kept many of them for months or years in legal limbo without recourse to counsel or communication with the outside world.[30] Many have claimed that they were taken to other countries and tortured. It is widely known that the CIA has engaged in "extraordinary rendition", that is, the arrest and transport of terror suspects to countries that allow torture.[31] From Abu Ghraib to Guantanamo to secret prisons around the world, victims and witnesses have lived to tell of degradation, sexual abuse, and torture suffered at the hands of U.S. service personnel, contract interrogators, private security guards, or others acting on behalf of the U.S. military. Even U.S. citizens have been classified as enemy combatants and caught up in this web.

Governments are responsible to guarantee the human rights of all people, as stated in the United Nations' Universal Declaration on Human Rights. The principle of *protecting human rights* is basic to our hope for a better world. These rights include civil and political rights, as well as economic, social, and cultural rights. The U.S. government has become a repressive force both globally and domestically, and has strayed far from the principle of protecting human rights.

As we explore the relationship between the U.S. prison/industrial complex and the war on terror, we cross into territory where domestic policy and foreign policy meet in the arena of national security. The government provides paramilitary training in security tactics to foreign governments, as it does domestically. The United States uses the same computer technology in its war on terror at home as it does abroad. Its surveillance satellites are directed not only at enemy or "rogue" nations, but also at Americans.[32] U.S. arms dealers export the same militarized weapons and equipment that they sell to domestic police forces, much of it subsidized by the government, paid for by tax dollars, in the form of vouchers for purchasing weapons from corporate arms dealers. The U. S. Government hires the same private paramilitary firms to provide "security" in other countries as it does at home. Troops from the private security firm Blackwater USA, who serve as mercenaries in Baghdad, patrolled the streets of New Orleans after Hurricane Katrina, dressed in full battle gear, with guns strapped to their legs, carrying automatic assault weapons, with authority to make arrests or use lethal force.[33]

We will look at U.S. foreign policy in the next chapter, but it is important to note that the corporate security state, though in some ways distinct from foreign policy, is part of the same apparatus, meant to establish control. As inequity grows, both in the United States and around the world, more of the surplus populations left behind by unfettered free-market capitalism need to be controlled. More and more, security tactics used domestically resemble the military tactics used abroad, and the separate functions of police and military become intertwined. The primary aim of the interlocking network of institutional Powers that make up the corporate security state is this: to survive and extend its reach by creating a domestic base of support for its now-global policies and to enforce the unjust global and domestic order that originates in, centers upon, and proceeds from the United States.

As the domestic-security apparatus casts its net ever wider and tightens the net around more of us, several things could happen. Fear for ourselves or our loved ones could keep us in check and a sense of powerlessness could keep us apathetic. On the other hand, with such widespread, extreme, and repressive policies, dissent could grow, and with it, resistance. This, to me, is the direction of hope. Otherwise Martin Niemöller's warning, written as poetry in 1945, could come true in our day:

> First they came for the communists, and I did not speak out—
>   because I was not a communist;
> Then they came for the socialists, and I did not speak out—
>   because I was not a socialist;
> Then they came for the trade unionists, and I did not speak out—
>   because I was not a trade unionist;
> Then they came for the Jews, and I did not speak out—
>   because I was not a Jew;
> Then they came for me—
> and there was no one left to speak out for me.[34]

CHAPTER FOURTEEN
The Iron Fist:
Enforcing Corporate Globalization

> Today even the inoculation of baptism has not prevented our
> being sucked up into mass possession. Why else are we pay-
> ing our taxes to purchase ever more lethal weapons of mass
> suicide? Why else are we—to be sure, disquieted, disturbed,
> even perhaps outraged—yet still so supine, so compliant, so
> innocuous? Why, when it comes right down to putting our
> bodies on the line, do we draw back—unless we are in the grip
> of a Power that has us enthralled?
>
> —Walter Wink[1]

I began my career as an activist in 1979 when I realized the extent
of the danger of nuclear war and became involved with the Nuclear
Weapons Freeze Campaign. One morning I was at home by myself,
cleaning house while I listened to a tape of Helen Caldicott talking about
the psychological effects of nuclear war on the survivors of Hiroshima
and Nagasaki, known as hibakusha. Listening to the stories about what
these people had suffered over the years, I imagined my own family going
through what they had gone through and I began to weep.

Suddenly, I was struck with the thought: How must God feel
about all this? How must God feel about what we human beings have
done to each other, and about what we intend to do, as we stockpile
nuclear weapons? I fell to my knees, praying for forgiveness, overcome
with a sense of the depth of pain that God must bear because of the
horrors we human beings create for each other. To this day, I believe
that God weeps for the harm we do to each other.

WHY NOT A PEACE DIVIDEND?

> When peace arrived, the swords were not beaten into plow-
> shares, as the prophet Isaiah envisioned. The swords, one
> might say, were beaten into capital gains. A "peace dividend"
> did appear after the Cold War ended. It was distributed to
> shareholders of the major defense companies.
>
> —William Greider[2]

> If we bomb Iraq, we will be creating a hell on earth in Baghdad.
> —Daniel Ellsberg[3]

I recently attended a candlelight vigil commemorating the three thousand five hundred members of the U.S. military who as of this writing have died in Iraq and the deaths of hundreds of thousands of Iraqis. The strategy of "shock and awe," which the U.S. government threatened would create a "Hiroshima-like effect," has become an ongoing occupation. Over time U.S. policy has brought unspeakable harm to Iraqis through bombing, sanctions, destruction of the country's infrastructure, contamination with depleted uranium, and the ongoing violence of military action, insurrection, and terror. To date there is no exit strategy or clear plan for "victory." And while Pentagon officials say that the U.S. military is already overstretched with its commitments in Iraq and Afghanistan, the Bush administration continues to threaten military action against Iran.

Why is the United States, the only remaining superpower, not leading a major diplomatic effort toward disarmament, peacemaking, and sustainable development in the Middle East, in the former Soviet Union, and elsewhere? Would this not create a far more secure world? Why are our nuclear weapons still on high alert? Why are we not helping Russia to secure its nuclear material? Why, in an age when terrorists could smuggle nuclear weapons (or simply knives) in a suitcase, are we trying to build an elaborate nuclear shield to prevent an unlikely attack by a "rogue nation"? Why do we continue to develop increasingly accurate and useable first-strike nuclear weapons? Why are we using every available technology to create obscenely imaginative weapons of mass destruction, and why are we opposing treaties that limit such technologies?

The only way this makes sense is in the overall scheme of corporate globalization. The U.S. military is the primary enforcer of the emerging global economic system. This military wing of corporate globalization reveals the true nature of the Powers at work in our world today.

At the end of the Cold War, there was widespread discussion of a "peace dividend," a diversion of public funds from military to social spending. People hoped that their yearning for world peace would finally become reality. But people's dreams of peace were not realized.[4] Around the world, factions that had been armed by the rival superpowers continued their armed conflicts. In spite of the dissolution of the Soviet Union, the United States continued to produce weapons that had been designed for Cold War purposes. Indeed, more progress was made toward disarmament during the last years of the Cold War than in the ten years that followed.[5]

Long before the terrorist attacks of September 11, 2001, and before George W. Bush became president, a neoconservative think tank called Project for a New American Century issued a report entitled "Rebuilding America's Defenses," which outlined its goals: to expand the military budget by $15 to $20 billion per year, institute a regime change in Iraq, establish a permanent military presence in the Middle East, create a missile defense system, strengthen U.S. nuclear weapons capability, and create a Pax Americana, a U.S. empire that would dominate the world.[6]

After the terrorist attacks on the World Trade Center and Pentagon there was a no-holds-barred approach to instituting these policies. Congress dramatically increased military spending, with the military budget rising from $310 billion in 2001 to $343.2 billion in 2002, $396.1 billion in 2003, and $441.6 billion in 2006.[7] These figures do not include funding for the Afghan or Iraq wars, which by early 2006 had cost an additional $300 billion. The military budget request by the Bush administration for fiscal year 2007 is $462.7 billion.[8]

Within a year of the 9/11 attacks, the Bush administration had disregarded or withdrawn from several international treaties, including the Kyoto Protocol and the Anti-Ballistic Missile (ABM) Treaty. In October 2002, President Bush announced the rationale that had guided his administration's policies from the beginning, based on the document mentioned above, "Rebuilding America's Defenses", which "outlines the ideas behind global dominance and empire in the form of a global Pax Americana." [9] The "Bush Doctrine" made clear that the goal of the United States was to dominate the world politically, economically, and militarily into the foreseeable future. The United States would no longer focus on the "nonproliferation" of weapons, but instead on "counter-proliferation".[10] In other words, the United States would have such powerful and advanced weapons that no country would ever be able to catch up, and it would act unilaterally and preemptively in order to protect its interests.

The justification and ethos behind this doctrine is that the United States is on the side of good and should lead the world and enforce its will, since it has the power to do so. But where, exactly, is the United States leading the world? And who is actually doing the leading?

ENFORCING CORPORATE GLOBALIZATION

> **The hidden hand of the market will never work without a hidden fist.**
>
> —Thomas Friedman[11]

Government officials justify military spending as necessary for national security. But the overarching goal of U.S. military planning is not simply the defense or protection of its citizens. The current push toward U.S. political, economic, and military dominance is directly related to the goal of an integrated capitalist global economic system. U.S. military policy has historically supported corporate interests. The government sees its survival and the expansion of its power as linked with the survival and expansion of U.S. corporations. U.S. military power paved the way for U.S. corporations to establish themselves throughout Latin America and in nations around the world. U.S. goals have long included establishing a base in the Middle East to ensure U.S. access to oil. This goal continues to shape U.S. relationships with other Middle East countries, including our relationship with Israel. Protecting U.S. interests means not only protecting U.S. citizens and military installations but also preserving the access of U.S. corporations to natural resources, cheap labor, and foreign markets around the world.

This function of the U.S. military as the enforcer of corporate globalization is apparent even at the highest levels of advanced weaponry and strategic planning. A primary rationale for developing the "Star Wars" Missile Defense System is to secure the global economy. According to the U.S. Space Command's long-range plan, "Vision for 2020," the United States intends to "dominate the earth from space in the 21st century" in order "to protect national investments—both military and economic." The document goes on to say,

> The United States will remain a global power and exert global leadership. . . . Widespread communications will highlight disparities in resources and quality of life—contributing to unrest in developing countries. . . . The global economy will continue to become more interdependent. Economic alliances, as well as the growth and influence of multi-national corporations, will blur security agreements. . . . The gap between "have" and "have not" nations will widen—creating regional unrest. . . . One of the long acknowledged and commonly understood advantages of space-based platforms is no restriction or country clearances to overfly a nation from space.[12]

Space warfare is computerized warfare. Handheld computers enable troops to engage in ground operations that are guided by satellite. Satellite technologies allow unmanned missiles to be launched from remote locations. According to a spokesperson from Lockheed Martin, this capability prevents U.S. deaths and enables the military to wage wars where "the national image is at stake and not necessarily the national security. . . . It's kind of the CNN factor."[13] Image is important in empire.

Satellite-linked computers allow those who launch attacks from U.S. bombers to hone in on their targets as if they were playing video games. Indeed, a military-recruitment television commercial includes outreach to those who have grown up on war-fighting video games. The theme of the ad is: "We've been waiting for you."[14]

"Vision for 2020" shows that the Missile Defense System, although publicly portrayed as purely defensive, is part of a larger U.S. plan to "wage war in, through, and from space." The plan is not simply to create a missile defense shield, but to dominate the world from space and to protect the global economic order by establishing a global satellite surveillance and positioning system and space-based weapons including lasers, not only for defensive but also for offensive purposes. According to "Vision for 2020," this strategy will enable the United States to gain the "ultimate high ground" of space in order to enforce its will. The goal is: "Dominating the space dimension of military operations to protect US interests and investment. Integrating Space Forces into warfighting capabilities across the full spectrum of conflict."[15]

The war on terror has given those who are in power the opportunity to ruthlessly pursue this long-established imperialistic vision: to establish U.S. global dominance and to integrate the rest of the world into the global capitalist system. It is a vision of empire. This is where the United States is leading the world.

This vision may appeal to those who have faith that the United States is on the side of the good and that political leaders make policy decisions freely for the well-being of the people. But who actually sets military policy? Concerned public officials who are simply trying to create safety for the nation's people? Hardly.

Of course, most elected officials are sincerely concerned about peoples' security. But setting national-security policy involves far more than making reasoned decisions based on heartfelt concern for the common good. Other factors include political pressures, economic interests, military scenarios, and worldview. No matter how good-hearted they are as individuals, politicians deal with institutional pressures that define and limit their choices. They deal with what has come to be called "the real world."

It is important at this point to be spiritually grounded, to remember that the "real world" is actually the earth in all its diversity and splendor, revealing the glory of God. The global system of economic, political, and military domination is not "real" but is an institutional construct based on a deeply flawed worldview whose values are directly at odds with spiritual values. This system does not bring security to the earth and its people, but slavery and death.

Yet it is within this system that national security decisions are made. Debates take place within a milieu that takes for granted a certain worldview shared by most political, military, and corporate leaders. Except for the occasional "radical" position taken by a few brave souls, their decisions are limited by the existing network of political, economic, and military institutions—the Domination System—to which they are beholden and of which they are a part. Simply stated, U.S. military policy is largely determined by the Powers. The military-industrial complex is the most powerful expression of the Domination System that the world has ever seen and the most obvious manifestation of the reign of death working through the Powers.

THE IRON TRIANGLE

This is Eisenhower's nightmare. The military-industrial complex is dug in to defend economic interests that have nothing to do with national defense.

—Gary Hart[16]

In 1961, President Dwight Eisenhower, in his farewell address to the nation, warned of the "grave implications" of "the conjunction of an immense military establishment with a large arms industry" in the country: "In the councils of government, we must guard against the acquisition of unwarranted influence . . . by the military-industrial complex. The potential for the disastrous rise of misplaced power exists and will persist."[17]

The term "Iron Triangle"[18] has been used to describe the three distinct institutions that make up this overarching system known as the "military-industrial complex:" the U.S. government, the U.S. military, and U.S. corporations that manufacture weapons and otherwise profit from war. The government is the political wing of this system, consisting of the congressional, executive, and judicial branches that supposedly safeguard U.S. democracy with a system of checks and balances. The military wing, which has so much influence that it essentially serves as a fourth branch of government, includes the Pentagon, government weapons labs, military installations, weapons systems, and military personnel that have been deployed around the world. And although Congress controls the federal purse, by following the money we can see that the economic wing of the Iron Triangle consists of corporations that manufacture weapons and use their earnings to influence the political process and military policy.

Through a complex network of relationships and interactions, these three major types of institutional systems (government, military, corporate) control U.S. military policy. A "revolving door" within this system enables people to move through leadership positions from one of its institutions to another. For instance, one can retire from military service and go directly into a lucrative position in a weapons firm or into service as a political appointee. Or one can move from public office into a position as a lobbyist for a weapons firm, maintaining connections in seeking to influence former government colleagues.

The networks between these three wings of the Iron Triangle are complex and interwoven, allowing people to influence decision making in more than one of these institutions at a time. Actually, in the administration of George W. Bush, the door doesn't revolve—it stays open, for corporate executives and government leaders are one and the same.

Many in the Bush administration have close ties to the weapons industry. Dick Cheney is a former member of the board of TRW[19] and his wife, Lynne Cheney, is a past board member of Lockheed Martin. While Norman Augustine was CEO of Lockheed Martin he also served as chair of the Pentagon's Defense Science Board, as president of the politically influential Association of the United Sates Army, and as chair of the Defense Policy Advisory Committee on Trade, which guides the Secretary of Defense on issues related to arms exports.[20] Haley Barbour, after serving as chair of the Republican National Committee, served as a lobbyist for Lockheed Martin.[21] The Bush administration is guided by a foreign policy articulated by Bruce Jackson, a former vice president of Lockheed Martin. "I wrote the Republican Party's foreign policy platform," he boasts.[22] Jackson also co-founded the Committee for the Liberation of Iraq and is a current director of People for a New American Century. Many of these people not only help set domestic, foreign, and military policies, but also personally benefit from such policies.

It may be tempting to focus blame on individuals within the Bush administration or some other government or corporate leaders, but as I pointed out earlier, this is somewhat beside the point. It is the system itself that is defective—I will go so far as to call it "evil." The people who are currently in power did not arrive at such positions of authority by accident, but because they serve the institutional purpose. The vast and complex system of interrelated bureaucracies that make up the military-industrial complex has its own momentum, its own ethos, and its own purpose: to survive and extend its power. William Stringfellow, in writing about the Vietnam War, went so far as to say that the purpose of the war was the survival of the Pentagon:

> The principalities have great resilience; the death game which they play continues, adapting its means of dominat-

ing human beings to the sole morality which governs all demonic powers so long as they exist—survival. To put it very plainly, concealed within the public rhetoric justifying the Southeast Asian war . . . has been the purpose of supporting and serving the Pentagon and the whole array of war principalities which the Pentagon symbolizes. To speak of the Indochinese war in terms of the relation of principalities and human beings is, bluntly, to expose the survival of the Pentagon and its satellite or adjoining principalities as the purpose of the war.[23]

U.S. military policy is developed within a context that has already been determined. The institutions that make up the Iron Triangle have already set the overall focus of war fighting and the primary direction of domination. The rhetoric and policies of the U.S. government and military are based on acceptance of the utility of war. The military-industrial complex devours resources that could be used for beneficial purposes, growing ever bigger and more ready to wage total war. The major institutions of the world's richest and most powerful nation, the nation that dominates the world, are geared toward war. The interlocking network of institutions that rule our world today (Wink's "Domination System") is moving us toward death.

Although individuals who are highly placed within these institutions can influence policy, those who have the authority, whether politicians, generals, or CEOs, have generally risen to power by accepting the dominant ethos and playing by the rules of the system as a whole. In theological terms, as Stringfellow notes, "There is unleashed among the principalities in this society a ruthless, self-proliferating, all-consuming institutional process which assaults, dispirits, defeats, and destroys human life even among, and primarily among, those persons in positions of institutional leadership. They are left with titles but without effectual authority; with the trappings of power, but without control over the institutions they head; in nominal command, but bereft of dominion."[24]

The point is not that such individuals are without power. Occasionally a courageous politician, military dissenter, or corporate whistleblower will risk all for the sake of conscience, and now, of all times, we need people who will do so. But rare within the system is the individual who has the insight and courage to resist. Most who serve in positions of authority accept the overall system, adopt its ethos, and carry its agenda forward. It is the system itself that needs to be changed.

Martin Luther King, Jr., made the point in a more positive way. He spoke of seeking to defeat evil systems, but of loving those who are caught up in such systems: "When you rise to the level of love, of its great beauty and power, you seek only to defeat evil systems. Individuals who happen to be caught up in that system, you love, but you seek to defeat the system."[25]

WHO DECIDES MILITARY POLICY? WHO BENEFITS?

[Iraq] has two rivers, it's fertile, it's sitting on an ocean of oil. Iraq ought to be a major player in the world. And we want to be working for them long term.
—Cliff Mumm, Bechtel's head of Iraq operations[26]

The government buys weapons with our tax dollars and uses them in our name. They can do so only by convincing the public that such weapons are necessary for national security. But how do new weapons systems come to be approved? Elected officials do not simply decide what weapons are needed to protect the people and then proceed to purchase them. Political, military, and economic Powers work together to continually raise military spending.

Weapons manufacturers themselves have significant input into these decisions. The ideas for new weapons systems often come from military research labs and military contractors, who dream up new weapons based on what is technologically feasible. Weapons designers in corporations and in government research institutions envision, research, and develop plans for new weapons and then present their suggestions, based on what is possible, to the Pentagon. Lockheed Martin's Dr. Arman J. Chaput explains it this way: "My job is not to determine what the government wants but what the government will need and will want only it doesn't know it yet."[27]

The process can also work in reverse. For instance, the government is seeking applications for the development of a specialized weapon using nanotechnology to create an insect installed with video or other surveillance features that could then be controlled by their handlers.[28]

After designing new weapons systems, these labs and corporations promote them at the Pentagon. The Pentagon, always on the lookout for increasingly sophisticated high-tech weapons, presents its wish list to Congress and lobbies Congress to fund them. Weapons manufacturers lobby Congress as well, spending millions to persuade its members to vote for specific weapons systems. For instance, in 2005 Lockheed Martin spent over $8 million for lobbying.[29] Northrop Grumman spent over $13.6 million.[30] Campaign contributions also provide motivation for public officials to support particular weapons. In 2006 the four largest weapons manufacturers contributed more than $5 million in campaign contributions, favoring Republicans but providing financial incentives to politicians in both parties to support their demands.[31]

In congressional debates, this issue is closely linked with concern for jobs. Congressional representatives champion weapons systems that are manufactured in their districts, motivated not simply by security concerns, but by the political implications of jobs gained or lost. They know that people who work for major weapons corporations in their areas will be more likely to vote for them the next time around if such contracts go through. This dynamic can account for such regularly occurring anomalies as defense budgets approved by Congress that include billions more than the Pentagon requests.[32] For example, Congress debated a 2006 Defense Appropriations Bill that included at least $12 billion for weapons and research programs for which the Pentagon did not ask.[33]

Clearly, factors other than security are at play. One way that weapons manufacturers cultivate congressional support is by locating research and production facilities in many congressional districts. Lockheed Martin, for instance, maintains facilities in all fifty states.[34]

The problem also works the other way. There are pressures on weapons corporations to continue and expand existing programs even if some of them are inefficient or obsolete. They often keep factories open in several locations, even if it would be cheaper to consolidate production at a single factory. Military contractor consultant Bob Paulson explains:

> The CEO at Lockheed Martin needs to build a new fighter plane. He's got all of these factories, and none of them is full. So where does he put the work? Ideally, ignoring the politics, the CEO would like to put all of the work in one or two of those factories and close the others . . . and save a lot of money. But that requires him to tell at least half of the congressmen who are supporting him: "I'm closing the plant in your district. I'm laying off all those loyal workers who used to applaud your speech at the ceremony where we roll out the new plane, workers who have always voted for you and contributed to your campaign." Defense contractors are very loyal to Congress. They would never embarrass a congressman who supports them because the people who give out the contracts can also take them away.[35]

When the time to vote for corporate subsidies comes around, these corporations lobby for their approval. The government often picks up the initial costs of research and development of major weapons systems. They often allow corporations to develop weapons systems in factories owned by the government, rent-free, even those that are being made for export and private profit.[36] With such arrangements, corporate earnings can be almost pure profit, with U.S. taxpayers picking up the tab for everything except labor and materials.[37]

Weapons corporations even influence congressional debates about foreign-policy decisions, especially policies that will result in increased weapons sales. Weapons manufacturers successfully lobbied Congress to lift the arms ban on Latin America and other foreign military sales.[38] Bruce Jackson, mentioned above, was president of the U.S. Committee to Expand NATO, which included representatives of many arms dealers and which lobbied successfully for the expansion of NATO after the fall of the Soviet Union.[39] According to Dr. Helen Caldicott:

> Despite official rhetoric to the contrary, the expansion of NATO was entirely about weapons sales, the bill for which will run in the range of 500 billion dollars over twelve to fifteen years—2,500 dollars for every American household, since America ends up bankrolling much of this military expenditure. Sales to foreign governments are particularly lucrative for weapons manufacturers, since by the time the weapons are ready for export, all research, development, and initial production problems have been covered by the U.S. taxpayer.[40]

This kind of corporate influence on foreign and military policy casts suspicion on the announced intentions of U.S. foreign and military policy throughout the world.

For Bush administration officials, economic and geopolitical goals came together in Iraq. The president, vice president, and secretary of state are all former energy-company executives or board members, and they maintain their close ties to the industry. Vice President Cheney's secretive Energy Advisory Board included representatives of the petroleum, natural gas, coal, nuclear, construction, and electricity industries.[41]

Although plans for war against Iraq were set long before, momentum grew in the Bush administration after the September 11 terrorist attacks. At the same time, corporate pressures to launch an attack against Iraq mounted. Weapons contractors, including Lockheed Martin, oil giants like Chevron, and engineering, construction, and energy service firms like Halliburton and Bechtel employed think tanks to lobby the government and to influence public opinion through the media. Under the leadership of Richard Perle, the Defense Policy Board (DPB), a government advisory board to the U.S. Department of Defense, advocated preemptive military action to combat terrorism and overthrow Saddam Hussein. Nine members of the DPB were connected with companies that received $76 billion in defense contracts in 2001 and 2002, and several won contracts in Iraq, including Bechtel.[42]

In 2002 Bruce Jackson left his position as vice president of Lockheed Martin to found the Committee for the Liberation of Iraq (CLI) with other members of the Project for a New American Century, mentioned above. In the lead-up to war, CLI members wrote articles in leading newspapers, made speeches, and appeared on radio and television talk shows, making the case that Iraq had weapons of mass destruction, supported terrorism, and was an immediate threat to the United States.[43] Many CLI members had connections to corporations that later made huge profits in the U.S. war against Iraq. Randy Scheunemann, CLI's first president, is credited with writing the Iraq Liberation Act. At the same time, Lockheed Martin was a client of Scheunemann's lobbying firm. CLI member George Schultz wrote convincingly of the danger posed by Iraq, while neglecting to mention his long-standing ties to Bechtel or the company's role in providing Saddam Hussein with the means to produce chemical weapons.[44]

The corporations that lobbied so zealously for war have extraordinary profits to show for their efforts. In 2003, the twenty-nine major U.S. oil and gas firms earned $43 billion in profits, rising to $68 billion in 2004. In 2005, the top three companies alone earned nearly $64 billion. Chevron nearly doubled its profits between 2003 and 2004 to $13.3 billion, rising again in 2005 to more than $14 billion. Bechtel's profits rose from $11.6 billion in 2002 to $16.3 billion in 2003 and to $17.4 billion in 2004.[45] Between 2000 and 2005, Lockheed Martin's sales increased by $13 billion to over $37 billion, over 80 percent paid for by U.S. taxpayers, and the value of its stocks tripled. In just three years, between 2003 and 2006, Halliburton's stocks have nearly quadrupled.[46]

Many who were involved in lobbying and setting policy have personally benefited financially from the Iraq War. For instance, Vice President Cheney holds stock in both Lockheed Martin and Halliburton.[47] As stated earlier, the system is designed for the results it is getting, and it is paying off for those for whom it is designed.

PRYING OPEN THE ECONOMIES OF THE MIDDLE EAST

> The fact that no two countries have gone to war since they both got McDonald's is partly due to economic integration, but it is also due to the presence of American power and America's willingness to use that power against those who

would threaten the system of globalization—from Iraq to North Korea.

—Thomas Friedman[48]

While WTO negotiations and the U.S.-led free-trade agenda has stalled in many places, Iraq and the Middle East as a whole can be counted as a success in terms of the corporate agenda to pry open economies in the name of trade liberalization. In Antonia Juhasz's book *The Bush Agenda: Invading the World, One Economy at a Time*, she claims that the goal of the Bush administration in Iraq is "the creation of a U.S. corporate haven that will act as a model and jumping-off point for the rest of the region."[49]

The Bush administration continues to claim that its policies, including the Iraq War, will make Americans safer. But as Antonia Juhasz points out, "The only thing that the war effort has made definitively safer is U.S. corporate access to Iraq, Saudi Arabia, Morocco, Bahrain, and Oman, while the rest of the Middle East races to open its doors. . . . It is the ultimate lie of Pax Americana: World peace will prevail as long as the United States can spread its military and economic dominance without impediment."[50]

While Paul Bremer III was head of the Coalition Provisional Authority in Iraq, he issued one hundred orders that locked in a restructuring program for Iraq's economy that is far more radical than the most extreme IMF structural adjustment program. Several of the orders nullified sections of the prewar Iraqi constitution. Order #1 removed 120,000 of Iraq's best-educated professionals from their positions because they were members of the Ba'ath party.[51] Order #2 dissolved Iraqi "entities," including the army and intelligence service, which threw another half-million men out of work.[52] By June, 2006, 59 percent of Iraq's labor force was unemployed and 31 percent held only temporary or seasonal jobs.[53] Meanwhile, between 2005 and 2006, fuel and electricity prices in Iraq increased by 58 percent; food by 26.6 percent; rent by 37.5 percent, and transportation/communication by 119.4 percent.[54]

Order #39, instituted on September 19, 2003, privatized Iraq's 192 state-owned enterprises, including "everything from water to electricity, schools to hospitals, factories to airlines, newspapers to television stations, food to housing programs."[55] It also gave foreign (that is, U.S.) corporations unprecedented rights to own Iraqi businesses and take all profits out of the country, without being required to hire any Iraqi workers or work with Iraqi firms.[56] The result has produced windfall profits as mentioned above for U.S. corporate war profiteers.

In the midst of this radical economic restructuring, the IMF has stepped in, offering to cancel Iraq's debt, most of which should be considered odious debt, since it was contracted during the rule of Saddam Hussein. But as is usual with the IMF, the terms under which the debt may be cancelled can only cause greater suffering to the Iraqi people.[57] The IMF is calling on the Iraqi government to exercise "fiscal discipline" by cutting pensions, limiting wages of public employees, establishing no public-works programs that could reduce unemployment, and further liberalizing the economy. At the same time, the World Bank is helping Iraq to "reform" its public distribution system of food rations. Food rations under the program have already been significantly reduced.[58]

Meanwhile, the Bush administration and corporate America are proceeding with their plan to restructure the whole Middle East through political and economic pressure and the threat and use of military force. The U.S. Congress is loath to object, since these policies are being undertaken in the name of the war on terror. One by one, countries are being pressured to form bilateral and trilateral free-trade agreements with the United States in preparation for the U.S.-promoted Middle East Free Trade Area (MEFTA), which would greatly benefit foreign, especially U.S., corporations. Juhasz links the Iraq War to corporate globalization, and criticizes the goal, strategy, and results of this form of U.S. domination:

> The individual Middle East Free Trade Area agreements are paving the way for a radical, thoroughly U.S.-centric corporate globalization agenda for the Bush administration to carry from country to country in the Middle East and then well beyond. . . . Governments the world over are forced to adopt economic policies that benefit the growth and power of one nation with a threat of military action if they do not accede, all in the name of "world peace." The result for the people of the Middle East will likely be increased subservience to U.S. corporations rather than the "freedom" promised by Bush. The result for the people of the United States and its allies has already been revealed since the economic invasion of Iraq: intensified anti-U.S. sentiment, increased insecurity, and escalating acts of deadly violence.[59]

The bloodshed in Iraq continues. Five thousand Iraqis are dying each month. Over thirty-five hundred U.S. troops have died, and over 22,000 have been injured. This number does not include the many private "security" and paramilitary forces that also serve at the behest of the U.S. military. Over $8.8 billion of U.S. taxpayers' money is unaccounted for.[60] By any measure, the U.S. war against Iraq has been a failure. By any measure, that is, except corporate profits and the goal of extending the system of corporate globalization.

GOING GLOBAL

> Because we are a US defense contractor, our board members
> will have to have security clearance. As we move in an inter-
> national direction, we will have to find ways—the US govern-
> ment will have to find ways—of dealing with that.
>
> —Philip Condit, Boeing Chairman[61]

Under current accounting methods, war is good for the economy.
The U.S. Gross National Product (GNP) is boosted by the profits of
U.S. arms manufacturers. The United States is by far the largest arms
exporter in the world. U.S. corporations sell weapons, including
advanced military weaponry, subsidized by the U.S. government, on the
open market to countries around the world. The region that buys the
most U.S. weapons is the Middle East. The leading customers are
Egypt, Israel, Saudi Arabia, Kuwait, and Oman, which spent $16.3 bil-
lion between them between 2001 and 2004.[62] Far more is given in U.S.
military aid, paid for with taxpayer dollars. Israel alone receives approx-
imately $2 billion in military assistance each year.[63] The revenues of U.S.
arms dealers from foreign military sales in 2006 was $21 billion, nearly
double that of 2005.[64]

The United States often provides arms to both sides of various
conflicts, as when we armed both sides during the Iran/Iraq war. A
joke was going around when the Bush administration insisted that Iraq
still had weapons of mass destruction before it launched the attack on
Iraq: "We know that they have weapons of mass destruction. We have
the receipts." The global arms trade does not make the world safer, but
more dangerous. Since countries that have been armed by the United
States can turn against us, we have to continually develop more
advanced weapons in order to maintain a military advantage. In other
words, the United States is in an arms race with itself.

Or rather, as Helen Caldicott says, "Lockheed Martin is in an
arms race with itself."[65] The major weapons contractors design, develop, lobby for, and aggressively market weapons that need to be continually upgraded in order to be useful in a war against earlier models.

Furthermore, the major weapons manufacturers are "going
global"—merging, buying stakes in foreign companies, and forming
corporate alliances in order to become globalized firms with networks
of factories, designers, and jobs that extend around the world.[66]
William Greider says: "Imagine a military-industrial complex that is
truly multinational in scope and scale and able to play governments off
against each other. Imagine a global arms market that claims to be
above and beyond the political control of mere nations."[67]

As weapons manufacturers become truly transnational, based in many different nations and selling weapons to many different purchasers, where will their loyalties be? In such a situation, how could the U.S. government exert even minimal control over the defense industry that it originally created? On the other hand, such a powerful industry could exert tremendous influence on national governments and on global institutions, directing the world toward a future that no one wants to see.

Meanwhile, in the real world, God's world, "the earth lies polluted under its inhabitants," and the poor and victims of war and oppression cry out to God. But the cries are growing louder, joined by people around the world who have glimpsed the hell being prepared for us and have caught another vision, who see beyond the institutions that seem to limit human choice and are working to develop life-giving alternatives to the present structures. Meanwhile, the forces gather, a global resistance movement creating its own momentum away from war and destruction toward creative new possibilities of life and hope. And meanwhile, the peacemakers are blessed. They shall be called children of God.

WE ARE RISING UP

What we look for is no longer the Pax Romana, the peace of imperial Rome, nor is it simply the Pax Humana, the peace among humans, but the Pax Gaia, the peace of earth and every being on the earth. This is the original and the final peace, the peace granted by whatever power it is that brings our world into being. Within the universe, the planet Earth with all its wonder is the place for the meeting of the divine and the human.

—Thomas Berry[68]

I was invited to speak at a Christian women's conference in Japan in 2003. While there, I visited Hiroshima. Walking through the Memorial Museum, I wept as I looked at the burned clothing of children, the stories and artwork of survivors, the charred remains of a tricycle that a father buried in his backyard with his beloved child.

I watched as a busload of Japanese elementary-school children poured into the museum and surrounded the two main exhibits on the first floor: a model of Hiroshima before the blast, with roads and houses, parks and trees, churches and other buildings like any other city; and Hiroshima after it had been reduced to indistinguishable rubble for miles around. I saw in the serious faces of the children what I can only now articulate: shock and awe.

As I walked through the Hiroshima Memorial Museum, I was struck by the power of the evil that destroyed that city. What happened there seemed to me to be so against life, against all that I love. It is like an "anti"-power, a power that is opposed to all creation and contrary to all that God, who is love, intends.

I also found many signs of hope there. The museum itself has been dedicated to peace. Groups from around the world have erected memorial statues in the Peace Park. Countless individuals have visited the museum and have left written statements that give voice to their desires and intentions for peace.

One museum display was a Phoenix tree. After the bomb was dropped on Hiroshima it was predicted that grass, plants, and trees would not grow there for seventy-five years. But within six weeks a Phoenix tree began to send out green shoots. This tree has become a symbol of hope in the midst of overwhelming destruction and despair.

A woman I met at the conference in Japan told me that her friend, a Hiroshima survivor, had given up hope in those early days after the city was destroyed. She had wanted to die. But one day she saw a tree with a green shoot going out, and from that time on she decided to live. Perhaps it was a Phoenix tree.

This experience gave new meaning to a resistance song that I learned in the streets from fellow protestors during demonstrations against the Iraq War:

> We are rising up like a Phoenix from the fire,
> So brothers and sisters spread your wings and fly higher.
> We are rising up
> We are rising up
> We are rising up
> We are rising up

This song of empowerment is about rising up from a sense of despair, helplessness, and hopelessness, and finding courage and hope in resistance and action. And it's true. People around the world are rising up, organizing, joining together with others who are working for a peaceful, just, and sustainable world.

When my husband and I spoke to an English class at Kanseigakuin University, the students were amazed and glad to hear that many Americans opposed the war against Iraq. (They also appreciated our Salsa dance demonstration.) We taught them the song about the Phoenix. In their written responses to us about our presentation, one young man wrote: "I am still singing the words to the song you taught us. I feel like I am rising up even now."

To me, it is a resurrection song.

PART THREE
SHAKING THE GATES OF HELL

Faith-Led Resistance

"In resistance persons live most humanly. No to death means yes to life."
—William Stringfellow

CHAPTER FIFTEEN
The Triumph of God over the Powers

In Christ every one of God's promises is a "Yes."

—2 Cor. 1:20

In preceding chapters we have explored the social and ecological challenges of our day and the underlying network of institutional Powers that have fostered these challenges. As we have seen, the problem is not simply that we have deliberately engaged in harmful, unethical, or sinful behavior. An even greater problem is that we have relinquished our responsibility for the common good. We have given over our authority to the institutional Powers that now dominate the earth. In the milieu of the Powers, we forget who we are. The Powers shape our very identities as we assume the role of beneficiary, enabler, or victim. At times, resistance does seem futile, and we fall into cynicism, apathy, hopelessness, and despair. We are tempted to give up, to stand on the sidelines, to relinquish the playing field to the major players, to those who we think really can make a difference in the world—in other words, to the Powers.

No matter how daunting our challenges are, our starting point cannot simply be the problems facing the world, but rather the reality that precedes the problems—that is, God's creation. As discussed in chapter 1, the creation reveals the beauty, mystery, and magnificence of the Creator. We are children of the earth, interdependent with all other parts of creation. The Spirit of God is within us and "in [God] we live and move and have our being" (Acts 17:28). As Matthew Fox says, we are part of the "original blessing"[1] of creation. In resistance, we are not simply seeking to negate what is going on, but to bring things into alignment with God's intention for the world, beginning with ourselves.

The challenge, then, is a spiritual one. We are called to remember who we are, children of the earth imbued with the Spirit of God. That is our identity. We are called to accept our human freedom and to assume our full responsibility as moral agents, allowing God to work through us to bring hope to the world.

This requires faith in the ultimate goodness of God and God's creation, including human beings. For Christians, it requires faith in the good news that Jesus brought and in his promise of abundant life.

So our starting point is positive: "In Christ every one of God's promises is a 'Yes.'" God's "yes" in Christ is the foundation for our "no" to corporate globalization and empire. "Yes" to abundant life includes a "no" to all that would diminish or destroy life. For Christians, the "no" of resistance is based on the "yes" of discipleship.

This chapter addresses how the gospel of Jesus Christ can help us understand what it means to be faithful and to become more fully the people God created us to be. We will begin by considering the life of Jesus of Nazareth. The Bible does not give us a clear, harmonious picture of the historical Jesus, because the four Gospels are written not as history but as faith accounts of what each author witnessed, heard, and understood. Each Gospel has its own theological perspective, as do the writings of Paul and the other New Testament authors.

Walter Wink goes so far as to speak of "the myth of the human Jesus." This is not a claim that the Jesus of history did not exist, but that the symbolism, interpretation, and meaning that people find in his story have attained mythical significance

For the past two thousand years Christians have continued to interpret and assign meaning to the stories of Jesus' life, death, and resurrection. Scholars have shed light on some aspects of his life and the world in which he lived, but it is impossible to uncover a universally accepted or objective picture of who Jesus was. For us, even more than for the Gospel writers, Jesus is a figure we come to know through faith.

Though we can glimpse who Jesus was, we do so through various lenses—theological, artistic, literary, cultural. In order to gain theological perspective on today's global crisis, it is crucial that we explore the social, economic, and political context in which Jesus lived, and examine his relationship with the institutional Powers of his day. As we do, we meet the Jesus who modeled the compassionate nonviolent resistance practiced by Mahatma Gandhi and Martin Luther King, Jr. And we discover a way to live in hope and bring about a more hopeful future in the presence and grace of God.

JESUS, RESISTER

> To free people from the powers that possessed them was central to [Jesus'] struggle to undercut the domination System in all its forms, spiritual as well as physical, personal as well as political.
> —Walter Wink[2]

Who was Jesus? New Testament writers and Christians through the ages have referred to him as the "Son of God." But what does this mean?

During Advent and Christmas, people around the world celebrate the stories surrounding Jesus' birth in pageants and liturgies. Literalists insist that these stories must be taken as historical fact, especially the story of Jesus' divine conception by the Holy Spirit and subsequent birth to a virgin. In other words, they believe that Jesus is the Son of God biologically. Some see the literal understanding of this story as a crucial test of faith.

Though Jesus used the intimate term *Abba* when addressing God, he never claimed the exclusive title "Son of God" for himself. He usually referred to himself as "the Son of man," better translated as "the son of the man" or "the human being." According to Walter Wink: "'The son of the man' is the expression Jesus almost exclusively used to describe himself. In Hebrew the phrase simply means 'a human being.' The implication seems to be that Jesus intentionally avoided honorific titles, and preferred to be known simply as 'the man,' or 'the human being.' Apparently he saw his task as helping people become more truly human."[3]

Paul referred to Jesus as the "Son of God," but not because Jesus was born to a virgin. Rather, Paul claimed that Jesus was "descended from David according to the flesh and was declared to be Son of God with power according to the spirit of holiness by resurrection from the dead" (Rom. 1:3-4).

A literal belief that Jesus' mother was a virgin is not crucial in understanding who Jesus was. What the birth stories symbolize, however, is the incarnation of the divine in human life. Matthew Fox expands the concept of incarnation to include all life: "God has become incarnate—made flesh—not just in the historical Jesus and certainly not just in the two-legged creatures but in all of us. All of us are incarnations—home and dwelling-places for the Divine—all people, the poor no less than the comfortable. All races, all religions, all sexes, all sexual orientations, and all beings—four-legged, the winged, the rock people and tree people and cloud peoples—all are dwelling places of the Divine."[4] God is present in matter, indwelling all creation.

According to Walter Wink, the question for us is: "Before he was worshiped as God incarnate, how did Jesus struggle to incarnate God?"[5] We might also ask: What can Jesus show us about how human life can be lived fully and deeply in the light and presence of God?

The stories of Jesus' birth and infancy are important because they shed light on how the Gospel writers understood the significance of Jesus. Some of these stories are overtly political and provide compelling evidence that the authors understood the revolutionary significance of Jesus' life.

According to the "infancy narratives" in Matthew and Luke, Jesus was born to a poor, young, unwed mother under extremely difficult circumstances. When Mary was well along in her pregnancy (so the story goes), the Roman Empire issued an edict forcing all Jews to register for the census in their own hometowns. Mary and Joseph traveled a long distance from their home in Nazareth to Bethlehem, Joseph's hometown, where Mary gave birth to Jesus in a stable (Luke 2:1-7).

Mary and Joseph were poor. When they traveled to Jerusalem for their purification, to present their firstborn son to God, instead of offering the standard sacrifice they offered the poor peoples' alternative: "a pair of turtledoves or two young pigeons" (Luke 2:22-24, Lev. 12: 6-8). Mary and Joseph later fled with their infant son into Egypt as political refugees to escape King Herod's genocidal attempts to hold onto his throne (Matt. 2:13-15).

During her pregnancy, Mary proclaimed the remarkable words of hope for the poor and oppressed that have come to be called the "Magnificat" (Luke 1:46-47, 51-53):

> My soul magnifies the Lord,
> and my spirit rejoices in God my Savior . . .
> He has shown strength with his arm;
> he has scattered the proud in the thoughts of their hearts.
> He has brought down the powerful from their thrones,
> and lifted up the lowly;
> he has filled the hungry with good things,
> and sent the rich away empty.

Mary's words could hardly have been more political, or threatening to the Powers.

Though they differ in sequence and details, all four Gospels tell of Jesus' baptism by John the Baptist, whose message contained a similarly overt political theme. John challenged the rich and powerful and called people to repent in preparation for the immanent coming of the Messiah. By submitting to baptism by John, Jesus affirmed John's message. He also incorporated elements of John's message into his own.

At the time of his baptism, Jesus had a vision of "the heavens opened," the Holy Spirit descending on him as a dove, and God claiming him as a beloved Son (Matt. 3:16-17). Immediately after this revelation, the Spirit led him (or "drove" him, according to Mark 1:12) into the wilderness, where he was tempted to follow a calling that would allow him to gain worldly status, wealth, and power. In other words, he was tempted to take on the role of the Messiah for whom people were waiting. They were expecting a powerful king, along the lines of his ancestor David, who would oust the Romans from their land and establish a worldly kingdom with God at the apex of political, economic, and military power. Instead, Jesus chose a path of voluntary poverty, relinquishment of worldly power, and nonviolent resistance to the Powers.

Jesus emerged from the wilderness strong and clear about his vocation. He announced his public ministry in the synagogue in his hometown of Nazareth, by reading from the prophet Isaiah (Luke 4:18-19):

> The Spirit of the Lord is upon me,
> because he has anointed me to bring good news to the poor.
> He has sent me to proclaim release to the captives
> and recovery of sight to the blind,
> to let the oppressed go free,
> to proclaim the year of the Lord's favor..

Note that this message, which is essentially Jesus' mission statement, is strikingly political. The people were delighted and amazed to hear him—at first. But their perception of him quickly soured when Jesus challenged them on their racial prejudice and their expectations of privilege. They turned against him and tried to kill him, foreshadowing his death (Luke 4:28-30). Jesus then moved on and began to share his message of personal and social transformation throughout the region.

Jesus lived simply. He refused to seek wealth, status, or worldly power, and was homeless by choice. He lived close to the earth and used metaphors from nature in his parables. He used common elements such as bread and wine to demonstrate God's grace. He enjoyed simple food and drink. Jesus was not an ascetic, however. People even accused him of being a glutton and drunkard. He enjoyed a good party—he celebrated life.

Jesus also sought solitude, spending hours alone in prayer. His life, ministry, and message were based on an intimate relationship with God, and he called others to a similar relationship.

Jesus' ministry took place when Israel was under occupation and rule by the Roman Empire. The stability of the Roman occupation of Israel depended upon the collaboration of the elite Jewish religious establishment. Rather than risk their privileged positions or the security and continued existence of the Jewish nation, the religious leaders accommodated to and cooperated with the empire, as religious institutions often do.

But Jesus' response was different. He proclaimed and demonstrated the coming of an alternative "kingdom," where the sick would be healed, the hungry would be filled, and those in bondage would be freed. He created a new community, "not of this world" (John 18:36)—that is, as Wink says, "not of the systems of this world"—that embodied a different set of values and demonstrated the egalitarian, nonhierarchical kingdom of God he was talking about. This community was largely made up of marginalized, poor, outcast, sick, sinful, and demon-possessed people who were seeking or had found healing through their relationship with him. Jesus challenged the patriarchal structures of his day, crossing gender boundaries in order to include women. He even welcomed children, who in that culture had no status at all.

Jesus taught and demonstrated a view of economics based on radical trust and dependence on the God who cares for all parts of creation, including the birds of the air and the lilies of the field. People in his community and in the early church shared everything in common and gave to those who were in need. It may be that the miracles of feeding several thousand people with a few loaves and fish were not miracles of multiplication, but miracles of sharing that took place when, through Jesus' example, people who had provisions shared with those who had none.

His teaching on economics was radical, directly opposed to the general understanding of the majority of people of his day and ours. He did not simply tell people to stay spiritually unattached to their worldly treasures, but not to store them up in the first place. When a rich young man who had followed all the religious rules asked what more he needed to gain eternal life, Jesus advised him to "go, sell your possessions, and give the money to the poor, and you will have treasure in heaven; then come, follow me" (Matt. 19:21). According to Luke, Jesus says, "Blessed are you who are poor, for yours is the kingdom of God" (Luke 6:20), then goes on to say, "Woe to you who are rich, for you have received your consolation" (Luke 6:24). The parables of the sheep and the goats (Matt. 25:31-46) and of the rich man and Lazarus (Luke 16:19-31) harshly condemn those who refuse to share what they have with those who are in need.

The ruling authorities were irritated and enraged by Jesus' vision, teachings, popularity, and the community he created. The political and religious leaders, though often at odds over other issues, were united in their opposition to him. They considered the movement he led to be a very real threat, and they considered various ways to discredit or eliminate him in order to stop it.

Jesus expressed his resistance to the Powers through noncooperation with unjust and discriminatory religious rules and civil laws, which overlapped in his culture. He refused to obey the purity codes, which separated respectable religious people from the poor, who could not afford and whose lifestyles would not allow the elaborate hand washing and separation from people or things considered unclean.

Jesus healed on the Sabbath, claiming that compassion is more aligned with God's will than is the literal upholding of the Law. When the authorities challenged him about these healings, they were not simply making petty, legalistic charges against Jesus. They were upset because he refused to acknowledge their authority and their Law. He threatened the status quo by dramatically demonstrating the power of God to heal people from physical, emotional, and mental illness. Such healings gave more validity to Jesus' message and caused his popularity to grow.

The movement Jesus led was so successful that the Jewish religious leaders were afraid that the Romans would destroy the whole nation because of it. At a specially called meeting of the council of religious leaders, the chief priests and Pharisees said, "If we let him go on like this, everyone will believe in him, and the Romans will come and destroy both our holy place and our nation" (John 11:47). The high priest, Caiaphas, responded to the gathered assembly: "You know nothing at all! You do not understand that it is better for you to have one man die for the people than to have the whole nation destroyed" (John 11:50). Or, in the words of the King James Version, "It is expedient for us, that one man should die for the people, and that the whole nation perish not." It was expedient. This kind of justification for political violence is still going on today.

When Jesus came riding into Jerusalem on a donkey's colt, crowds gathered along the road and celebrated the coming of the Messiah. People hailed him as king (Luke 19:29-40). This further inflamed those who opposed him.

Jesus' conflict with the authorities went beyond noncooperation to direct action, culminating in his overturning the tables of the moneychangers in the temple, thus directly challenging the economic system upon which the whole religious hierarchy was built (Luke 19:45-46). He damaged, or at least created disarray and threatened, the private property of people who were commercializing the sacred, profiting at the expense of the poor, and turning a holy place into a "den of robbers," a place where religious experience and worth before God could supposedly be bought and sold. For the Powers, this challenge to the economic order was the last straw.

Jesus could see where his resistance actions were taking him. When he prayed on the Mount of Olives, his sweat was like great drops of blood (Luke 22:44). He knew he had a choice, a very real choice. He could have turned around and gone away from the confrontation that awaited him in Jerusalem to freedom and obscurity. But he refused to be intimidated. He refused to back down. Instead, he submitted to arrest, where he faced certain death at the hands of the governing authorities. He was taken into custody as a political prisoner, charged with sedition, tried, beaten, mocked, and finally crucified by the Roman Empire. Biblical scholar Allen Callahan says: "Why was Jesus killed? The Roman answer is good enough for me. He was causing trouble. He constituted a security risk and he was dealt with the way the Romans always deal with security risks in the provinces. This was a matter of not even so much politics, as policy. This is how the Romans handled trouble-makers, even if they didn't intend to make trouble . . ."[6] According to biblical scholar L. Michael White: "The plaque which names him as Jesus, the king of the Jews, suggests that the charge on which he was executed was one of political insurrection. A threat to the Pax Romana but he's also now a victim of the Pax Romana."[7]

Jesus stood for what he believed, directly challenged those who were in power, and refused to back down even when he could see that those who were in power were trying to kill him. He resisted, nonviolently, to the point of death.

In short, Jesus and the movement he founded threatened the network of religious, economic, political, and military Powers, so they executed him, as they had so many others. It was a matter of national security. His death, however, did not put an end to the movement. His disciples, having witnessed his brutal death, became convinced that he had risen.

"We have seen the Lord" became a rallying cry for a movement that spread quickly. Early Christians followed what they called the "Way." They sought to reflect the values of the kingdom of God that Jesus proclaimed and to demonstrate, as Jesus did, how human life can be lived in close relationship to God, under the power and influence of the Holy Spirit, in loving community and in resistance to Powers that would degrade or destroy life.

It wasn't long before distinctions were made, lines were drawn, creeds were developed, and hierarchies established in the early church. Under Constantine, Christianity became a religion of empire, and to this day Christianity in many of its forms has cooperated with the ruling Powers. Wars have been fought and genocide carried out under the banner of the cross. This is one of the great ironies of history, since its founder nonviolently resisted empire at the cost of his own life.

But for the first three centuries, Christians were a persecuted minority, living in nonviolent resistance to the Roman Empire, refusing to bow to the emperor or serve in the Roman army. Many were martyred, courageously following the example of Jesus, who demonstrated the nonviolent, self-giving love of God.

Both Gandhi and King pointed to Jesus as the inspiration and model for their movements of organized nonviolent resistance. In this age of corporate globalization and empire, Jesus' unwavering spirit of resistance and hope for transformation can give us a sense of the depth of courage and commitment that is possible in a human life lived in faithfulness to God.

No matter how difficult our challenges, no matter how powerful the forces against us, we have the example of Jesus, who selflessly stood up to the forces of oppression with courage and love. We who are his followers are called to do the same, to live as he lived, to follow his values as best we can. That may be difficult to discern and even harder to carry out in our current context, but it is still our calling. This brings us further in our question of how Christian faith can inspire and empower us to respond to the great social and ecological challenges of our day.

FOLLOWING JESUS

> Happy are the simple followers of Jesus Christ who have been overcome by his grace, and are able to sing the praises of the all-sufficient grace of Christ with humbleness of heart. ... Happy are they who know that discipleship simply means the life which springs from grace, and that grace simply means discipleship.
>
> —Dietrich Bonhoeffer[10]

For this book to stay true to its purpose, namely, to articulate a practical theology of resistance and hope for the sake of the world, our discussion here must relate directly to the problem of sin and the Powers. In chapter 8, we saw how social sin and institutional evil have grave and far-reaching effects. We identified idolatry and injustice as primary expressions of such sin within a society. We looked at the effects of these twin evils on individuals, as well as on society and the world, and at how the Powers teach and reinforce them.

We have also considered the dehumanizing inner effects of the Powers of our age, including apathy, the captivity of the conscience, and loss of moral agency, that is, inability to take right action. We saw how we relinquish our humanity when we give to the Powers the allegiance that we should be giving to God (idolatry) and when we serve the Powers instead of serving our neighbors (injustice).

How can we live humanly, as free and responsible human beings, enmeshed as we are in a global system that is diverting the life-force of human beings and siphoning off the gifts of God's creation for idolatrous and unjust purposes that threaten the future? This question brings us around again to resistance, for, as Stringfellow said, in times of great tyranny, "resistance [becomes] the only human way to live."[11]

For the topic of personal transformation to be relevant here, it must address these issues. In other words, How does the message and way of Jesus Christ help us to become free of idolatry and injustice? How do they help us to become free, fully human, faithful to God, more completely the people God created us to be?

First, it is essential not to lift the story of Jesus' death on the cross out of the context of his life, teachings, and ministry, or out of the time, place, and political situation in which he lived. In the words of Charles Campbell: "The cross cannot be plopped down out of the blue as a magical transaction between God and individual sinners. Rather, Jesus' resistance to the powers of the world leads to his crucifixion and gives the cross its distinctive meaning."[12] Jesus' death was a continuation of the way he lived his life. It was also the consequence of living in faithfulness to God and in resistance to the Powers.

Second, those who would follow Jesus can expect the same. There is no promise of safety, no corner of ease or complacency in which to hide. Jesus said, "If any want to become my followers, let them deny themselves and take up their cross and follow me" (Matt. 16:24). In the words of Dietrich Bonhoeffer, "When Christ calls a man, he bids him come and die."[13]

Third, Jesus makes us a wonderful promise that will be fulfilled, if we are willing: "For those who want to save their life will lose it, and those who lose their life for my sake will find it" (Matt. 16:25). Jesus promises that if we follow him without reservation we will be given back our lives, our humanity, ourselves.

But how? Following Jesus isn't easy. In fact, it is impossible without divine aid. Fortunately, this is just what is offered. For those who would follow Christ, this aid comes through an ongoing relationship with the Creator, through the tangible activity of the Holy Spirit, and through the presence of the Christ within and among us. Christian faith does not just offer us an example to follow, but a "way." And ironically, the cross, an instrument of torture and oppression, has become a symbol of the way of Jesus Christ, which transforms human life.

NEW LIFE IN CHRIST

I have been crucified with Christ; and it is no longer I who live, but it is Christ who lives in me. And the life I now live in the flesh I live by faith in the Son of God, who loved me and gave himself for me.

—Gal. 2:19b-20

The cross does not just symbolize the death and resurrection of Jesus, which happened so long ago. It also symbolizes the lived experience of generations of his followers who, in a spiritual sense, have died and risen with Christ. Nor does it simply signify the promise of life after death. Following Christ offers a new way of being, a resurrected life, a new life in Christ now. Albert Schweitzer called this way of being "Christ mysticism", and described it as follows: "In everything they [who experience this new life] are like men who have been buried with Christ and now live in a new state of existence. . . . they are men who have been dead and have been made alive. . . . As their life-power they have the Spirit of God, which is also the power which lives in Jesus and goes forth from Him. Christ Himself is in them. Since the life-power of His resurrection state of existence is also theirs, they are a new creation."[14]

This state of being is expressed in many ways in the New Testament: as living in fellowship with Christ, belonging to Christ, being one with Christ, putting on Christ, and so on. But the bottom line is this: I have new life in Christ because I live in Christ and because Christ is alive in me. I experience this new life in many ways, to the degree that I surrender my self will and say "yes" to this unmediated fellowship with God through Jesus Christ. I live in faith that I am forgiven, accepted, and loved to the degree that I allow forgiveness, acceptance, and love for myself and others to flow through me. I experience hope to the degree that I plant seeds of hope by taking positive action in the world. Freedom, too, comes to me, but also through me, to the degree that I live not by the law, according to human constructed rules and regulations, but by the Spirit. For life in the Spirit is not characterized by moralist legalism, but by compassion and creativity.

What is the antidote to the twin evils of idolatry and injustice? Jesus, the "Great Physician,"[15] offers us the cure: love God above all and your neighbor as yourself. In this time of ecological awareness, we have learned to include the nonhuman community of life as neighbors within our circle of love and concern.

To return to the opening quote of this book, when we "fear nothing but sin" we seek to live in just relationship with all parts of creation, and when we "desire nothing but God" all competing loyalties fade. Idolatry is transformed into faithfulness and injustice into compassion for all living things. This transformation is not something that we can do for ourselves. We experience this new life only by the grace of God.

New life in Christ is lived not in isolation, but in community. Paul likens the church of Jesus Christ to a human body. This is not the same as the institutional church, but is a mystical body of Christ animated by the Holy Spirit. We might like to identify this community with a particular group or denomination, but that is not possible. The true church is not static. The faithful church, the followers of Jesus, appear not once and for all within a particular institution but, in Stringfellow's words, "here and there and now and then."[16] Nevertheless, we are called, however imperfectly, to live out the faith, carry the message, share the Spirit, and follow Christ.

In humility, we are called to create communities that live in the spirit of Christ and carry out the values of the kingdom of God (some call it the "kin-dom" of God[17]) that Jesus lived and proclaimed. According to Marcus Borg, the church is called to be an "alternative culture where the Spirit is known" and that is characterized by compassion as Jesus was.

If we live in Christ and are animated by his Spirit, we will be motivated and willing to follow in the direction he leads, which is directly into the heart of the struggle for a better world. The Powers do not like that. They hold up modern, death-dealing equivalents of the cross to intimidate us. But fear need not hold us back, for the Powers that rule the world today are not ultimate, though they pretend to be. We may not know the immediate outcome of our actions, but we do know what side of the struggle we are on—the only side that offers hope for humanity and hope for the earth, the side of self-giving love, the love of God.

THE TRIUMPH OF GOD OVER THE POWERS

He disarmed the rulers and authorities and made a public example of them, triumphing over them in [the cross].
—Col. 2:15

The power of God, at work in the life, death, and resurrection of Jesus, transforms hearts and lives. But for those of us who see the earth dying and hear the cries of suffering humanity, personal transformation is not enough. We long for major social change, revolutionary change, change that shakes the foundations and turns the world upside down. We long for a new community, for the "upside down kingdom"[18] that Jesus initiated, where the hungry will be fed, the naked clothed, the oppressed set free, and slaves released. We hear the groans of the earth, and we ourselves groan inwardly, in labor for the day when the whole creation is set free from bondage and we enjoy together the glorious liberty of the children of God (Rom. 8:21). We look not only for personal transformation but also for transformation of the world.

According to Scripture and tradition, the divine power at work through the birth, life, teachings, death, and resurrection of Jesus is not limited to changing the lives of individual human beings. Early Christians believed these were cosmic events that shook the very foundations of reality, turning everything upside down.

According to Gustaf Aulén, author of *Christus Victor*,[19] this was the "classical" view of the atonement, the view held in the early church and revived by Martin Luther. Through his "victory" on the cross, Jesus Christ triumphed over the Powers of this world. The powers of sin, death, and hell were vanquished. The decisive battle of good over evil had been won.

In postmodern language we could say that the crucifixion and after-death appearances of Jesus brought about a paradigm shift in the evolution of human spirituality. The apostasy of the ruling Powers are no longer disguised by wealth and power they claim God bestows upon them. Jesus' death on the cross exposed the Powers as being in blatant rebellion against God and, by so doing, spiritually disempowered them. As his followers carried on his message and way of life, claiming that Jesus had risen and lived among them, death was shown to be a hollow threat. In the words of Walter Wink, "Christ was the 'victor' who overcame the Powers by exposing them for what they were, trumping their final sanction, which is death."[20]

But as we look at the situation in our world today, it is hard to see how God has triumphed over the Powers at all. The network of institutions that dominate the global empire is so extensive, complex, and entrenched that at times resistance does seem futile. Their domination of the earth seems almost complete. Governing as they do through propaganda, economic sanctions, violence, and intimidation, we might ask: Does God really have any power over them at all? Is there any hope for global transformation? Does the earth stand a chance?

For many, the die is cast. People feel powerless, and so they give up. Since there seems to be no hope for the world, they become apathetic, escapist, or materialistic. But this is just what the Powers want. It sets up a self-perpetuating cycle that supports worldly systems and interferes with the liberating purposes of God.

God is eternal, so in a sense God always triumphs over the limited and finite. Even if life as we know it on planet Earth is extinguished through nuclear war or ecological catastrophe, something new will evolve over eons of geologic time. But shall we resign ourselves to this possibility in apathy, helplessness, and despair? Shall we forfeit the precious lives of our children and our children's children, the heritage of our ancestors, the love incarnate here on earth? Shall we abandon the other creatures with whom we share the planet and the beauty of the natural world? Are these things of such little value that we place our comfort above their loss? Shall we avoid our personal responsibility by insulating ourselves through denial in our own lives? Are we letting the Powers deceive us into thinking that we can do nothing, or that we don't have enough knowledge, money, influence, or power to stop their rampaging destruction? Shall we allow them to play God in our lives that we may avoid the cross?

If so, this is bondage of the mind, heart, and will. It is alienation from God, creation, self, and other. It is sin.

This bondage of mind, heart, and will has a remedy that is found in the gospel of Jesus Christ. As I accept the unconditional blessing, forgiveness, and love that God offers me through Jesus Christ, I am transformed. As God sets me free to change, I recover my moral agency.

Here is where the personal transformation offered by the good news of Jesus Christ of a personal and intimate relationship with God intersects with hope for world transformation. Even when considering the fate of the earth, it comes down to a very personal question: "Whom do I serve by my thoughts, words, and actions, God or the Powers?"

We are called and empowered today, in the midst of our present circumstances, to live as God's people and to follow Jesus, no matter what the cost, even to the cross. In this way we participate in Christ's saving work and God's triumph over the Powers.

NAMING, MASKING, AND ENGAGING THE POWERS

When activists reframe a significant cultural context, they're like the child who shouts that the emperor is wearing no clothes. They expose a whole belief system for what it is—a belief system, not the natural order of things, not reality. . . . Then people who never before doubted the status quo, who took it as God-given and utterly legitimate, start to ask their own questions.

—Paul Ray and Sherry Anderson[21]

The three volumes of Walter Wink's trilogy on the Powers are aptly entitled: *Naming the Powers, Unmasking the Powers,* and *Engaging the Powers.*[22] The concepts of naming, unmasking, and engaging help shed light on our human responsibility in relation to the institutions of our day. All three require humility, courage, spiritual discernment, and prayer.

Naming and unmasking the Powers primarily involve spiritual discernment and thought, in a process of identifying, analyzing, and articulating their reality. But according to Wink, that is just a beginning: "The ultimate issue . . . is not whether we comprehend the Powers, but whether we confront them with their apostasy. . . .

Understanding the Powers is but a step toward encountering them. We unmask them only in order to engage them, in the spirit and power of . . . the truly Human Being incarnated by Jesus."[23]

So far we have focused primarily on naming the Powers, that is, the ruling institutions of our time. Matthew Fox frames (that is, names) the demonic aspect of institutional (specifically, corporate) power in this way: "Not 'Word was made flesh,' but the 'Devil is made fleshless.' Yes, a Devourer of Flesh—of the flesh of rainforests and indigenous peoples, of ordinary citizens, of the future. . . . They are the Flesh Eaters. . . . They lack incarnation. They are angels—bad angels, unfortunately. As in the Book of Revelation, there is only one question here: Who rules the universe: economic fleshless imperialists or the incarnated ones?"[24]

We are the incarnated ones. God, the Creator and Spirit of the universe, can work through us. As living human beings, we are the only ones who can name, unmask, and engage the "economic fleshless ones" and the other disembodied, institutionalized dealers of death. We are the ones with the power, ability, and responsibility to bring change.

This generation has a window of opportunity in which to act. We have been given prophets to point us in the direction of healing, human faculties with which to deal with the great challenges we face, spiritual gifts that the earth so desperately needs. We have every tool we need to name, unmask, and engage the ruling Powers that are propelling us toward a living hell.

Engaging the Powers begins with our personal refusal to bow to them. As we have seen, the Domination System of our day, with its interlocking network of powerful institutions, depends upon our fear of death, or its mental, emotional, financial, or spiritual equivalents, to keep it in place. The power of the state is coercive, and depends upon its final sanction, which is death. Economic power, too, is coercive, pursuing profits at the cost of people's lives and ecological destruction. Religious institutional power can also be coercive, providing moral support to the dominant political, military, and economic Powers through active consent or silent complicity. Some churches even use the threat of eternal torment to keep people in line.

When we refuse to live in fear of and obedience to the Powers, their stratagems no longer work. When the Powers can no longer count on fear, selfishness, and apathy to keep us in line, they cannot do business as usual.

But how can we know whether we are still dominated by the Powers, especially if we are benefiting from the system and are not in harm's way? We can go to where the damage is being done. We can enter into solidarity with people who are suffering and risk speaking and acting on their behalf. In this way we give voice to the voiceless and take our stand with, as Matthew Fox says, "God being crucified anew by impersonal, rational, abstracted, mostly fleshless powers and principalities."[25] If God in Christ is in solidarity with the victims of injustice and oppression, so should Jesus' followers be. In the words of Dorothee Soelle: "To attain the image of Christ means to live in revolt against the great Pharaoh and to remain with the oppressed and the disadvantaged. It means to make their lot one's own."[26]

We are called to engage the Powers by taking actions that expose them for what they are, so they can no longer mislead, distort, and hide. We are called to reveal (unmask) their true nature, their idolatry and injustice, their worship of death, their rebellion against God. Our words and actions can show that the dominant system is bereft of morality and based on lies.

What kind of actions? Those that are undertaken under the guidance and motivation of the Spirit, that demonstrate God's power that is made perfect in weakness, the power of nonviolent love, the power of the cross. Such actions are baffling to the ruling Powers. The "weakness" and "foolishness" of cruciform love makes no sense to those who dominate through violence and intimidation. "None of the rulers of this [or any] age understood this; for if they had, they would not have crucified the Lord of glory" (1 Cor. 2:8), nor the millions of other innocent victims killed on the altars of wealth and worldly power.

But others, even some in positions of power, will see and understand. Courageous nonviolent actions have a way of lifting peoples' hearts and spirits, giving them hope that change is possible, and inspiring them to take courageous actions of their own.

We are called to confront the "flesh eaters" in actions that demonstrate their Achilles heel, that is, their utter powerlessness to dominate the earth without the consent of the people. For engaging the Powers exposes not only their evil effects, but also their folly. When we refuse to live in denial and instead speak truth to power, the lies and pretensions of the Powers are exposed. When we challenge their morality, the Powers lose their legitimacy. When we choose lifestyles that reflect creative, life-giving values, the Powers lose their ability to dominate culture. When we enter actively into solidarity with the poor and oppressed, with victims of war and unjust social and economic policies, the brutality of the Powers is exposed. When we take part in organized actions of nonviolent resistance, the futility of their attempts to rule through domination is exposed. When we refuse to live in fear and are willing risk even jail or death, the ability of the ruling Powers to govern life through violence and intimidation is lost, and the triumph of God's love is revealed.

AND DEATH SHALL HAVE NO DOMINION

> God put this power to work in Christ when he raised him from
> the dead and seated him at his right hand in the heavenly places,
> far above all rule and authority and power and dominion ...
>
> —Eph. 1:20a

Ultimately, God triumphs over the Powers of this world; that is not in question. The "rule and authority and power and dominion" of this age is not ultimate—God is. Empires rise and fall. Today's global corporate empire shows serious signs of overreaching itself. Eventually this system, too, will collapse or disintegrate. The ground of being, the source of all creation, the love at the heart of this and every universe is eternal.

As we surrender to God, moving from spiritual death to life, we celebrate God's triumph over the Powers in our own hearts and lives. The fear of death diminishes or disappears and we are set free to continue on in a lifelong process of growing in the grace of God and actively participating in hopeful actions in faith, hope, and love.

What hope is there for changing the systems of the world? The only way to triumph over the violence that is so pervasive in our culture is through nonviolent, self-giving love. By demonstrating such love in his life, death, and continuing presence, Jesus shows us that divine love is possible in human life. As we "die to the Powers," we are set free from our enthrallment to them. As we allow Christ to live in us and love through us, we demonstrate the present reality of the power of divine love. The "myth of redemptive violence" is shown to be the self-perpetuating, bankrupt sham that it is, as nonviolent alternatives are revealed. The myth of the market as God is unmasked as unjust and idolatrous as justice and compassion are allowed to take root and flourish.

In our lives and communities, we demonstrate to ourselves, each other, and the world that the "wisdom" and "power" of the world (that is, of the system) are no match for the "foolishness" and "weakness" of God. The God who suffers the violence that human beings inflict on each other and the earth also waits for prodigal sons and daughters to return and lavishes upon us all the riches of divine love. This love is our birthright to which we are entitled by virtue of being children of God and part of the original and ongoing blessing of creation.

As we experience, practice, and reinforce these spiritual truths, the life of Christ is manifest in our lives, in our communities, and in the world. For there to be a more compassionate world we need to be a compassionate people. For there to be a more peaceful, just, and sustainable world we need to be peaceful, just, and willing to live in ways that are sustainable. In order for the world not to be dominated by deadly institutions we must refuse to be dominated by such institutions and willing to call them to account. Only in this way will God's triumph over the Powers be manifest in the world of human affairs.

So hope for the transformation of the systems of the world depends upon us. It does not begin or end with us, but it depends upon us. We cannot sit idly by. The saving work of God in Christ takes place in the hearts and through the lives of human beings.

This seems like a tall order. But as we are transformed and witness transformation in others, as we create communities of transformation and stand in solidarity with other such communities, we become agents of change in the world, claiming our full authority as children of God. And lo and behold, we begin to see signs of God's triumph over the Powers everywhere, people around the world rising up in resistance and creating beautiful and compassionate alternatives to the system of corporate globalization. Global transformation becomes not only possible, but within reach.

We become hopeful. Hope becomes a movement, a direction, a way of being in the world.

HOPE FOR THE EARTH

The creation waits with eager longing for the revealing of the children of God . . .
—Rom. 8:19

Jesus said, "The kingdom of heaven is within [or among] you" (Luke 17:21). Deep fulfillment in the present is possible when life is lived in the light and presence of God. The reign of God is present here and now, within and among Jesus' followers and wherever the Spirit enlivens and moves people to acts of compassion, courage, justice, and love.

But there is also a sense in which the reign of God is not yet realized, that is, not fully manifest in the world. We pray, "Thy kingdom come, Thy will be done on earth as it is in heaven," because it is not yet so. There is a future orientation to Christian faith, an orientation of hope.

An historical symbol of Christian hope has been the concept of the "second coming." Early Christians expected Jesus' imminent return, and later biblical passages demonstrate their struggle to retain hope and make sense of his delay. At different points throughout the past two thousand years, people have claimed that the time is at hand, that the day of Christ's return is near. In modern times, however, for many mainline Christians, the idea of the second coming has slipped into the background, eclipsed by the focus on existential experience and rational thought.

With the rise of Christian fundamentalism since the 1970s, the concept of the second coming has again come to the fore, accompanied by the claim that we are living in the "last days," that Jesus will soon return and usher in the "rapture," when believers will be taken up bodily into heaven. Biblical literalists support these views by lifting Bible passages out of the context of the times and situations in which they were written, and then piecing them together in a strained attempt to make one harmonious whole, a prophecy that supposedly applies to us today.

It is easy to understand why so many people foresee unprecedented global destruction when they consider the prospects for the future of life on earth. Many of the apocalyptic images in the book of Revelation seem remarkably appropriate when describing current events. In the words of James Douglass: "There is no sensitive conscience which can confront the global organization of power today, and its apparently uncontrollable technology, without seeing that the people are . . . drowning everywhere, and they are going down fast. If the horsemen of the Apocalypse continue to gallop faster, there will soon be no stopping their sweep across the entire world, beating into dust and bones every illusion which human beings have managed to sustain to this point in history . . ."[27]

Humanity certainly faces grave threats, many of which I have outlined in this book. But claims that the last days are now unfolding according to God's plan are deterministic, pointing to a God that ordains a violent end to the world (war in the Middle East or even nuclear war), and are built upon fear. Such predictions could even become self-fulfilling prophecies, since people act out of their beliefs.

Such views rob people of the spirit to help bring about a peaceful, just, and sustainable world. Why waste your time if the Bible says that things will just get worse and worse? Better to focus on the return of Jesus, which will be any day now, and where you will spend eternity. The focus of such teachings is not on life here and now, but on life after death. This preoccupation with death is a rejection of the gift of life we have been given and a denial of the incarnation ("God with us").

Christian hope is not simply hope for life after death, but also for the future of this world, for the time when "the earth will be filled with the knowledge of the glory of the Lord, as the waters cover the sea" (Hab. 2:14). Hope does not lie in the anticipation of being saved out of this world, but in the yearning for God's reign. Albert Schweitzer, the great biblical scholar who wrote *In Search of the Historical Jesus*, criticized all Christian doctrines of redemption that focus solely on the individual and that neglect the coming of the kingdom of God: "To be a Christian means to be possessed and dominated by a hope of the Kingdom of God, and a will to work for it, which bids defiance to external reality. Until this comes about Christianity will stand before the world like a wood in the barrenness of winter."[28]

How we view the future affects the future, because our expectations affect our actions and our actions affect the outcome of events. It makes a difference whether we live in fear, denial, or expectation of global catastrophe, or by faith in the power of God to bring change. In the words of Jürgen Moltmann:

> In apprehension and in hope, we anticipate the future and adapt ourselves to it in the present. The people who today despair and say "no future" are anticipating the end and destroying the lives of other people. However, Christians anticipate the future of the new creation, the kingdom of justice and freedom, not because they are optimists, but because they trust the faithfulness of God. We cannot dispense ourselves from preserving this world for God's future, because we can also annihilate it. There is no salvation without this earth.[29]

Hope is directly related to faith: "Faith is the assurance of things hoped for, the conviction of things not seen" (Heb. 11:1). As we grow in faith, we also grow in conviction, and we come to trust and see evidence that the power of God that has transformed our lives is active in the lives of others and behind the scenes in world events, bringing transformation in mysterious ways that we do not comprehend. At the same time, as Jim Wallis notes, "Faith leads to hope, hope leads to action, and action leads to change."[30] As we entrust ourselves to God and see our lives transformed, we become more hopeful, and willing to take action for change.

In his book *The Coming of the Cosmic Christ*, Matthew Fox updates the concept of the second coming, reclaiming it as a symbol of hope for the world. He writes of a spiritual second coming in which we participate, a "New Pentecost" where the Holy Spirit is poured out on all flesh, ushering in a new age of widespread spiritual transformation, a "Great Awakening" of the peoples of the earth. Furthermore, Fox says, this global transformation is already in process, as evidenced by a revival of interest and activity in spiritual things, in traditional religious practices, in Native and earth-centered spiritualities, in the revival of creativity and the arts, in ecological awareness and action, and in movements of justice and peace. This hope relies upon the Spirit of God but requires human beings to be active participants in the creative process of transforming the systems of the world.

James Douglass understands hope for the world in a different, but perhaps complementary, way. In *Resistance and Contemplation*, he uses convincing scholarship to make the case that things turned out differently than Jesus had first anticipated. Jesus' goal was not to die on the cross, but to usher in the kingdom of God, a new community that reflected the values that he taught and lived. Douglass believes that Jesus was deeply disappointed in the failure of his initial mission. As Jesus' understanding of his situation deepened, he began to point to the coming of the Son of man as his hope. However, Jesus was not promising that he himself would personally return. Rather, says Douglass, "Son of man" is better understood as "The New Humanity," a humanity transformed and living in the light and presence of God:

> The Second Coming envisioned by the accused revolutionary standing alone before the high priest was to be the communal coming, "from now on," of a suffering, faithful people, empowered by God in their history to break through to a non-violent Humanity, the kingdom of God. Abandoned by his followers, alone before his judge, anticipating execution, Jesus still saw that total divine revolution coming from within Humanity. He knew that God would somehow make it happen, and he was determined to embody it by his own death. He did, and the nonviolent coming of God took over.[31]

Throughout the past two thousand years there have been people and communities that have lived out the vision of the new humanity that Jesus exemplified, claiming that the Holy Spirit is present with them, that the risen Christ lives among them. That vision is still alive today, demonstrated in nonviolent resistance and self-giving love.

Living in hope does not mean passively waiting for the future to manifest itself. We may need to wait for clarity and guidance, but it is important to know that God is not holding out—we are. God has provided everything we need to bring about a changed world. We don't need to wait for God to act. "We are the ones we have been waiting for"[32] and we are the ones the creation eagerly awaits.

IN RESISTANCE IS THE SECRET OF JOY

Moral commitment alone and organization alone do not build breadth. Shared delight, heavy laden with creative signs of a coming alternative future—this is what invites the many,

encourages them to stand up in new solidarity to powers that
rule by their spectacles of terror.

—Mark Lewis Taylor[33]

Moving from despair to hope is a primary form of struggle in
resistance to the Powers that would crush the heart and spirit of life
out of human beings. Hope for the future is countercultural. It
requires spiritual resistance to the mind-numbing and heart-harden-
ing distractions and excesses of modern life. Despair is easy—painful,
but easy, for it enables us to excuse inaction. On the other hand,
despair can become a hole so deep and so dark that anything would be
better than continuing our descent into our own personal hell. When
we hit bottom, we are at a turning point, a point of decision. The
choice is to stay as we are or to take responsibility for ourselves and
our world and become willing to take action. Our "no" to despair is
based upon our "yes" to life.

In resistance to the institutions and systems that destroy the
earth and crush the life out of people, hope comes alive. As we withdraw our consent to these Powers, practicing noncooperation, finding
or creating life-supporting alternatives, what has seemed impossible
becomes possible because we are willing to pay the price to make it so.
It is like the difference between being a spectator in the stands and
being a player on the field. As Dorothee Soelle says, "Only when we
ourselves enter the game and bind our own life inextricably to the
game's outcome does hope arrive."[34]

In *nonviolent* resistance, we leave behind not only our validation of
the ruling Powers, but their "stratagems," which are violent to the core.
In *faith-led* resistance, instead of reacting out of old patterns into which
we have been socialized and acculturated, we go deeper. We open ourselves to the Spirit of love that resides in our hearts and at the heart of
the universe. In prayer and meditation, the Spirit touches us and we
groan inwardly together with all creation "as in the pangs of childbirth,"
for freedom from bondage, for the "glorious liberty of the children of
God." Our hearts reach out in solidarity to all who suffer, to victims of
the Powers near and far, to God in Christ, who is crucified in our neighbors and in the earth, and who is crucified in us as we face our own pain
and darkness and as we share the world's suffering. We enter into something deeper than the influence and socialization by the Powers. We
begin to live intuitively rather than automatically, to live in community
rather than as part of an unthinking collective, and in so doing we allow
God to triumph over the Powers in us. We change.

As we begin the process of breaking free, we recognize others
engaged in the same process and we see that change is not only possi-

ble, but is happening now. Then, in spite of the risks, losses, and even sacrifices, the struggle becomes joyous, even fun. Fun? Yes, fun, energizing, inspiring, hopeful.

In his book *The Executed God*, Mark Lewis Taylor speaks of how important it is to counter the "spectacles of terror" presented by the Powers by creating a "theatrics of counterterror" through creative, empowering, joyful, public actions. Many are creating such a "theater, as many are doing in small acts of witness and in mass demonstrations for the pageant of empowerment . . . the triumph of God, will be not only deep, it will also be wide, galvanizing an array of diverse forces."[35] In this way, "The many who are either terrorized or mesmerized by lockdown America will take note. They will wake up, and the wider power will join the deeper power in one pageant of empowerment, in a kind of triumph of God most needed."[36]

It is a gift to participate in the saving work of God in the world. It is poignant and painful, yet satisfying, to stand in solidarity with the poor and oppressed, to cast our lot with "the least" (Matt. 25:45) of Jesus' brothers and sisters, and so with him. It is a privilege to struggle in solidarity with people around the world, to throw off the oppressive weight of institutions that ruin people's lives. It is here that we find hope. In James Douglass' words:

> Here, among the most radically powerless and oppressed of the world, is where the nonviolent coming of God begins, at that moment when faith catches fire in their hearts. . . . No empire has ever had the power to stand against such faith. The British had as little success with Jesus' Hindu successor, Gandhi, as the Roman Empire had with Jesus and the early Christians. The nonviolent coming of God is a growing force in Humanity that will not be denied its full flowering in the world.[37]

What a blessing it is when such faith catches fire in our hearts, enabling us to live in hope. By living in hope and taking hopeful actions, we actually make the world a more hopeful place. We make positive change more likely when we manifest hope, when we embody hope. We live hope into being.

How do we embody hope? By becoming who we really are, by coming into our own as human beings, by defining our own identity. The Powers try to convince us that we are primarily consumers, motivated by competition, self-interest, and personal gain. They would teach us to be realistic on their terms, to believe that violence and domination are basic to who we are. Like Caiaphas, they would have us accept that it is expedient for there to be winners and losers, that some people are expendable. They would have us believe that the consolidation of the current global order is inevitable, and that we are powerless to stop it.

But who are we really? We are children of the universe, brought to this amazing moment here and now through a process of evolution that has taken billions of years. We are children of God, alive, breathing, embodied human beings in whom God lives and through whom God can act. We are children of humanity, humanity's hope in this generation when change must come. We carry the legacy of the saints and prophets through the ages, as well as the hopes and dreams of mothers and fathers from time immemorial for the well-being of future generations. And we are the brothers and sisters of Jesus the Christ, the human being, who shows us what God is like and what human life can be when lived in the light and presence of God.

CHAPTER SIXTEEN
A Better World Is Possible: The Movement for Global Justice

> History is governed by those overarching movements that
> give shape and meaning to life by relating the human venture
> to the larger destinies of the universe. Creating such a move-
> ment might be called the Great Work of a people.... The his-
> torical mission of our times is to reinvent the human—at the
> species level, with critical reflection, within the community
> of life-systems.
>
> —Thomas Berry[1]

In June of 1992 I traveled to Rio de Janeiro as part of a United
Methodist delegation during the United Nations Conference on
Environment and Development (UNCED), where 178 heads of state
gathered to address issues related to poverty and the global environment. Around the world people were filled with hope that world leaders would finally address these pressing problems.

Several official documents emerged from this "Earth Summit,"
but corporate influence weakened the Framework Climate
Convention, the Biodiversity Convention (which the United States
refused to sign), and Agenda 21, the Rio Declaration on Environment
and Development.[2] In addition, corporate leaders promoted a vision of
environmental protection and sustainable development based on open
markets, economic growth, and free trade. Sadly, in Rio, world leaders lost an opportunity to transform national and global institutions
and set them on a path toward a sustainable future.[3]

But at the same time, in large tents along the beach in another
part of Rio, another set of negotiations were taking place among members of civil society who had gathered for a parallel "Global Forum."
Tens of thousands of people had come from throughout Brazil, South
America, and around the world to connect with each other, to celebrate diversity, to discuss shared concerns, and to create a peoples'
agenda for change. During the day I attended educational events and
forums, visited colorful displays, witnessed an amazing variety of creative initiatives, and made new friends. When darkness fell, brightly

dressed Samba dancers took to the stage, and music and dancing continued long into the night.

Many of us labored over various citizens' documents. These efforts resulted in a set of alternative treaties, including the "Earth Charter," which outline principles, strategies, and commitments to working toward a truly just, equitable, and sustainable world.[4]

COMPETING PARADIGMS

> A convergence of imperative and opportunity unique to the present moment in the human experience sets the stage for an intentional collective choice to put the way of Empire behind us as we live into being a new era of Earth Community.
> —David Korten[5]

The values and worldview that dominated negotiations at the official Rio Conference differed greatly from those of the participants of the peoples' Global Forum. This divergence of values and worldview is still at work today.

Martin Khor of the Third World Network points out that as we work for change we need to be aware that there are two alternative paradigms functioning today. One is the current system of corporate globalization, while the other is more local, community–based, people–friendly, and earth–centered than the dominant global system.

Most of us still participate in the dominant system to some degree, so we must work to make it fairer, less damaging, and more sustainable. But Khor warns that "even as we work in that system and make it more fair for all the participants, that system may not last very long because of ecological limits." The challenge, says Khor, is to "infuse the second paradigm into the first paradigm as a kind of transition."[6]

David Korten identifies these two competing societal models as "Empire" and "Earth Community." The dominant paradigm is anthropocentric. The emerging paradigm is earth–centered. The first is the paradigm of the present world order, in which we must work for laws that promote justice for workers, aid the poor, conserve critical habitats and endangered species, limit corporate power, reverse harmful energy policies, create more equitable tax laws, protect public services like education and health care, reform the prison system, reign in military spending, and so on. Work at this level requires energy and stamina, since the dominant system's momentum is moving in precisely the opposite direction. Such work assumes a continuity of the world's power structure, but it is urgent and necessary in order to contain damage and constrain the Powers.

At the same time, we must live the coming "new paradigm" into existence as Jesus did in his day when he created a community that lived out the values of the kingdom of God that he proclaimed. A paradigm shift is taking place in human consciousness, which is being actualized "here and there and now and then" in communities around the world.

In the paradigm of Earth Community the work requires us to go deep within, to draw from the wells of Spirit, to ground ourselves in the source of life, love, and creativity. Many people emphasize the importance of story in this process of humanity's transformation into a new way of being. The amazing story of the unfolding universe is our story, and the nature of reality being revealed through genetics, geology, astronomy, and quantum physics sheds light on our nature.

Our institutions have not yet caught up with the scientific paradigm shift that has taken place and is breaking through into human consciousness. The institutional Powers that continue to demand human loyalty and sacrifice are supported by social characteristics such as domination, hierarchy, competition, and exploitation. Such characteristics and associated attitudes and values have long been identified as male, and are foundational to the current patriarchal culture.

The emerging paradigm is decidedly feminist. Its values, attitudes, and characteristics include cooperation, partnership, intimacy, and nurture. Work on this level involves creating and nurturing communities with these characteristics into existence, and working to bring new and parallel institutions into being that are humanizing, truly democratic, and ecologically responsible. But we must remain vigilant, for any institution can become dehumanizing. Participatory democracy requires ongoing discernment, resistance to inertia and dehumanization, and individual responsibility for the common good.

Most major institutions continue to function from the dominant paradigm, including the media. Mainline press coverage takes for granted the perspective of the Empire paradigm. For this reason, dissenting views, actions of resistance, and alternatives that better represent the Earth Community paradigm rarely make it to the evening news, or even to the back page of the newspaper. When such stories do appear, they are presented as isolated, chaotic, unrelated events, which are then downplayed and misrepresented by establishment "experts" who are immersed in the dominant worldview. News coverage rarely presents alternative viewpoints or proposals for change.

Although global civil society is diverse and activist groups are largely autonomous, they often hold common values and a shared worldview. Several common themes unite people who are working to resist corporate globalization and to create alternative, life-affirming social structures. The International Forum on Globalization (IFG) has identified ten principles for sustainable societies:[7]

- Participatory Democracy: Systems of governance must ensure that people can hold their governments accountable and that their governments serve people and communities rather than corporations.
- Subsidiarity: Governments must be able to set policies that protect their people and the environment. The current top-down system must be reversed to favor local self-rule; decision making should move up to the next level only when necessary.
- Ecological Sustainability: Economic, social, and operating systems such as transportation, communication, agriculture, and manufacturing must enable people to meet their genuine needs while preserving the earth's biodiversity and its ability to support future generations.
- Common Heritage: The commons must be protected. The earth's water, land, air, forests, and fisheries, upon which life depends, are part of a natural heritage that must be available to all and preserved for future generations. Likewise, health care, education, and other basic services based on culture and knowledge constitute a cultural heritage that must be available to all.
- Human Rights: Governments are responsible to guarantee human rights as stated in the United Nations' Universal Declaration on Human Rights. These include civil and political rights, as well as economic, social, and cultural rights of all people.
- Livelihood: The right to a means of livelihood must be protected, along with the right of workers to organize independent trade unions. Policies that cause unemployment and displace people from communal lands upon which they subsist must be reversed.
- Food Safety and Food Security: Nations must have the right to protect local food production, limit food imports, set and enforce food safety standards, and restrict the sale of foods based on the precautionary principle.
- Equity: The inequity caused by corporate globalization must be reversed so that wealth is distributed more equitably both within and among nations. This will require the cancellation of the debt of poor nations.
- Biological and Cultural Diversity: The rules of the global economy must be changed to protect the world's cultural, biological, social, and economic diversity.
- Precautionary Principle: Products or practices that are potentially harmful to human health or the environment should be restricted, even in the absence of scientific certainty, until they are proven safe.

These core principles overlap with those outlined in the people's Earth Charter developed in Rio. They have emerged in varied combinations among groups organizing to address different issues in places around the world. Core principles such as these unite autonomous peoples' movements that are resisting corporate globalization and pursuing a more hopeful future. For this reason, this growing network of autonomous grassroots groups cannot simply be called an "antiglobal-ization" movement. It is truly a movement for global justice. Its theme has become "a better world is possible."[8] This idea is consistent with Christian hope. In the words of Jürgen Moltmann:

> God's promise is not for another world, but for the new creation of this world, in all its material and worldly reality. The whole of creation . . . will be transformed in God's new creation. Christian [hope] is therefore the hope that the world will be different. . . . Because it is hope for the future of this world, its effect is to show present reality to be not yet what it can and will be. The world is seen as transformable in the direction of the promised future. In this way believers are liberated from accommodation to the status quo, and set critically against it.[9]

Although today's dominant institutions are as outmoded and harmful as rule by emperors and kings, few institutions, including the church, have made a complete transition to the new paradigm of Earth Community. But many individuals have begun the transition and are working in various ways to create sustainable communities that nurture life. Though tactics may differ among individuals, our common principles unite us, as does our common hope for a peaceful, just, and sustainable future. We learn from each other and gain strength in solidarity.

COMMUNITIES OF RESISTANCE AND TRANSFORMATION

> **Thus it seems that the quest for an alternative vision and alternative movements to build a future that can include the poor majority of the world must arise, for this majority will not accept being consigned to slow death. It is only here perhaps that we can see the face of the true God at this time, not in the boardrooms and council chambers of empire, but rather in the stubborn refusal of millions of people in small networks to accept death and destitution as their fate, and who begin, however modestly, to create communities of solidarity and survival.**
>
> **—Rosemary Radford Ruether[10]**

In contrast to the horrendous violence of the last century, there were also many peoples' movements that brought about amazing and positive change through nonviolent resistance. These include the movement led by Gandhi to oust the British Empire from India, the civil rights movement in the United States, the South African struggle against apartheid, the Solidarity Movement, and other struggles in Central and Eastern Europe that led to the breakup of the Soviet Union. All of these involved organized nonviolent struggle on the part of many people. Walter Wink's book *Engaging the Powers* includes a list of successful campaigns of nonviolent resistance that goes on for many pages, an inspiring reminder of the power of nonviolent struggle.[11]

Similar movements are going on today in various communities around the world. People who are negatively affected by corporate globalization are organizing in resistance and creating viable alternatives, supported by networks of others who, in solidarity, reject the Powers' idolatrous claim of inevitable assimilation and absolute power. I mention only a few of these movements for change. These examples "are simply ripples on a moving river of alternative systems that are operating, growing, and being imagined around the world."[12]

On January 1, 1994, the day on which NAFTA went into effect, indigenous people in the state of Chiapas in southern Mexico rose up to challenge the new trade agreement, which they called "a death certificate for the ethnic people of Mexico."[13] Since then, the Zapatista resistance movement has created an autonomous system of regional indigenous self-government. Without support of the Mexican government the Zapatistas have elected county councils, created schools and clinics, established an autonomous justice system, and developed an agrarian economy based on indigenous values such as community and collective work. Their movement inspires people around the world.

In 1999, following advice from the World Bank, the government of Bolivia privatized Cochabamba's municipal water system and contracted with Bechtel, which gained rights to all the water. It even became illegal to use rainwater, which people in this poor desert region had traditionally captured, stored, and used. Bechtel immediately raised prices dramatically, leaving many without access to water. In response, the people formed the Coordination in Defense of Water and Life. People from throughout Bolivia marched to Cochabamba and shut down the city through a mass mobilization, using slogans like "Water Is God's Gift and Not Merchandise" and "Water Is Life." The government at first responded with deadly force, but after four months of protests Bechtel abandoned the project. The government reversed its water privatization program and cancelled its contract with Bechtel. Bechtel responded with a $25 million lawsuit against Bolivia for "lost profits" under a trade agreement similar to NAFTA. Meanwhile, water services in Cochabamba are being administered successfully by workers, citizens, and local officials in a way that favors people's access, not profits. Cochabamba has become a symbol of resistance to corporate globalization and the privatization of water.

When the Bolivian government moved to privatize the energy sector in 2003, people all over Bolivia again took to the streets, demanding that the president step down. Indigenous leader Evo Morales was elected to the presidency on a platform that explicitly rejected the neoliberal policies that had ravished the country. He has since nationalized the country's energy resources, which had long been dominated by foreign oil companies.[14]

Oil companies have long operated in Nigeria, extracting profits without sharing the benefits with the people while polluting the air and water. In July 2002, over 150 Nigerian women, some with children on their backs, brought oil exports to a standstill when they occupied ChevronTexaco's main oil export terminal for ten days. ChevronTexaco officials finally agreed to give jobs to at least twenty-five residents. They also agreed to provide electricity and water to villages in the region and to help build schools, clinics, town halls, and fish and chicken farms.[15] Company officials had no recourse but to negotiate with the women, who had threatened to use a powerful traditional shaming method by removing their clothes, which would have humiliated the oil company in the eyes of the community. This nonviolent "weapon" had more of an effect than any act of violence, for violence is a language the Powers understand and in which they excel, while creative acts of nonviolence confound them, reveal their impotence and immorality, and offer the potential of bringing about real change.

Argentina was a poster child for the IMF, having undergone many IMF structural adjustment programs. Then, in 2001, its economy crashed. Banks closed, its stock market plummeted, and corporations abandoned factories. The people marched through neighborhoods banging on pots and pans, calling out, "Que se vayan todos" ("They all must go"). Without a functioning government or economy, people organized themselves according to a new model called horizontalism. Workers formed cooperatives, took over hundreds of abandoned factories, and began production. A network of diverse movements now functions through direct democracy, including hundreds of neighborhood kitchens, arts and independent media collectives, indigenous communities, neighborhood assemblies, and unemployed workers movements. Five consecutive presidents took office and were forced to resign before the people elected Nestor Kirchner, who then unilaterally cancelled the country's IMF debt and "forced northern bondholders to accept only 25 cents of every dollar Argentina owed them."[16]

In 2004 Wangari Maathai won the Nobel Peace Prize for her work in creating the Greenbelt Movement, which she founded to avert desertification in her native Kenya. Thousands of members, mostly women, have planted over twenty-five million trees. The movement provides work for thousands of women who plant seedlings and offer them for sale. All group members are trained in land management, organic farming, and the values of indigenous food crops. Maathai, the first environmentalist and the first African woman to win the Nobel Peace Prize, had been called "a mad woman" and a "threat to the order and security of the country." She now serves in the Kenyan parliament. When she was notified of the award, she celebrated by removing her jewelry, kneeling, and planting seeds of a Kenyan tree known as the Nandi Flame in the soil in the foothills of Mount Kenya.[17]

Likewise, in 2006 the Nobel Peace Prize was awarded to Muhammad Unus, a Bangladeshi, and the Grameen Bank he created three decades ago to offer small loans to the poor, mostly women, to enable them to establish income-generating projects. The bank now has over six million borrowers and over two thousand branches. Its model of microcredit has been duplicated in over one hundred countries, including small communities in the United States.

In India, the Vavdanya ("nine seeds") movement facilitates the conservation and exchange of traditional seed varieties, and links small organic farmers with urban consumers. It has initiated a nationwide campaign of education related to WTO rules, loss of genetic diversity, and diminishing food security.[18] Sri Lanka's Sarvodaya Shramanda ("awakening through sharing") movement involves nearly four million people working in ten thousand villages in a people's democratic movement focused on meeting basic human needs such as food, water, clothing, shelter, energy, education, and health care.[19] Pusspaindo, a biodiversity organization in Indonesia, promotes farmers' independence by protecting local rice varieties, indigenous wisdom, and traditional food-production systems.[20] In Bangladesh, the Nayakrishi Andolon farmers' movement involves sixty-five thousand farmers in reviving traditional crops through saving, storing, and sharing seeds. Their movement rejects monoculture and plants local tree varieties to reestablish biodiversity and food security. Many communities in the United States and other developed countries are also experimenting with locally based initiatives that encourage support for small businesses, organic farms, environmental protection, and regional food self-sufficiency.[21]

In short, there are countless avenues through which people are organizing to resist corporate globalization and create communities and networks that are life–sustaining and offer hope for the future. Movements for change are active in every country and on every continent the world over:

From Kentucky to Kenya, from Bangladesh to Bolivia, and from Indonesia to Italy, the communities listed here are only representative of countless others that are directly challenging the "inevitability" of economic globalization by reclaiming their rights to land, healthy food, water, dignity, biodiversity, political autonomy, and a safe and sustainable environment, or simply the right to live in harmony with one another. Each has established meaningful and powerful alternatives that make clear that a better world is not only possible, it is here.[22]

New Foundations

> The powerlessness we experience is not a sign of personal failings, but reflects the incapacities of our institutions. We need to reconstruct those we have or create new ones.
>
> —Anthony Giddens[23]

In *Runaway World: How Globalization Is Reshaping Our Lives*, Anthony Giddens argues that people feel increasingly powerless because of our outdated institutions. He joins many others in calling for extensive reconstruction of old institutions or creation of new, open, accountable governing institutions based on democracy and human rights, institutions that will end poverty and inequity, protect the environment, structure a sane economy, and promote national and global security and peace.[24]

When describing the global economy I pointed out that "the system is designed for the results it is getting. If you want different results, you will have to redesign the system."[25] Redesigning the system is just what we are talking about here.

I have presented some suggested alternatives to our current institutions and systems earlier in this book. They include establishing alternative accounting methods, instituting a tax on short-term speculative financial transactions, forming democratic structures to facilitate debt cancellation, establishing systems that facilitate government control over corporations, creating democratically accountable trade, development, and finance institutions, building on existing international treaties, and developing a global networking process for creating new international agreements led by civil society.

The International Forum on Globalization (IFG) has done extensive work on the topic of alternatives to our present institutions and systems. Its comprehensive report, *Alternatives to Economic Globalization: A Better World Is Possible*, presents detailed, practical ways to structure our institutions so that they serve the needs of humanity and preserve the earth. The book includes principles upon which to organize and presents alternatives to institutions such as the IMF, World Bank, and WTO. It also suggests ways to administer vital goods and services for the common good instead of for private gain and provides examples of alternative policies, methods, structures, and operating systems that are already in use in communities around the world.[26] David Korten, who helped write the IFG report, explained some of its suggestions in a presentation to the National Council of Churches in Seattle in 2003:

> A chapter on international institutions calls for dismantling the World Bank, the IMF, and the WTO and replacing them with new institutions under the United Nations with mandates exactly the opposite of the institutions they will replace. In the place of a World Bank coaxing Southern countries into ever deeper international debt and dependency, we call for the creation of a UN International Insolvency Court responsible for helping countries work their way out of international debt. In the place of an IMF that prohibits countries from exercising essential oversight over the flow of goods and money across their borders, we call for a UN International Finance Organization to help countries put in place mechanisms to maintain balance and stability in their international financial relationships. Instead of a World Trade Organization preventing governments from holding corporations accountable to the public interest, we propose a UN Organization for Corporate Accountability to work with citizens groups and nation states to break up concentrations of corporate power and hold all corporations with operations in more than one country to a high standard of public accountability.[27]

The authors of *Alternatives to Economic Globalization* also point out that in addition to our major institutions, society's primary operating systems must also be changed, including our energy systems, manufacturing systems, agricultural and food systems, and the global media, for "they are all part of a single integrated megastructure that is the global economy, which extends into our nations and communities. It will not be possible to build more sustainable international structures without redesigning many of the world's key operating systems."[28] There are many alternatives to our current ways of organizing these systems, and much of the work to create sustainable operating systems is already being done, often on a relatively small scale, in various communities and regions. A large part of what remains to be done is to create the political will to shift society's resources away from subsidizing harmful systems and to begin financing the shift to a more just and sustainable world. If the hundreds of billions of dollars in government subsidies were shifted away from unsustainable and damaging institutions, processes, and systems, many of our problems would be on the way to being solved.

The work of recreating our governing institutions and operating systems to reflect the emerging paradigm of Earth Community is crucial to our time. As we do so, we share in the biblical promise of Isaiah 58: "Your ancient ruins shall be rebuilt; you shall raise up the foundations of many generations; you shall be called the repairer of the breach, the restorer of streets to live in."

GLOBALIZATION FROM BELOW

> In nature, change doesn't happen from a top-down, strategic approach. There is never a boss in a living system. Change happens from within, from many local actions occurring simultaneously.
>
> —Meg Wheatley[29]

The task ahead may seem daunting, and the people working for change too isolated and diverse. But let us look again, for what may seem weak and foolish in the eyes of the dominant culture may well be the wisdom and strength of the global movement for change.

In September 2003, WTO negotiations in Cancun collapsed when delegates of southern nations walked out of the talks, effectively stalling the efforts of the United States and other wealthy nations to extend the free-trade agenda on a global scale. The neoliberal agenda was further thwarted two months later when the majority of delegates from North, Central, and South American nations and the Caribbean who gathered in Miami failed to approve the U.S.-led plan to create a new Free Trade Area of the Americas (FTAA), which would have extended the provisions of NAFTA to all of Central and South America and the Caribbean, excluding Cuba.

That same year tens of millions of people had gathered in towns and cities around the world to demonstrate their opposition to U.S. plans for war against Iraq. Since that time, the legitimacy of U.S. global leadership has eroded even further, largely due to the ongoing war and the domination and mismanagement of Iraqi reconstruction by U.S. corporations. It is rare these days, even in the corporate media, to hear the gushing praise of corporate globalization that was ubiquitous in the late 1990s. What Thomas Friedman calls the "Americanization of the world" through political, economic, and military domination no longer looks so inevitable—or so hopeful.

Instead, as we have seen, in contrast to the dominant, hierarchical, top-down global system, people around the world are developing alternative systems of organizing that are small scale and locally based and that depend upon the networking of autonomous groups to form voluntary, cooperative, and interdependent webs of mutual support, modeled upon the natural systems of the earth. I have participated in this form of organizing for mass protests, where spokespersons from autonomous affinity groups gather to make decisions through a consensus process on basic tactics and principles agreed to by all participants. Decentralized, grassroots organizing from the ground up has also been effective for work on issues of global concern.

Around the world, concerned individuals are forming what David Korten calls "communities of congruence"[30] to work on specific issues. These small, local, human-scaled groups are joining together to form networks of support on issues of common concern. In turn, networks are reaching out in solidarity to form coalitions across regional and national boundaries. Some of these networks have become truly global, such as the church-led Jubilee Movement to cancel the debt of poor nations; the student-led movement to eliminate sweatshops and child labor; the Rainforest Action Network and other environmental groups that help indigenous groups and others resist the destruction of forests; union movements that reach out in solidarity beyond national boundaries; the Fifty Years Is Enough Campaign and the World Bank Bonds Boycott movements that focus on the IMF and World Bank; the global network that rose up to defeat the proposed Multilateral Agreement on Investments (MAI); and the global peace movement.

These and other networks coordinate with each other, sometimes in mass demonstrations, sometimes in joint statements, sometimes in international gatherings such as the annual World Social Forum, which is now attended by over 150,000 people. Together they form a global movement based on grassroots organizing and popular support. This global justice movement, decentralized, diverse, creative, and engaged in various struggles around the world, is truly a form of globalization from below. Together these networks are very powerful. As UN Secretary-General Kofi Annan said when speaking of the antiwar movement, global civil society has become the world's "other superpower."[31]

David Korten, in his book *The Great Turning*, says of this kind of organizing: "Although the leadership styles of Earth Community may seem chaotic and diffuse to those accustomed to the dominator styles of Empire, they fit the pattern by which all healthy living systems self-organize. This pattern of self-organizing distributed power gives contemporary social movements their distinctive vitality and makes them nearly impossible to suppress."[32]

Although global civil society is diffuse and self-organizing, according to Korten its many and varied actions and expressions reveal an implicit strategy in the work of bringing society into alignment with the new paradigm of Earth Community. This strategy includes four "essential imperatives" that take place sequentially, each step preparing the way for the next, but also simultaneously, as each contributes to the whole:

- Accelerate the awakening of cultural and spiritual consciousness.
- Resist Empire's assault on children, families, communities, and nature.
- Form and connect communities of congruence.
- Build a majoritarian political base.[33]

In this book's final chapter, we will explore how people within faith communities can contribute to each of these tasks. People of faith have a distinct part to play in the movement for global justice, for what is at stake is the future of life on earth and the soul of humanity. We must join with others in this common struggle, but to do so we must be standing on a firm foundation. As James Douglass said, "The people are . . . being drowned by a system which submerges humanity beneath enormous power apparently controlled by a few but perhaps by no one. For the sake of everyone's humanity, a response is necessary. But to . . . resist the power of that system without a rock to stand on is simply to jump in the water and drown with the people."[34]

For Christians, that rock is Jesus Christ. Faith-led resistance as a way of life is a life of discipleship. Our challenge is to listen to the Spirit of God for direction in order to discern where, specifically, the Spirit calls, and to act in faith, trusting in the living presence and activity of God in the world. This will be the focus of the next chapter.

CHAPTER SEVENTEEN
Faith-Led Resistance as a Way of Life

> In my view the liberating practice of resistance is itself the
> moment of spiritual fulfillment. For it is only in the act of
> resistance, when we embrace that which is most disturbing
> not by accepting but by seeking to overcome it, that we can
> know ourselves as fully one with all of reality.
> —Roger S. Gottlieb[1]

In this book, we have considered the great global challenges of our day. We have peered into the future and seen that we are careening toward a living hell on earth, accompanied by death and destruction all around. We have considered the Powers that be, those systems, institutions, and individuals in authority ("rulers") that dominate and benefit from the global system. We have seen that these Powers function only with the consent of the people and that actions of organized non-violent resistance can "shake the gates of hell," changing the course of events in powerful ways. We have also explored a few of the many alternatives, both local and global, to the system of corporate globalization, and have seen that the current political, economic, and military order is not inevitable, that there are many alternatives.

As people of faith, we have glimpsed our hope: that the Spirit of love who brought all creation into being continues to act in ways that bring light out of darkness and life out of death. The way to keep this hope alive is to embody it ourselves in life-sustaining actions that stop and reverse the institutional momentum toward death. In short, hope requires resistance, resistance grounded in faith.

This chapter will focus on faith-led resistance as a way of life. Many books give concrete suggestions of actions that people can take to help bring peace, justice, and environmental healing. I will not duplicate such efforts here. Instead I will focus on unique ways that those who seek to follow Jesus Christ can contribute to what Thomas Berry calls the "Great Work" of our time.[2]

The church is entrusted with the task of sharing the stories of Jesus, proclaiming the message of the gospel, and embodying the Christian "Way" for each new generation. Dominant forms of Christianity have often been culturally bound and, by not living in resistance, have supported the powers and principalities of their times. But throughout history there have also been many examples of faithful followers of Jesus who have walked the same path as he did in relation to God and the Powers. It is this kind of radical faithfulness that we are called to in this and every age.

This is the direction to which I aspire. I believe it is the narrow way to which Jesus calls us. I myself see only the bare beginnings of the path, and I am grateful to others who have walked the path before me and who point it out to me.

From this vantage point we can consider what it would mean to step out into a life of discipleship, resistance, and ongoing transformation. We can count the cost. For grace is free, but it is not cheap. In the words of Dietrich Bonhoeffer: "Such grace is costly because it calls us to follow, and it is grace because it calls us to follow Jesus Christ. It is costly because it costs a man his life, and it is grace because it gives a man the only true life. It is costly because it condemns sin, and grace because it justifies the sinner. . . . Costly grace is the Incarnation of God."[3]

By following Christ, we become more truly who God intends us to be. By refusing to be held hostage to the cultural gods of our age we find our freedom and regain our humanity. The point is that we refuse to be held hostage to the Powers—not by our fears, our possessions, our jobs, or even our families. In the words of the great hymn by Martin Luther:

> Let goods and kindred go,
> this mortal life also;
> the body they may kill,
> God's truth abideth still;
> His kingdom is forever.[4]

What does it mean to follow Jesus in the midst of the global crises facing the world today? Where is the Holy Spirit leading us? How can we, as followers of Christ, contribute to the great work of personal, social, and global transformation in our day?

In addressing these questions, I return to the four strategies identified by David Korten that can move us along the path toward a more hopeful future, but for my own purposes I will change the order as follows: (1) Accelerate the awakening of cultural and spiritual consciousness; (2) form and connect communities of congruence; (3) build a majoritarian political base; (4) resist empire's assault on children, families, communities, and nature. We will now look at a few ways in which people of faith can contribute in each of these arenas to the work that is already being done by so many people throughout the world. I focus in this chapter primarily on churches in the United States, because that is my context and because my hope is for their widespread conversion to a consciousness that is grounded in the emerging paradigm of Earth Community.

ACCELERATE THE AWAKENING OF CULTURAL AND SPIRITUAL CONSCIOUSNESS

> The precondition for an ecological reform of modern industrial society is a spiritual and cultural conversion, which has its roots in a new religious experience of the reality of God and nature. The church must become the temple for the whole creation.
>
> —Jürgen Moltmann[5]

I spoke earlier about the need to ground our "no" of resistance in the "yes" of faith. It is essential that we recognize the true context and foundation of our lives in the midst of God's good creation, and that we develop an ongoing sense of the sacred in everyday life. We return now to where this book began—to the earth, our home and our primary source of revelation. As we practice active democracy that furthers globalization from below, we must not forget who we are: children of Spirit, but also children of the earth, dependent on God for life and breath and all things and interdependent with the whole community of life. Thomas Berry reminds us of the extraordinary gifts offered to us through the creation, and of our responsibility to care for the earth, our home:

> The natural world tells us: I will feed you, I will clothe you, I will shelter you, I will heal you. Only do not so devour me or use me that you destroy my capacity to mediate the divine and the human. For I offer you a communion with the divine. I offer you gifts that you can exchange with each other. I offer you flowers whereby you may express your reverence for the divine and your love for each other. In the vastness of the sea, in the snow-covered mountains, in the rivers flowing through the valleys, in the serenity of the landscape, and in the foreboding of the great storms that sweep over the land, in all these experiences I offer you inspiration for your music, for your art, your dance.[6]

In addition to being grounded in the earth, we must also become aware of how we relate to the dominant institutions of which we are a part. We see how ruling institutions foster a sense of powerlessness, distort the truth, dampen the Spirit, nullify conscience, and impair moral agency. These inner effects of the Powers prevent people from rising up in clear and concerted resistance to these harmful systems and demanding change.

Recognizing the reality of social sin and institutional evil does not relieve conscience or excuse us from personal responsibility, but it does add another dimension to our understanding of the human condition. Just as we are dependent on God for life and breath and all things and interdependent with the rest of creation, we are also embedded in institutions and systems that affect us and that we affect through our passive acceptance, active participation, or actions of resistance and transformation. We are called to resist being taken over by the forces of a culture that would have us believe that comfort, pleasure, ease, and looking good are the most important things in life. We are called to refuse to worship our culture's dominant gods of money and domination, to resist the lure of materialistic values that keep so many enthralled, and instead to value human life and the natural world. By so doing, we plant seeds of hope and honor the Creator.

Prayer is crucial in this process. Prayer is an act of humility, a way to acknowledge our utter dependence on God and our gratitude for the new life we have received in Christ. In prayer, we open ourselves to the clarity, guidance, and empowerment that only the Holy Spirit can bring. Prayers of intercession and petition have immeasurable effects on our lives and on lives around us. Prayer "with the Bible in one hand and the newspaper in the other,"[7] as Karl Barth recommended, helps us develop the ability to discern God's activity in current events. Contemplative prayer and meditation can help us stay grounded in the present moment and give us a sense of freedom from time. Prayer can also enable us to discern the inner effects of the Powers. Regular ongoing prayer can help us resist collective thinking and to understand our own inner dynamics, so that we can know which of our impulses are anger- or fear-based, and which are Spirit-led, guiding us in the direction of God's call and empowering us to move toward creative transformation. As Karl Barth said, "To clasp the hands in prayer is the beginning of an uprising against the disorder of the world."[8]

If we neglect to nurture our relationship with God through prayer, we lose ourselves in outward activity and we forfeit what peace, freedom, and clarity we have attained. The inner journey and the outer journey together constitute the spiritual life. Prayer is essential. So is action. In *Resistance and Contemplation: The Way of Liberation*, James Douglass writes of the inner and outer journeys as two sides of a mountain, as two parts of a whole way of life:

Contemplation is an encounter on the dark side of the mountain, in the soul. Contemplation, the struggle to experience reality as it is, in the life-giving water of the One, is the acceptance of the upward wind of the Spirit and the disciplined loss of my self-control. I struggle for the power of the powerless, where I would lose my self, where only the Spirit moves. . . .

Resistance, on the bright slope, is the struggle to stand against a murderous collective self and to express communally the living unity of all . . . in the One. Resistance is active opposition to the death forces discernible in every modern state. The confrontation of resistance therefore takes place on the bright side of the mountain, in the sunlight of public or collective consciousness, where people struggle with the powers of war, racism, exploitation.[9]

Contemplative prayer and other spiritual practices can equip us for resistance against social, political, and economic "death forces" in the outer world. Such practices repudiate the values of domination, violence, and greed. They also constitute resistance in their own right. Douglass sees contemplation itself as a form of resistance: "The Spirit is received through a painful resistance to, and renunciation of, the claims of the self on the climb into greater darkness. Contemplation receives by resisting. At its center contemplation is receptivity to the wind of the Spirit, but it is conditioned by my active resistance to the fears and claims of the self: claims of comfort, security, self-control."[10]

Walter Wink, too, speaks of the spiritual journey in terms of resistance. He points to the myth or archetype of "The Human Being" as exemplified by Jesus, which "defines as human, not prowess in battle or beauty of body or achievement of high office, but that which is left when the desire for these has been crucified"[11] and which "offers us the secret of our individuality."[12] Yet in spite of the promise of a deeper relationship with God and a more fulfilled humanity, we often find ourselves seduced by the lesser gods of comfort, familiarity, cultural accommodation, and ease, which we must resist: "The Human Being cracks open the shell of something new. But human beings are terrified by the sound of that scratching deep inside. The sound reminds them of their deprived humanity, which they know instinctively cannot be recovered without painful inner resistance and a massive reaction from the Powers . . ."[13]

As we move into new ways of being, in faithfulness to God and in resistance to both the inner and outer effects of the Powers, we find that the struggle becomes at once more costly, more satisfying, and more real. For in the words of Wink, "to take on those who have power over our lives inevitably will require that one 'suffer and be treated with contempt' and be 'rejected by this generation.'"[14] At the same time, resistance motivated by the Spirit enables us to face the very great suffering of our time, to repent for our part in it, to move toward transformation, and to find hope.

Faith-led resistance both begins and ends in prayer. In Richard Foster's book *Prayer: Finding the Heart's True Home,* he writes: "The true prophetic message always calls us to a spiritual defiance of the world as it now is. Our prayer, to the extent that it is fully authentic, undermines the status quo. It is a spiritual underground resistance movement. We are subversives in a world of injustice, oppression, and violence."[15]

Another form of "spiritual defiance of the world as it now is" is the practice of simplicity. Foster speaks of the necessity of cultivating this traditional spiritual discipline in another book, *Freedom of Simplicity.*[16] Living simply is a basic form of spiritual resistance to commercial pressures to over-consume.

It is not easy to make careful and conscientious choices in the areas of food, clothing, recreation, housing, child rearing, and transportation. Everyone's life circumstances are different, and lifestyle decisions are deeply personal. Each person must decide how to live and what actions to take. Those of us who are immersed in the dominant culture may experience extreme pressures, both inner and outer, as we seek to extricate ourselves from cultural domination by the institutional Powers and to practice new ways of living into the future that we want to see. But there will also be rewards. Through the practice of simplicity we exercise our moral agency and develop our integrity, both of which are necessary if we are to rise to the challenge of taking action in the larger world. As Hendrik Berkhof put it in his classic work, *Christ and the Powers,* "We can only preach the manifold wisdom of God to Mammon if our life displays that we are joyfully freed from its clutches."[17]

FORM AND CONNECT COMMUNITIES OF CONGRUENCE

There is a radicalism to the alternative community of Jesus, and only if it incarnates that radicalism can it be "the city set on a hill whose light cannot be hid." It can do this only by being a community grounded in the Spirit.

—Marcus Borg[18]

In August 2006, Elvira Arellano, an undocumented immigrant living in Chicago, was ordered to report for deportation. Instead she went to Adalberto United Methodist Church, where she was a member.[19] The church took her in and declared itself to be a sanctuary for Ms. Arellano and her seven-year-old son, Saul. Each day a church member escorts Saul to school. Ms. Arellano does not leave the premises. Within the first twenty days of declaring itself a sanctuary, the church had over seven thousand visitors. Some groups came to Chicago to protest the church's stand, including the anti–immigrant Minuteman Project, which tried to disrupt a Sunday worship service but were kept outside by church members.[20] Chicago Area Bishop Hee-Soo Jung stated: "While as Christians, we may disagree over the best way to fix the nation's broken immigration system, we affirm that the Bible directs us to care for the foreigners in our midst (Exodus 23:9) and reminds us that we too are sojourners (Lev. 25:23)."[21]

Adalberto United Methodist Church did not just take this action out of the blue. It was already a community committed to justice for immigrants and the poor. It was a relatively new congregation, founded less than a decade ago in the predominately Puerto Rican Humboldt Park neighborhood by residents who were frustrated because nearby churches showed little support for the daily struggles of immigrants. They named the congregation after a young gang member who had turned his life around. Elvira Arellano had been an active member of the church and was an outspoken advocate of the rights of immigrants. In early 2006 she had gone on a twenty-one-day hunger strike to support demands for a moratorium on immigration raids and deportations. It may be that immigration authorities took action against her because of her activism. By providing support and sanctuary, Adalberto United Methodist Church not only provided support for Ms. Arellano and Saul but witnessed to the love of God and the Spirit of Jesus Christ at work in acts of solidarity, justice, and compassion.

Resistance based in Spirit requires a support system and network of solidarity. Local churches or small groups within churches can form "communities of congruence" that are grounded in the Spirit as an alternative to the dominant culture. Marcus Borg says: "Taking the vision of Jesus seriously calls the church to be an alternative culture in our time. . . . The dominant values of contemporary American life—affluence, achievement, appearance, power, competition, consumption, individualism—are vastly different from anything recognizably Christian. . . . Our existence has become massively idolatrous."[22]

Small groups within churches can provide spiritual support for lifestyle change and for taking action in the larger world, while Bible studies, book studies, workshops, and educational forums can raise peoples' consciousness about relevant issues. Faith communities can sponsor creative, celebratory events that nourish the spirit, demonstrate alternatives to consumer culture, and bring hope and joy. Such experiences are spiritually renewing and enable us to stay in the struggle for the long haul. Worship services and rituals can be held outside in places of natural beauty or can incorporate story, symbol, and art to cultivate reverence for God's creation.

Local churches can institute programs that enable them to be a witness and model of institutional conversion by eliminating toxic chemicals, creating a community garden, landscaping with native plants, or becoming more energy efficient. At the same time, churches can provide space for support groups, present educational forums, host community meetings, provide tutoring or job training, and offer food for the hungry and shelter for the homeless. Congregations can serve fair-trade coffee, provide sanctuary for immigrants, support conscientious objectors to war, host interracial or interreligious gatherings, offer interfaith services for peace, or organize meetings for local campaigns.

Congregational members can work within their denomination to raise issues of concern. Some faith communities have exerted economic pressure through boycotts, shareholder actions, and divestment campaigns. For example, the World Council of Churches has called on its member denominations to divest their pension funds and other investments from companies that profit from the Israeli occupation of Palestine. Many have responded.

Churches in the United States and around the world are taking actions that support the human community and the larger community of life. In these ways, as Borg notes, we "live the alternative values generated by life in the Spirit and become a witness to compassion by incarnating the ethos of compassion" and become "an alternative culture where the Spirit is known."[23]

Work for change within the local church is rarely easy. It requires a willingness to go against the flow, for the church, too, is an institutional Power that tends to take on a life of its own. Even churches have grown up and found their niche in the dominant (and dominating) paradigm. As Borg says, "We live in a modern Babylon, one largely unrecognized as such and all the more seductive because of its mostly benign and benevolent face. Indeed, to a large extent, Babylon also lives within the church, so thoroughly has it (through us) been infected with the 'spirit of this age.'"[24]

Sadly, even within our churches, those who seek to bring about needed change must be prepared to be "rejected and treated with contempt," as Jesus was. But such work is absolutely essential, for the church that carries the name of Jesus Christ must be reminded again and again, whenever it forgets, of his message and his way. The church has an important role to play. According to Larry Rasmussen: "Whether Israel or the Church, the vocation is the same: To witness to God's hope for all by living as communities of visibly redeemed creation. The believing community is to display in its own life the justice-doing and peacemaking of God. It is to be an anticipatory community of creation-made-new, a taste or aperitif of the reign of God. Differently said, it is to be a restored society."[25]

In forming communities of congruence, our circles of concern extend far beyond the walls of our faith communities, and so do our opportunities for connection and action. We must join hands with all people who are working to create a more just, humane, and ecologically sustainable world.

One of the primary problems of our current global system is that the size, scope, and complexity of our dominant institutions make them almost impossible for humans to control. As we have seen, people feel so powerless that they shrink back from public involvement, and democracy suffers. One of the solutions to this dilemma is to develop sustainable communities that function with smaller-scale, locally based institutions where people have power to influence regional decision making through participatory democracy. In the words of Jürgen Moltmann: "If people in our society are going to be able to live in a more humane way again, we shall have to build up communities from below, and recognize that human beings can develop their personhood only in relationships and groups. The alternative to poverty is not property. The alternative to poverty and property is community. The principle of life is 'mutual help.'"[26]

We can "build up communities from below" by supporting local businesses, organic farmers, and organizations that are working to create a just and sustainable community. As we find ways to become less enmeshed in the global economy and to focus on local means of sustenance, we begin to ground ourselves in the real economy, the economy of the earth.

There are countless creative ways that people can organize locally and regionally around issues as diverse as land use, habitat restoration, energy self-sufficiency, public transportation, community credit unions, low-income housing, protection of public water services, or alternative currencies. Anyone can begin to help transform their own community in a number of ways. By joining with interfaith and secular organizations that are working toward these ends, we participate in building coalitions that can express the "power of the people" in effective ways.

BUILD A MAJORITARIAN POLITICAL BASE

The "politics of compassion" did not lead Jesus to withdraw
from culture, but to a passionate mission to transform the culture of his day.

—Marcus Borg[27]

In the mid-1990s I was among a group of clergy and other religious leaders who were invited by California State Senator Tom
Hayden to give a press conference on behalf of the Endangered
Species Act, which was under attack by "property rights" (that is, corporate rights) activists, and in danger of being weakened or dismantled. When we began speaking, a hush fell on the room, as each of us
spoke in turn from our own faith tradition about the intrinsic value of
every part of God's creation. News coverage was extensive, and follow-
up articles reported on "green religion." The large religious coalition
that supported a strong Endangered Species Act was widely credited
with helping to maintain the Act. When people speak an authentic
word of hope for the future, we can trust that people will listen.

In this age of globalization, no matter how involved we are in
alternative local structures, we cannot avoid the larger issues of our
world. The global political/economic/military juggernaut can destroy
local movements, ignore them, or simply reframe and seek to contain
such movements as a niche within the dominant paradigm. For this
reason, it is imperative that we educate ourselves on global issues and
speak out on public policy. Although campaigns can focus on any
aspect of public policy there is an overarching issue that ties all these
issues together: the domination of life by a powerful network of undemocratic institutions that restricts human freedom and prevents governments from acting on behalf of the common good. While the challenge posed by this reality seems far greater than with any single issue,
it also has the potential to unite us all in a single purpose: to resist spiritual, cultural, economic, political, and military domination by the
institutional Powers and to demonstrate an alternative reality based on
nonviolence, justice, compassion, and the beauty of creation, which
includes human love.

People of faith have a profound opportunity and responsibility to
lend aid to this struggle, for it is the primary spiritual issue of our day.
As such, we must be willing to step out beyond our comfort zones and
to pray for the willingness to take actions beyond those condoned by the
Powers. Because democracy has been so undermined, creativity will be
required in challenging the corporate domination of global institutions,
national governments, media, and culture. Voting every two years and

contacting government representatives, as essential as these actions are, will not suffice to bring about the great transformation that is needed. A major effort will be required to create the political will to shift society's vast resources away from deadly and outdated institutions and toward institutions that nurture the human and earth community. This transfer of resources is unlikely until such new institutions, communities, and ways of being are shown to be viable.

But as we have seen, they are viable! Part of the problem is that alternatives are largely unseen by the majority of people, since most television channels, radio stations, and newspapers are controlled by the very corporations that have risen to such dominance. Today all the major media are owned and controlled by a handful of transnational corporations, which transmit their messages around the world, subsuming local media, creating artificial desires, shaping public opinion, and drowning out independent voices and alternative views. This situation gives new meaning to the biblical reference to the demonic "ruler of the power of the air" (Eph. 2:2), perhaps better put in modern terms as "ruler of the power of the airwaves." It is an act of faith-led resistance simply to speak truth in contrast to the babel that pervades the media portrayal of contemporary culture.

For this reason, it is important to write letters to the editor, speak on the radio or community television, support or create independent media, or take actions that the mainline media cannot ignore. We must create our own news! Large-scale, visible protest and nonviolent direct action will be necessary in order to highlight the global crisis and the extremity of our situation. Only then will creative alternatives become newsworthy, and only then will the public support a major shift in resources away from empire and toward more equitable, just, and sustainable policies that are based in the emerging paradigm of Earth Community.

In 2004, the West Michigan Annual Conference of the United Methodist Church passed a resolution to continue supporting a citizen boycott of fourteen brands of bottled waters sold by the Nestlé Corporation, including Perrier. The resolution instructed the Conference Board of Church and Society to notify Michigan's governor to pursue legislation that would make it illegal for fresh water to be bottled or sold for profit in the state without establishing a public process for determining its social, environmental, economic, and social consequences.

A small number of area residents, including several United Methodists, hired a lawyer and filed suit against Nestlé Waters, which was represented by nine lawyers. Nevertheless, in November 2003 Judge Lawrence Rood ordered Nestlé to stop extracting the spring water. The judge ruled that Nestlé's overpumping had caused the surface levels of water to drop two inches, leading to a loss of 75 percent of open water in area wetlands and a six-inch drop in local lake levels. The state has allowed the pumping to continue in order to "save jobs" and develop a comprehensive water policy. The struggle continues.[28]

In addition to working locally and regionally, people can align themselves with progressive ecumenical or interfaith groups. By becoming a part of the Network of Spiritual Progressives,[29] the Covenant for a New America,[30] the National Religious Campaign to End Torture,[31] Earth Justice Ministries, or other faith-based advocacy groups, our individual voices are amplified and more likely to be heard by society as a whole.

Both the National Council of Churches and the World Council of Churches provide resources in support of peace, justice, and caring for creation and have comprehensive statements related to economic globalization that witness to the Powers that be. The World Council of Churches is among the groups represented at the World Social Forum, which began in Porto Alegre, Brazil. The theme that the WCC used as its focal point at the 2003 Forum was "Another World is Possible: A Spirituality of Resistance." Rogate Mshana, director of the WCC's economic justice program, explained: "We are witnessing the development of a spirituality that supports the powers responsible for the current unjust and unsustainable process of corporate globalization. For that reason, we need to recover the long tradition of a Christian spirituality that is critical of power. It is a spirituality which has given those without power the strength and courage to oppose those who abuse it."[32]

Some may not feel called to be involved directly in political action. But as Marcus Borg points out, "Taking the politics of compassion seriously would make a difference in the kind of 'politics' Christians would support."[33] So, as Richard Foster says: "In holy boldness we cover the earth with the grace and the mercy of God. . . . We throw caution to the wind and pray not just for individuals but also for nations, not just for the renewal of the Church but also for the transformation of the world. We pray for and work of the kingdom to come on earth—on all the earth—as it is in heaven."[34]

RESIST EMPIRE'S ASSAULT ON CHILDREN, FAMILIES, COMMUNITIES, AND NATURE

Will we stand up to imperial power, or bend down to, submit to, or tolerate, its victimizing ways? The cross of the one executed by empire is our crossroads.

—Mark Lewis Taylor[35]

The U.S. war against Iraq has become a primary focus of resistance to empire. In 2004, fourteen-year-old Ava Lowery started her Web site, peacetakescourage.com, because she "couldn't, and wouldn't, reconcile the U.S. war in Iraq with the Christian faith she learned from her parents." On one part of her Web site a child sings "Jesus Loves Me" as slides show photographs of wounded Iraqi children. The Peace Takes Courage campaign has brought national attention to Lowery. She has been interviewed on CNN and mentioned in the *New York Times* and *Rolling Stone*. She has also been threatened with violence and death. "Peace Takes Courage has evolved into a multimedia campaign to tell the truth about the harsh realities of the U.S. war in Iraq, and its contradiction with the teachings of Jesus Christ."[36]

On June 11, 2006, the administrative council of the First United Methodist Church in Tacoma, Washington, voted unanimously to declare the church a sanctuary for members of the armed forces who are questioning the morality of their participation in military activities. The church is producing leaflets to pass out to people who serve on nearby military bases, inviting them to call the church to speak to a counselor if they are struggling with questions of conscience. The outreach is particularly geared toward service personnel who question the legitimacy of orders to fight in Iraq.[37]

On January 11, 2007, several Christian Peacemaker Teams (CPT) trainees entered the U.S. Federal Courthouse in downtown Chicago dressed in orange jumpsuits and black hoods. They knelt in silence, supported by others who held a banner saying, "Charge them or release them." They were there to protest the indefinite detention and inhumane treatment of detainees in Guantanamo Bay, Cuba. Many of the 435 Guantanamo detainees had been there for five years without charges or access to legal counsel. The United Nations and international human rights organizations have called for the closure of Guantanamo due to the grave human rights abuses that have taken place there.[38]

CPT is a nonmissionary organization that sends teams into areas of war and conflict to serve as witnesses and to diffuse violence. Teams in Iraq have documented the abuse of Iraqi detainees and have worked with the families of prisoners. Long before the media revealed the abuse taking place at Abu Ghraib, CPT publicly denounced the torture of Iraqi prisoners at the hands of U.S. forces.[39] In November 2005, four CPT members were kidnapped in Iraq and held hostage. Their captors killed the only American, Tom Fox, and released the others after four months.[40] On the CPT Web site the question is asked, "What would happen if Christians devoted the same discipline and self-sacrifice to nonviolent peacemaking that armies devote to war?"[41]

In supporting Elvira Arellano and her son Saul the Adalberto United Methodist Church is resisting "the assault of Empire on children, families, and communities." In its acts of nonviolent direct action, witness, and solidarity, Christian Peacemaker Teams resist the domination of empire through state-sanctioned torture and war. In their action to protect fresh water through their denomination, through boycott, through the court system, and through political action, United Methodists in the West Michigan Conference are resisting "the assault of Empires on communities and nature" and on behalf of future generations and the community of life. In countless ways, Christians and other people of faith and conscience are involved in actions of resistance that demonstrate hope in the midst of the darkness of our time. In so doing, they witness to the power of God at work in the world.

NONVIOLENT DIRECT ACTION

> **For the church to have said that following Jesus meant nonviolence would have made the church into a counter culture. Only occasionally has it been willing to be so since the time of Jesus and his earliest followers.**
>
> **—Marcus Borg[42]**

On Good Friday in 1982 I was arrested for the first time. The morning began with a worship service, where I sang and prayed with others at the foot of a rustic cross, looking out over colorful desert hills of the Nevada Test Site. After the service, I walked toward the fence with others who were willing to risk arrest. I reached out, separated the strands of barbed wire, and stepped through. As I strode out over the rough terrain in the direction of the test site I felt a sense of freedom that I had not felt before. I had faced my fear and had stepped out beyond the legal "fence" that had defined and confined me as a legitimate subject of the Powers up until that time.

When a security officer finally arrested me, I felt the presence of Jesus Christ. I felt solidarity with him, remembering that he was arrested, tortured, and killed for living in resistance to the Powers of his day, and I felt his solidarity with me. I could feel his strength, his "power made perfect in weakness" in me. As I quietly explained to the arresting officer why I took this action, I felt compassion for him, Christ's compassion in me.

Nonviolent direct action is an effective and viable form of active democracy. Many may prefer to take a less confrontational role, hoping that social change will come about gradually through education, negotiation, and advocacy. I have become convinced that there is nothing like nonviolent direct action to boost these very necessary activities to a whole new level of effectiveness. Disciplined, creative actions of nonviolent resistance have the potential to reveal the bankruptcy of the current system that dominates the earth, to awaken conscience, kindle hope, and demonstrate freedom and creativity.

Civil-rights-movement leaders recognized that calls for incremental change often merely stalled real progress and reinforced the status quo. As Martin Luther King, Jr., said: "You may well ask, 'why direct action? Why sit-ins, marches, etc.? Isn't negotiation a better path?' You are exactly right in your call for negotiation. Indeed, this is the purpose of direct action. Nonviolent direct action seeks to create such a crisis and establish such creative tension that a community that has constantly refused to negotiate is forced to confront the issue. It seeks so to dramatize the issue that it can no longer be ignored."[43]

Social change takes place not just gradually but in shifts that sometimes shake the foundations of society. As we address the urgent social and ecological issues of our day, major shifts are necessary, and these shifts must happen now.

A movement based on nonviolent resistance does not need to convince the majority of people to participate in mass protests or direct action in order to be successful. It simply needs the majority of people to be sympathetic. That is one reason why it is important for such actions to have the moral legitimacy of nonviolence. When support for oppressive Powers is withdrawn, their spell is broken. They may continue to use force, but they cannot maintain their rule without both inner and outer authority. Ken Butigan issues a call: "As Christians, our faith calls us now more than ever to join with one another to take powerful nonviolent resistance action to end war, to fashion economic and racial justice, to protect the earth and to champion the well-being and inclusion of all."[44]

Our spiritual work must include preparation and prayer that we will be ready and willing to do whatever it takes to bring about positive change at this time of global crisis. We can pray for the willingness to go wherever the Spirit might lead and to take whatever action is necessary, even if it requires personal sacrifice. We need not even fear death, for the one we follow shows us that some things are worth dying for and that even death is not the end.

THE WORD BEFORE THE POWERS

Prior to analyzing particular choices and actions, preaching first and foremost should seek to help people see the

world through the Christian story. Such new vision is a
critical step that helps build up the church as a community
of resistance. . . . Nothing is more revolutionary than a
transformation of the fundamental metaphors through
which we apprehend the world.

—Charles Campbell[45]

We have considered theological and spiritual foundations for
faith-led resistance, and we have explored some of the many arenas for
action and change. We return now to the challenge of changing spiritual and cultural attitudes, for there is still one point that needs to be
made—the importance of the church of Jesus Christ speaking a word
of truth, justice, and hope for our world today.

According to William Stringfellow, the "verbal" element is of
primary importance in the "stratagems" that the Powers employ to
enlist human beings in their service, because it is the human conscience and will that is being contested and because it is with words
that the struggle between truth and falsehood takes place. The verbal
tactics include distortion, doublespeak, denial, secrecy, exaggeration,
cursing, diversion, and harassment.[46] Sadly, the institutional church
has often employed these same stratagems and has enjoyed the fruits
of its message being distorted and barely distinguishable from that of
the other ruling Powers. In fact, many of our institutional churches
provide a moral front for empire and engender powerlessness in the
face of the grave challenges of our time by preaching a gospel of material abundance, cultural conformity, and fear. In Stringfellow's words,
some churches function as "American cultural productions or
Babylonian shrines."[47]

In *The Word before the Powers: An Ethic of Preaching*, Charles
Campbell stresses how important preaching is in the church's resistance to the dominant Powers. He goes so far as to say: "Preaching is
consciously the way of nonviolent resistance to the principalities and
powers; it is the way to set people free from their captivity to the powers of sin and death in the world."[48] Preachers and teachers of
Scripture have an important task, at times an unpopular and uncom-
fortable one, of challenging the myths and metaphors that form contemporary attitudes and values and upon which we build our lives. In
this area, the church, which is bearer of the story of Jesus, has a primary responsibility.

For this reason, both clergy and laity who seek to respond faithful-
ly to the call to preach and teach the biblical message have a challenge
and an opportunity. In Campbell's words: "The powers so shape the
world that their ways of death often seem like common sense. Exposing

them requires preachers to cut through ignorance, denial, and numbness and speak the truth in creative and powerful ways. Preachers take the place of the child in the 'Emperor's New Clothes,' who shouts, 'He's naked!' demystifying the crowds and setting them free."[49]

Finally, a word must be said about what constitutes the church's primary message, sometimes referred to as the Word of God. This Word is not identical with the Bible, though biblical literalists would have us think so. Even those who insist that the Bible must be taken literally still have to interpret its meaning and are usually all too happy to do so.

When I am in the pulpit I preface my Scripture reading and preaching with the words "Listen for the Word of God" rather than "Listen to the Word of God." For it is the Holy Spirit that brings the written or spoken word alive and allows it to become for us the Word of God in the midst of our present circumstances.

According to John 1:14, Jesus Christ is the Word of God, the Word made flesh, God's message to humanity incarnate in a human being. It is through Jesus that we come to know what God is like and what human life and community can be when lived in the light and presence of God. Therefore, when we preach or teach the Word of God we point beyond ourselves to the message of salvation and hope we have found in Jesus Christ, *as we understand it.* But this message is not static. No matter what authority we use to back us up, even the Bible, no one can speak objectively for God. We human beings speak for ourselves, from our own location in time and space.

But speaking for ourselves is no small thing. Indeed, the ability to discern spiritual things, interpret Scripture, speak the truth, and risk being wrong is part of mature spirituality. The fact that we are fallible does not mean that our message is simply subjective and relative, and therefore irrelevant, for the Holy Spirit is a reality that can be discerned by spiritual people (1 Cor. 2:6-16). Discernment is a primary gift of the Spirit and can be nurtured, practiced, and developed through prayer and faithful action. We are called to speak what the Spirit says and to follow where the Spirit leads as best we can.

Still, by the grace of God, "here and there and now and then" the church of Jesus Christ rises to its calling, and the Holy Spirit works in, among, and through us in our words and in our actions. The mystery of the Incarnation becomes a reality, and Christ comes alive in us. Through faithful preachers who "fear nothing but sin and desire nothing but God," God's Word comes alive, shedding light in a new way for our time. This Word has power to shake the gates of hell and inspire the creation of alternative communities of compassion, faithfulness, and hope for the kin-dom of God. This is the church against which the gates of hell shall not prevail (Matt. 16:18).

We are called to step out in faith, fully aware of our sin and short-comings, but with utter confidence in the power and wisdom of God as revealed in Jesus Christ. We are called to preach a Word that has power to open hearts and awaken conscience, a message of truth and hope that contrasts with the dominant "verbiage" of the Powers that be. As Stringfellow said,

> In the middle of chaos, celebrate the Word. Amidst Babel, speak the truth. Confront the noise and verbiage and false-hood of death with the truth and potency and efficacy of the Word of God. Know the Word, teach the Word, nurture the Word, preach the Word, defend the word, incarnate the Word, do the Word, live the Word. And more than that, in the Word of God expose death and all death's works and wiles, rebuke lies, cast out demons, exorcise, cleanse the possessed, raise those who are dead in mind and conscience.[50]

There is a way for each person, regardless of philosophy or religion or worldview, to resist domination by the ruling Powers. We all have different gifts to bring to the struggle to create a better world. In addition to our own unique gifts, followers of Christ have a particular contribution to bring: the story and way of Jesus. In the words of Walter Wink:

> All Christianity has to give, and all it needs to give, is the myth of the human Jesus. It is the story of Jesus the Jew, a human being, the incarnate son of the man: imperfect but still exemplary, a victim of the Powers yet still victorious, crushed only to rise again, in solidarity with all who are ground to dust under the jackboots of the mighty, healer of those under the power of death, lover of all who are rejected and marginalized, forgiver, liberator, exposer of the regnant cancer called "civilization"—that Jesus, the one the Powers killed and whom death could not vanquish. Jesus' is the simple story of a person who gambled his last drop of devotion on the reality of God and the coming of God's new world..[51]

CONCLUSION
By the Power
at Work within Us

Just look, the gates of hell they're falling, Crumbling from the inside out. He's bursting through the walls with laughter (Hah!) Listen to the angels shout. (Listen, Oh, listen)
—"The Victor" a song by Jamie Owens Collins[1]

PROTESTING THE WTO: FROM SEATTLE TO CANCUN

In September 2003, four years after the Seattle protests that made visible the effectiveness of grassroots opposition to the WTO, I was in Cancun with a delegation from Santa Cruz to witness and protest the WTO meetings taking place there. Ruth Hunter, who had been with me in Seattle, was also there. She was then eighty-seven, still determined to do everything in her power to bring change.

Cancun was very different than Seattle. The WTO meetings were held in the convention center in the Zona Hotelera, the hotel zone, which is an island strip lined with sprawling luxury hotels. Chain-link security fences and thousands of police and military personnel kept the majority of protestors on the mainland in Cancun City where teach-ins, organizing meetings, cultural events, and protests were held each day. During the week we met labor unionists, WTO delegates, small farmers, and activists from all over the world. We marched in demonstrations led by thousands of Mexican campesinos, many of whom had been driven off their land by the policies of NAFTA and the WTO.

Meanwhile, inside the convention center, WTO negotiations were deadlocked, with agriculture the most visible and contentious issue. While refusing to eliminate their own agricultural subsidies, the United States and European Union were pushing developing nations to remove subsidies and other protections against the dumping of cheaper subsidized foreign products. (Under existing NAFTA and WTO policies, cheaper subsidized U.S. corn was flooding the Mexican market, putting Mexican campesinos out of work and off the land.)

On the way to Cancun I read an article by U.S. trade representative Robert Zoellick, who articulated a lofty-sounding goal: "The United States wants to open global markets across-the-board, to expand a virtuous circle of trade and economic growth for developing and developed economies that can strengthen each other."[2] The most powerful nations, led by the United States, had arrived in Cancun with a detailed draft proposal to further their goals.

But poorer nations saw the agenda of these powerful nations in a different light. Brazil, India, China, and other developing nations joined together into a "Group of 21," representing over half of the world's population, to resist the draft proposal. India's WTO representative, Arun Jaitley, criticized the draft as "utterly incomprehensible and extremely insensitive to the large number of people living in poverty in developing countries. . . . It represents an attempt to thrust the views of a few countries on many developing countries."[3]

One day Ruth and I, together with Richard Snow, a Korean war veteran from Santa Cruz, were walking in downtown Cancun. As we approached an outdoor café we saw a man with an official WTO name badge sitting at a table. We greeted him and introduced ourselves. He in turn introduced himself to us. He was a delegate from Kenya named Peter. He invited us to sit and have lunch with him.

During lunch, we talked about how the WTO negotiations were going and shared ideas about alternative economic models that would encourage food security and fair trade. Peter explained that when delegates from poor nations negotiate with representatives of rich nations, "sometimes we feel like our brains are underdeveloped." He thanked us for demonstrating and said that street protests give delegates from poorer nations the will to stand strong in spite of great pressures. He also told us, "We can't agree to these unfair terms and go back to our people. It would be politically impossible." In other words, the people really do have power.

Ruth asked, "Peter, can you tell me why the developing nations don't just get up and walk out?" He smiled, and we discussed the idea for a while.

This idea did not originate with Ruth. We had seen protest signs saying, "Global South, walk out." Still, the next day we were stunned to hear that the Group of 21 developing nations had walked out of the talks, *led by the delegation from Kenya.*[4] It was later reported that a Kenyan delegate said publicly, "If it was not for the protestors outside on the street, we would not have been able to shut down these talks."[5] Was it Peter? We don't know. But we do know that the Kenyan delegation led the walkout, abruptly ending the negotiations of the WTO.

Newspapers put a negative spin on the story, making it seem that poor people in developing nations had lost out on the "virtuous circle of trade" promoted by the United States. But many around the world saw the walkout as a victory.[6]

That night, thousands of people in Cancun celebrated—Mexican campesinos, indigenous women and their children, elders and students, together with people who had come to Cancun from all over the world. In a downtown park a Mexican rock band performed "Redemption Song," the late Bob Marley's song of hope, first in Spanish and then in English. There in the public square I joined with hundreds of others, dancing and singing along, elated, caught up in the beauty of the song:

> Old pirates yes they rob I
> Sold I to the merchant ships
> Minutes after they took I
> From the bottomless pit
> But my hand was made strong
> By the hand of the Almighty
> We forward in this generation
> Triumphantly
> Won't you help to sing
> These songs of freedom
> 'Cause all I ever had
> Redemption songs . . .
>
> Emancipate yourself from mental slavery
> None but ourselves can free our minds
> Have no fear for atomic energy
> 'Cause none of them can stop the time
> How long shall they kill our prophets
> While we stand aside and look?
> Some say that's just a part of it
> We've got to fulfill the Book
> Won't you help to sing
> These songs of freedom
> 'Cause all I ever had
> Redemption songs . . .
> These songs of freedom[7]

BY THE POWER AT WORK WITHIN US

Did our conversation with Peter, the delegate from Kenya, have anything to do with the collapse of talks within the WTO? Was it simply a coincidence? Synchronicity? Divine providence? I don't know. But I do know that our actions, when combined with the actions of others, may have effects far beyond what we expect or imagine. We don't know how our prayers, words, and actions affect the whole. But we do know that God often works through people in mysterious ways that are beyond our ability to understand.

WTO negotiations have never gotten back on track since the collapse of talks in Cancun. Negotiations to form a Free Trade Area of the Americas (FTAA) have gone nowhere. Efforts to create a functioning Central American Free Trade Area of the Americas (CAFTA) have stalled. Nevertheless, when multilateral negotiations fail, the United States and other powerful nations use their power to negotiate bilateral and regional trade agreements that will benefit them. In spite of being blocked at times by citizen action and in spite of occasional breakdowns and collisions, the train of corporate globalization continues along, turning the gifts of the earth and human culture into commodities to be bought and sold. And many are blindly driving along in the same direction on the broad way against which Jesus warned, lured by the false promises of the gospel of materialism and their own need or greed, traveling the highway toward a hell on earth.

Is there hope for the earth? What does the future hold? We do not know, and there are no guarantees. In Jürgen Moltmann's words:

> Has the modern world any future? Its future is conversion. Will humanity survive the crises we have described? We cannot know, and we must not know. If we knew that humanity is not going to survive, we should not do anything more for our children but would say, "after us, the deluge." If we knew that humanity is going to survive, we should not do anything either, and by doing nothing we should miss our chance for conversion. Because we cannot know whether humanity is going to survive or not, we have to act today as if the future of the whole of humankind were dependent on us—and yet at the same time trust wholly that God is faithful to his creation and will not let it go.[8]

It all comes back to us, to our own personal choice and decision. What shall it be? Will we add to the institutional momentum toward global death through our conscious or unwitting complicity with the Powers? Or will we take responsibility for ourselves and for our relationship with the Powers, trusting that God can work through us as we set out on the narrow path that leads to life? Will we live in denial or take action for change? Which will it be: fear or faith? In the words from a poem by my husband, Guarionex Delgado:

> I can see the direction we're headed
> along a wide road
> an inevitable looking one

full of cars and malls
Disneyland and tv
paved as far as I can see
maybe to the moon, Mars and beyond
and everyone wants the same thing
to be happy and rich enough
not to suffer loss, a good life
free of the blues
as much as you can be
and it's almost like
there is no exit
except when you remember
you've got feet
and even though it's one way
you can walk over
to the shoulder
leave the pavement
and its noise behind
learn to walk along a new way
older than flesh and wood
as old as wind and water
narrow as the seed's sprout
steep as the dawn's breath[9]

As I have shown throughout this book, many people are awakening to the global crisis and rising up to meet the challenge. Many are resisting the current global system and the violence, injustice, and ecological destruction that it fosters. Many are adopting values, creating communities, and building alternative institutions that honor our interrelatedness with the human family and the rest of creation.

Won't you help to sing these songs of freedom?

No institution is invulnerable, not even a powerful institution like the WTO. No human-created system is ultimate, not even the current corporate-dominated global empire. No direction for human society is inevitable, unless the people relinquish their choice and responsibility and allow it to be so.

Won't you help to sing these songs of freedom? It's all we ever have... redemption songs.

As we set out on the path toward change, at times it may seem that we are fighting a losing battle. But we cannot lose—the stakes are too high. And we do not struggle alone. Though we cannot always see or feel it, we have tremendous support. A "great cloud of witnesses" (Hebrews 12:1) surrounds us and urges us on.

We are a part of the emerging global community of people engaged in struggles for peace and justice—people in Kenya and Mexico, Bolivia and Venezuela, and in countries around the world, working together, organizing locally and across borders to build a peaceful, just, and sustainable world. This global community supports us—we support each other. We are connected with those who have gone before, the martyrs and heroes, all the ancestors who invested themselves for the sake of future generations, and we are connected with those who will come after. They support us—we are their champions. We are related to the earth and all its creatures in a web that cannot be broken without injury to all—we are their advocates. We are connected to Jesus Christ, who reveals God to us, sends us the Spirit, and models courageous resistance even unto death—we are his followers.

We can act in hope, trusting that with God all things are possible. For the foundation of our hope is the source of life and love, the Creator of heaven and earth, who gives us new life through Jesus Christ and empowers us through the Holy Spirit, who is above all earthly rulers and authorities and powers and principalities, and who extends steadfast love to all generations.

"Now to the One who *by the power at work within us* is able to accomplish abundantly far more than all we can ask or even imagine, to that One be the glory in Christ Jesus and in the church and in the world to all generations, forever and ever. Amen."

-Eph. 3:20-21, adapted

NOTES

PREFACE
1. William Stringfellow, *An Ethic for Christians and Other Aliens in a Strange Land* (Waco, Texas: Word Books, 1974), 82.

INTRODUCTION: A Moment of Profound Choice
1. Words and music by Malvina Reynolds. Schroder Music Co.,www.sister-schoice.com/eartogroundlyrics.html.
2. Thomas Friedman, *The Lexus and the Olive Tree: Understanding Globalization,* updated and expanded ed. (New York: Farrar, Straus & Giroux, 2000), 9.
3. John Robbins, "The McAfrica Burger," from the Web site for his book *The Food Revolution: How Your Diet Can Help Save Your Life and the World* (Berkeley: Conari Press, 2001); http://www.foodrevolution.org/askjohn/38.htm (accessed Feb. 14, 2007).
4. John Wesley, John Wesley to Alexander Mather, August 6, 1777, in *The Letters of John Wesley,* Vol. 6, ed. John Telford (London: Epworth Press, 1931).
5. "Mohandas K. Gandhi," from the Web site Betterworldheros.com, http://www.betterworldheroes.com/gandhi.htm (accessed 2/14/07).
6. Notes from Nowhere, eds., *We Are Everywhere: The Irresistible Rise of Global Anti-Capitalism* (London/New York: Verso, 2003).
7. Richard Bauckham, "Jürgen Moltmann," in *The Modern Theologians: An Introduction to Christian Theology in the Twentieth Century,* Volume 1, ed. David E. Ford (Campbell, Mass.: Basil Blackwell, 1990), 299.

CHAPTER ONE: The Earth as Primary Revelation
1. Martin Luther, quoted in Sherwood Eliot and Kirston Beckstrom Wirt, *Living Quotations for Christians* (New York: Harper and Row, 1974), 95.
2. John Wesley, quoted in Richard Foster, *Celebration of Discipline,* rev. ed. (San Francisco: HarperSanFrancisco, 1988), 55.
3. Brian Swimme, *Canticle of the Cosmos,* audiotape 3, performed by the author, (Louisville, Colo.: Sounds True, 1996).
4. United States Conference of Catholic Bishops, "Renewing the Earth: An Invitation to Reflection and Action on Environment in Light of Catholic Social Teaching," A Pastoral Statement of the United States Catholic Conference, Nov. 14, 1991, http://www.usccb.org/sdwp/ejp/bishopsstatement.htm (accessed 3/2/07).
5. Luther, quoted in Eliot and Wirt, *Living Quotations for Christians.* 95.
6. John Wesley, *A Survey of the Wisdom of God in the Creation* (Briston: Printed by William Pine, 1763), 229.
7. Thomas Berry, *The Dream of the Earth* (San Francisco: Sierra Club Books, 1988), 45.
8. Ibid., 81.
9. "Sacrament: General Information," from "Sacrament, Ordinance, Mystery," on *Believe, Religious Information Source,* http://mb-soft.com/believe/text/sacramen.htm (accessed 3/2/07).
10. Jerry Mander, *In The Absence of the Sacred: The Failure of Technology and the Survival of the Indian Nations* (San Francisco: Sierra Club Books, 1992).
11. Berry, *The Dream of the Earth,* 81.
12. Ibid.
13. Thomas Berry, "Economics: Its Effects on the Life Systems of the World," *in Thomas Berry and the New Cosmology: In Dialogue with Gregory Baum,* et al., ed. Anne Lonergan and Caroline Richards (Mystic, Conn.: Twenty-Third Publications, 1988), 17.

14. Marjorie Hope and James Young, "Thomas Berry and a New Creation Story," *Christian Century,* Aug. 16–23, 1989, 750, http://www.religion-online.org/showarticle.asp?title=852 (accessed 3/2/07).

15. Chief Seattle, quoted on the Web site ThinkExist.com, http://thinkexist.com/quotation/humankind-has-not-woven-the-web-of-life-we-are/1573311.html (accessed 3/2/07).

16. John Wesley, quoted in Albert C. Outler, *Theology in the Wesleyan Spirit* (Nashville: Discipleship Resources-Tidings, 1975), 40.

17. Jürgen Moltmann, "Has Modern Society Any Future?" in Jürgen Moltmann and Johannes Baptist Metz, eds., *Faith and the Future: Essays on Theology, Solidarity, and Modernity* (Maryknoll, N.Y.: Orbis Books, 1995), 174.

18. Wendell Berry, "The Peace of Wild Things," in *The Selected Poems of Wendell Berry* (Washington, D.C.: Counterpoint, 1998), 30.

19. Leanne Hinton, "The Land Knows You're There," My Song Book Web site; http://www.mysongbook.de/msb/songs/50/landknow.html (accessed 3/2/07).

20. Guarionex Delgado, "I Write," in *Being Human: Poems of Resistance and Renewal* (Nevada City, Calif.: Rim of Fire, 2001), 5.

21. Swimme, *Canticle of the Cosmos,* audiotape 3.

22. T. S. Eliot, "Ash Wednesday," in *The Complete Poems and Plays,* 1909–1950

23. Ibid.,(New York: Harcourt, Brace and World, 1971) 66–67

CHAPTER TWO: Deforestation Is Hell

1. Chief Seattle, quoted in ThinkExist.com, http://thinkexist.com/quotation/humankind-has-not-woven-the-web-of-life-we-are/1573311.html (accessed 3/2/07).

2. Alex Kirby, "Biodiversity: " BBC News Online, Oct. 1, 2004, http://news.bbc.co.uk/1/hi/sci/tech/3667300.stm (accessed 3/2/07).

3. Ibid.

4. Thomas Berry, "Economics: Its Effects on the Life Systems of the World," in *Thomas Berry and the New Cosmology,* ed. Anne Lonergan and Caroline Richards (Mystic, Conn.: Twenty-Third Publications, 1988), 14.

5. See David Ulansey, Ph.D., "Mass Extinction Underway," The Current Mass Extinction, http://www.well.com/user/davidu/extinction.html (accessed 3/2/07).

6. Edward Goldsmith, et al., *Imperiled Planet: Restoring Our Endangered Ecosystems* (Cambridge, Mass.: MIT Press, 1990), 39.

7. Michael Lerner, "Surviving the Great Dying," *Yes! Magazine: A Journal of Positive Futures* (Spring 2003), http://www.yesmagazine.org/article.asp?ID=585 (accessed 3/2/07).

8. Associated Press, "EPA: Third of Survey Rivers Polluted," *Milwaukee Journal Sentinel,* Oct. 1, 2002, http://www.jsonline.com/news/nat/ap/oct02/ap-epa-water-needs100102.asp (accessed 3/2/07).

9. Janet Larsen, "Dead Zones in the World's Oceans," *The Globalist,* June 23, 2004, http://www.theglobalist.com/DBWeb/printStoryId.aspx?StoryId=3993 (accessed 3/2/07).

10. MSNBC.com, "Species disappearing at an alarming rate, report says," Nov. 17, 2004, http://msnbc.msn.com/id/6502368/from/ET/ (accessed 3/2/07).

11. Joby Warrick, "Mass Extinction Underway, Majority of Biologists Say," *Washington Post,* April 21, 1998, http://www.well.com/user/davidu/extinction.html (accessed 3/2/07).

12. Marsha Walton, "Study: Only 10 percent of big ocean fish remain," CNN, May 14, 2003, http://www.cnn.com/2003/TECH/science/05/14/coolsc.disappear-ingfish/ (accessed 3/2/07).

13. Warrick, "Mass Extinction Underway."

14. Michael Casey, "Survey: Waterbirds Species Are in Decline," *San Francisco Chronicle,* Jan. 23, 2007, http://www.sfgate.com/cgi-bin/article.cgi?f=/n/a/2007/01/23/international/i014653S70.DTL&hw=Many%2Bspecies%2Bof%2Bwaterbirds%2Bare%2Bin%2Bdecline&sn=001&sc=1000 (accessed 3/2/07).

15. Alex Kirby, "Third of primates 'risk extinction,'" BBC News Online, October 7, 2002), http://news.bbc.co.uk/1/hi/sci/tech/2306517.stm (accessed 3/2/07).

16. Alex Kirby, "UN's clarion call for great apes," BBC News Online, Nov. 26, 2003, http://news.bbc.co.uk/1/hi/sci/tech/3237726.stm (accessed 3/2/07).

17. BBC News, "Lions 'close to extinction,'" BBC News Online, Sept. 18, 2003, http://news.bbc.co.uk/1/hi/sci/tech/3119434.stm (accessed 3/2/07).

18. Chief Seattle, quoted in ThinkExist.com, http://thinkexist.com/quotation/humankind-has-not-woven-the-web-of-life-we-are/1573311.html (accessed 3/2/07).

19. Joanna Macy, "The Shift to a Life-Sustaining Civilization," The Great Turning, http//www.joannamacy.net/html/great.html (accessed 3/2/07).

CHAPTER THREE: The Heat Is On

1. Catherine Keller, "Talk about the Weather: The Greening of Eschatology," in Carol Adams, ed., *Ecofeminism and the Sacred* (New York: Continuum, 1993), 30–31.

2. James Saoulli, "Asthma Sufferers Fight for Breath," CNN, May 5, 2005, http://edition.cnn.com/2005/WORLD/europe/05/05/asthma/ (accessed 3/2/07).

3. Todd Zwillich, "Childhood Asthma Rise Remains a Puzzle," WebMD Medical News, Dec. 12, 2006, http://www.webmd.com/content/article/130/117795.htm (accessed 3/2/07).

4. Skin Cancer Foundation, "Skin Cancer Facts," http://www.skincancer.org/skincancer-facts.php (accessed 3/2/07).

5 Swetter, Susan. M., MD, "Malignant Melanoma," updated, March 29, 2007, E-medicine, from Web MD, http://www.emedicine.com/derm/topic257.htm. http://www.emedicine.com/derm/topic257.htm (accessed 4/3/07).

6. Skin Cancer Foundation, "Skin Cancer Facts."

7. Albert Gore, Jr., *Earth in the Balance: Ecology and the Human Spirit* (Boston: Houghten Mifflin, 1992) 87.

8. Bryan Walls, "Good News and a Puzzle: Earth's ozone layer appears to be on the road to recovery," Science@NASA, May 26, 2006, http://science.nasa.gov/headlines/y2006/26may_ozone.htm (accessed 3/2/07).

9. James Kanter and Andrew C. Revkin, "Climate-change report expected to project rising temperatures and sea levels," *International Herald Tribune,* Jan. 30, 2007, http://www.iht.com/articles/2007/01/30/news/climate.php (accessed 3/2/07).

10. Ibid.

11. Union of Concerned Scientists, "Early Warning Signs: Spreading Disease," http://www.ucsusa.org/global_environment/global_warming/page.cfm?pageID=508 (accessed 3/2/07).

12. Fred Pearce, "Instant Expert: Climate Change," NewScientist.com, Sept. 1, 2006, http://environment.newscientist.com/channel/earth/climate-change/dn9903 (accessed 3/2/07).

13. Kanter and Revkin, "Climate-change report."

14. Catherine Brahic, "Major climate change report looks set to alarm," New Scientist.com, Jan. 29, 2007, http://environment.newscientist.com/channel/earth/climate-change/dn11049-major-climate-change-report-looks-set-to-alarm.html (accessed 3/2/07).

15. Source Watch, A Project of the Center for Media and Democracy, "Climate Change and Hurricane Katrina," http://www.sourcewatch.org/index.php?title=Climate_change_and_Hurricane_Katrina (accessed 3/2/07).

16. Keller, "Talk about the Weather," 30–31.

17. Joseph Karliner, *The Corporate Planet: Ecology and Politics in the Age of Globalization* (San Francisco: Sierra Club Books, 1997), 95.

18. Ted Nace, *Gangs of America: The Rise of Corporate Power and the Disabling of Democracy* (San Francisco: Berrett-Koehler, 2003), 1.

19. Karliner, *The Corporate Planet*, 65.

20. Ibid., 78.

21. Ibid., 96.

22. Michael Klare, *Resource Wars: The New Landscape of Global Conflict* (New York: Henry Holt, 2001).

23. Kevin Danaher, "Corporate Globalization," speech at the Veterans Memorial Building in Santa Cruz, California, sponsored by the Resource Center for Nonviolence, March 20, 2003.

24. Karliner, *The Corporate Planet*, 97.

25. Bill McKibben, *The End of Nature* (New York: Random House, 1999), 10.

26. Dan Joling, "More pregnant polar bears denning on land," *San Francisco Chronicle*, Jan. 23, 2007, http://www.sfgate.com/cgi-bin/article.cgi?f=/n/a/2007/01/23/national/a153716S72.DTL&hw=More%2Bpregnant%2Bpolar%2Bbears%2Bdenning%2Bon%2Bland&sn=001&sc=1000 (accessed 3/2/07).

27. Global Climate Change Research Explorer, "Global Climate Change and Animal Populations," *The Exploratorium,* http://www.exploratorium.edu/climate/biosphere/data5.html (accessed 3/2/07).

CHAPTER FOUR: A Toxic Future?

1. Thomas Berry, *The Dream of the Earth* (San Francisco: Sierra Club Books, 1988), 33.

2. Hilary French, *Vanishing Borders: Protecting the Planet in the Age of Globalization, A Worldwatch Book* (New York: W. W. Norton, 2000), 76–77.

3. Ibid., 76.

4. Theo Colborne, Dianne Dumanoski, and John Peterson Myers, *Our Stolen Future: Are We Threatening Our Fertility, Intelligence, and Survival?* A Scientific Detective Story (New York: Penguin, 1996), 108.

5. Ibid., 105.

6. Ibid., 102–03.

7. Environmental Working Group, "The Most Poorly Tested Chemicals in the World," Chemical Industry Archives, http://www.chemicalindustryarchives.org/factfiction/testing.asp (accessed 3/2/07).

8. Colborne, Dumanoski, and Myers, *Our Stolen Future,* 28.

9. Ibid., 172–73.

10. Ibid., 185.

11. Breastcancer.org, "About Breast Cancer: Statistics, Causes, Symptoms, Surgery Options," http://www.breastcancer.org/press_cancer_facts.html (accessed 3/2/07).

12. Leslie Byster, ed., "Dioxins Everywhere and More Deadly than Ever," Silicon Valley Toxics Action 12, no. 4 (Winter 1994), 4.

13. Sandra Steingraber, *Living Downstream: An Ecologist Looks at Cancer and the Environment* (New York: Vintage, 1997), 41.

14. Ibid., 38.

15. Environmental Working Group, "Fact #4: Cancer rates are up, particularly for cancer that affect the young," Chemical Industry Archives, http://www.chemicalindustryarchives.org/factfiction/facts/4.asp (accessed 3/2/07).

16. Steingraber, *Living Downstream*, 38.

17. Byster, "Dioxins Everywhere," 1.

18. Ibid.

19. Colborne, Dumanoski, and Myers, *Our Stolen Future*, 11.

20. Ibid., 197.

21. Amy Goodman, "Treasury Secretary Nominee Lawrence Summers and Environmental Racism," Democracy Now! radio program transcript, June 16th, 1999, http://www.democracynow.org/article.pl?sid=03/04/07/044206 (accessed 3/2/07).

22. French, *Vanishing Borders*, 84.

23. Tom Athanasiou, *Divided Planet: The Ecology of Rich and Poor* (Boston: Little, Brown, 1996), 137.

24. Ibid., 138.

25. French, *Vanishing Borders*, 82.

26. Ibid., 80–81.

27. Ibid.

28. Ibid., 78–79.

29. Ibid., 77.

30. Steingraber, *Living Downstream*, 269.

31. French, *Vanishing Borders*, 77-78.

32. Marion Moses, M.D., *Designer Poisons: How to Protect Your Health and Home from Toxic Pesticides* (San Francisco: Pesticide Education Center, 1995).

33. Fagin, Lavelle, and the Center for Public Integrity, Toxic Deception, 11.

34. Environmental Working Group, "The Most Poorly Tested Chemicals."

35. Fagin, Dan, Marianne Lavell, and the Center for Public Integrity, *Toxic Deception: How the Chemical Industry Manipulates Science, Bends the Law, and Endangers Your Health* (Secaucus: Carol Publishing Goup, 1996), 16-17.

36. Bhagat, Shantilal P., *Your Health and the Environment: A Christian Perspective*, (New York: Eco Justice Working Group, National Council of Churches of Christ in the USA, 1998), 19.

37. Steingraber, *Living Downstream*, 270.

38. Colborne, Dumanoski, and Myers, *Our Stolen Future*, 249.

39. Bhagat, *Your Health and the Environment*, 5.

CHAPTER FIVE: Engineering the Future

1. Samuel Johnson, quoted on QuoteWorld.org, http://www.quoteworld.org/quotes/7250 (accessed 3/2/07).

2. Lisa Krieger, "Stanford gets OK to try human cells in mouse brain," *San Jose Mercury News,* Feb. 14, 2005, B1, 4, http://www.dana.org/books/press/brainnews/bitn_0205a.cfm (accessed 3/2/07).

3. Anthony Giddens, *Runaway World: How Globalization Is Reshaping Our Lives* (New York: Routledge, 2000), 46.

4. Silicon Valley Toxics Coalition, "Toxic Hot Spots," http://www.mapcruzin.com/svtc_maps/ (accessed 3/2/07).

5 Arthur Firstenberg, "Electromagnetic Fields (EMF): Killing Fields," *The Ecologist* 34, no. 5 (June 1, 2004), http://www.mindfully.org/Technology/2004/Electromagnetic-Fields-EMF1jun04.htm (accessed 3/2/07).

6. Robbie Collin, "Monitors give off deadly radiation—Digital Baby Monitors 'Raise the Risk of Cancer,'" *News of the World,* Feb. 19, 2006, 39, http://freepage.twoday.net/stories/1677124/ (accessed 3/2/07).

7. Robert Kubey and Mihaly Csikszentmihalyi, "TV Addiction—How does television harm your children?" *Labour of Love, The Web Magazine for Conscious Parenting,* June 3, 2004, http://www.labouroflove.org/tv-toys-&-technology/television/tv-addiction-%11-how-does-television-harm-your-children%3F/ (accessed 3/2/07).

8. "Research: Video Games Decrease Brain Activity," *Mainichi Daily News,* July 8, 2002, http://www.getnet.com/~elvis/news/news2002.07.08.html (accessed 3/2/07).

9. Evelyne Hong, "Novartis targets India's Patents Act," Third World Network, Jan. 9, 2007, http://www.twnside.org.sg/title2/health.info/twninfo-health064.htm (accessed 3/2/07).

10. Vandana Shiva, *Stolen Harvest: The Hijacking of the Global Food Supply* (Cambridge, Mass.: South End, 2000), 6–7.

11. Kathryn McConnell, "World Trade Agency Upholds Challenge of European Biotech Ban," U.S. State Department, International Information Programs, Sept. 29, 2006, http://usinfo.state.gov/exarchives/display.html?p=washfile-english&y=2006&m=September (accessed 3/6/07).

12. F. William Engdahl, "WTO, GMO and Total Spectrum Dominance," Global Research, Mar. 29, 2006, http://www.globalresearch.ca/index.php?context=viewArticle&code=20060329&articleId=2202 (accessed 3/2/07).

13. Melissa Moon, "Monsanto Wins GMO Pollution Case In Canadian Supreme Court," Inter Activist Info Exchange, May 31, 2004, http://info.interactivist.net/article.pl?sid=04/05/21/1652220&mode=nested&tid=21 (accessed 3/2/07).

14. Robert Schubert, ed., "Monsanto Still Suing Nelsons, Other Growers," *CropChoice News,* May 21, 2001, http://www.nelsonfarm.net/issue.htm (accessed 3/2/07).

15. Vandana Shiva, "The WTO and GMOs," presentation at First United Methodist Church, Seattle, Wash., Nov. 29, 1999.

16. Ranjit Devraj, "US Corporate 'Biopirates' Still Staking Claim On Basmati Rice," InterPress Service, Oct. 9, 2000, http://www.commondreams.org/headlines/100900-01.htm (accessed 3/2/07).

17. McKibbon, Bill, *Enough: Staying Human in an Engineered World* (New York: Henry Holt and Company LLC, 2003). 210.

18. Dorothee Soelle, *Against the Wind: Memoirs of a Radical Christian, trans.* Barbara Rumscheidt and Martin Rumscheidt (Minneapolis: Fortress Press, 1999), 77.

19. Mick Wilson, et al., *Nanotechnology: Basic Science and Emerging Technologies* (Boca Raton: Chapman & Hall/CRC, 2002), 4.

20. Ibid., 76.

21. Ibid., 29–30.

22. Jürgen Moltmann, "Has Modern Society Any Future?" in Jürgen Moltmann and Johannes Baptist Metz, *Faith and the Future: Essays on Theology, Solidarity, and Modernity* (Maryknoll, N.Y.: Orbis Books, 1995), 176.

23 Soelle, *Against the Wind,* 77.

24. Jim Thomas, "Future Perfect?" *Ecologist Online,* Jan. 5, 2003, http://www.theecologist.org/archive_detail.asp?content_id=186 (accessed 3/2/07).

25. Thomas Berry, *The Dream of the Earth* (San Francisco: Sierra Club Books, 1988), 18.

1. Carl Zimmer, "First Cell," *Discover* 16, no. 11 (November 1995), http://www.discover.com/issues/nov-95/features/firstcell584/ (accessed 3/2/07).

26. Carol Miner and Paula Della Villa, "DNA Music: Reverse translating proteins yields microbiological melodies," *The Science Teacher,* May 1997, http://whozoo.org/mac/Music/CarolMiner.pdf (accessed 3/2/07).

27. Thomas Berry, "The Great Community of the Earth," *Yes! A Journal of Positive Futures.* (Winter 2001), 45, http://www.yesmagazine.org/article.asp?ID=385 (accessed 3/2/07)

CHAPTER SIX: Race to the Bottom

1. Jared Diamond, *Collapse: How Societies Choose to Fail or Succeed* (New York: Viking, 2005), 524.

2. Jeremy Brecher and Tim Costello, *Global Village or Global Pillage: Economic Recontruction From the Bottom Up,* 2d ed. (Cambridge, Mass.: South End Press, 1998), 20–21.

3. William Greider, "A Globalization Offensive," *The Nation* (Jan. 29, 2007), 5.

4. Daniel Brandt, "The 'Information Superhighway' and Its Discontents," *NameBase Newsline,* no. 7, Oct.-Dec. 1994, http://www.namebase.org/news07.html (accessed 3/5/07).

5. Mark Weisbrot, et al., "Scorecard on Development: 25 Years of Diminished Progress," Center for Economic and Policy Research, Sept. 2005, 1, available in PDF format at http://www.cepr.net/index.php?option=com_content&task=view&id=112&Itemid=8 (accessed 3/5/07).

6. Ibid., 21.

7. Ibid., 23.

8. Ibid., 9.

9. Lester R. Brown, *Plan B: Rescuing a Planet under Stress and a Civilization in Trouble* (New York: W. W. Norton/Earth Policy Institute, 2003), 82.

10. Ibid., 85.

11. Weisbrot, et al., "Scorecard on Development," 10.

12. Brown, Plan B, 89.

13. The World Revolution, "Overview of Global Issues: Development and Poverty", http://www.worldrevolution.org/projects/globalissuesoverview/overview2/BriefPeace.htm (accessed 3/5/07).

14. Bread for the World, "Hunger Facts: International," http://www.bread.org/learn/hunger-basics/hunger-facts-international.html (accessed 3/5/07).

15. Mark Weisbrot, "'Globalization' for Americans is Really About Income Distribution," Center for Economic and Policy Research, Sept. 2, 2006, http://www.cepr.net/columns/weisbrot/2006_09_04.htm (accessed 3/5/07).

16. World Revolution, "Overview of Global Issues."

17. Public Citizen, "The WTO and the Developing World: Do As We Say, Not As We Did," quoted in Lori Wallach and Patrick Woodall, *Whose Trade Organization? A Comprehensive Guide to the WTO* (New York: The New Press, 2004), http://www.citizen.org/trade/wto/articles.cfm?ID=10447 (accessed 3/5/07).

18. Sarah Anderson and John Cavanagh, "Top 200: The Rise of Global Corporate Power," in *Corporate Watch: Holding Corporations Accountable,* 2000, on the Global Policy Forum Web site, http://www.globalpolicy.org/socecon/tncs/top200.htm

(accessed 3/5/07).

19. *Multinational Monitor,* interview with Edward Wolff, "The Wealth Divide: The Growing Gap in the United States Between the Rich and the Rest," *Multinational Monitor* 24, no. 5 (May 2003).

20. Barbara Casin, *Inequality and Violence in the United States: Casualties of Capitalism,* 2d ed. (Amherst, N.Y.: Humanity Books, 2004), 54.

21. Luisa Kroll and Allison Fass, eds., "The World's Billionaires," *Forbes,* Mar. 9, 2006, http://www.forbes.com/billionaires/ (accessed 3/5/07).

22. Matthew Miller and Tatiana Serafin, eds., "America's 400 Richest," *Forbes,* Sept. 21, 2006, http://www.forbes.com/lists/2006/09/21/americas-400-richest-biz_cx_mm_06rich400_0921richintro.html (accessed 3/5/07).

23. Casin, *Inequality and Violence in the United States,* 60.

24. Ibid., 55.

25. U.S. Conference of Catholic Bishops, "Poverty USA: The Faces of American Poverty," Catholic Campaign for Human Development, http://www.usccb.org/cchd/povertyusa/povfact2.shtml (accessed 3/5/07).

26. Ibid.

27. Jeff Green, "U.S. has second worst newborn death rate in modern world, report says," CNN, May 10, 2006, http://www.cnn.com/2006/HEALTH/parenting/05/08/mothers.index/ (accessed 3/5/07).

28. Tom Athanasiou, *Divided Planet: The Ecology of Rich and Poor* (Boston: Little, Brown, 1996), 220–21.

29. Diamond, Collapse, 517.

30. Albert Gore, Jr., *Earth in the Balance: Ecology and the Human Spirit* (New York: Penguin, 1993), 85.

31. Brown, *Plan B,* 86–87.

32. Maude Barlow and Tony Clark, *Blue Gold: The Fight to Stop the Corporate Theft of the World's Water* (New York: The New Press, 2002), 7.

33. Sierra Club, "Global Population and Environment: Population, Consumption and Our Global Footprint," http://www.sierraclub.org/population/consumption/ (accessed 3/5/07).

34. Lester R. Brown, "A New World Order," *The Guardian Unlimited,* Jan. 25, 2006, http://www.guardian.co.uk/print/0,,5382253-108142,00.html (accessed 3/5/07).

35. Associated Press, "China: Population grew last year to 1.307 b," *CHINAdaily,* March 13, 2006, http://www.chinadaily.com.cn/english/doc/2006-03/16/content_541863.htm (accessed 3/5/07).

36. Charles Wolf, Jr., "China: Pitfalls on Path of Continued Growth," Rand Corporation, http://www.rand.org/commentary/060103LAT.html (accessed 3/5/07).

37. Brown, "A New World Order."

38. Bill Blakemore, "Seeking Extra Planet Before 2050, Inquire Within," ABC News, Oct. 24, 2006, http://abcnews.go.com/Technology/story?id=2602568&page=1 (accessed 3/5/07).

39. James Howard Kunstler, The Long Emergency: Surviving the Converging Catastrophes of the Twenty-First Century (New York: Atlantic Monthly Press, 2005), 12.

40. Ibid., 44.

41. Ibid., 49.

42. Ibid, front book flap.

43. Mohandas Gandhi, quoted in "Quotations About Consumerism," *The Quote Garden,* http://www.quotegarden.com/consumerism.html (accessed 3/5/07).

44. Quoted in Maude Barlow, *Blue Gold: The Global Water Crisis and the*

Commodification of the World's Water Supply (San Francisco: International Forum on Globalization, 1999), 2.

45. Barlow, *Blue Gold: The Global Water Crisis,* 6.
46. Ibid., 22.
47. Ibid., 6.
48. Ibid., 2.
49. Barlow and Clark, *Blue Gold: The Fight to Stop,* 24.
50. Brown, Plan B, 88.
51. Barlow and Clark, *Blue Gold: The Fight to Stop,* 24.
52. Ibid.
53. Ibid., 2.
54. Ibid., 145.
55. Ibid., 2.
56. Ibid., 76.
57. Brown, *Plan B,* 7.
58. Earth Action, "2000: The International Year of Deserts and Desertification (IYDD)," http://www.earthaction.org/engl/actionalertc.html (accessed 3/5/07).
59. Peter N. Spotts, "10 years later: no plan to halt spreading deserts," *Christian Science Monitor,* Feb. 25, 1987, http://www.csmonitor.com/1987/0225/ades.html?s=widep (accessed 3/5/07).
60. Stephen Leckie, "Meat production's environmental toll: Wilderness destruction, soil erosion, energy waste, and pollution," Toronto Vegetarian Association, Feb. 1, 2006, http://www.veg.ca/issues/enintro.html (accessed 3/5/07).
61. Brown, Plan B, 7.
62. Lester Brown, et al., *State of the World, 1994: A Worldwatch Institute Report on Progress Toward a Sustainable Society.*
63. Juliet Eilperin, "World's Fish Supply Running Out, Researchers Warn," *Washington Post,* Nov. 3, 2006, A01, http://www.washingtonpost.com/wp-dyn/content/article/2006/11/02/AR2006110200913.html (accessed 3/5/07).
64. Diamond, *Collapse,* 3–6.
65. Ibid., 515.
66. Brown, *Plan B,* 104.

CHAPTER SEVEN: The Infernal Whirlwind

1. Walter Wink, "The Myth of Redemptive Violence," reprinted by UK Bible Society, http://www.biblesociety.org.uk/exploratory/articles/wink99.doc (accessed 3/5/07).
2. Felix Wilfred, "Religions Face to Face with Globalization," in *Globalization and its Victims,* ed. Jon Sobrino and Felix Wilfred (London: SCM Press, 2001), 35.
3. Os Guinness, *Unspeakable: Facing Up to the Challenge of Evil* (San Francisco: HarperSanFrancisco, 2005), 4–5.
4. Thomas L. Friedman, *The Lexus and the Olive Tree: Understanding Globalization, Updated and Expanded Edition* (New York: Farrar, Straus, Giroux, 2000), 239.
5. Wilfred, "Religions Face to Face with Globalization," 41.
6. Benjamin R. Barber, *Jihad vs. McWorld: How Globalism and Tribalism Are Reshaping the World* (New York: Ballentine Books, 1995).
7. Charles L. Campbell, *The Word Before the Powers: An Ethic of Preaching* (Louisville: Westminster John Knox Press, 2002), 46.
8. Chalmers Johnson, *The Costs and Consequences of American Empire* (New York: Henry Holt, 2000).

9. Ibid., 229.

10. Ibid., 8.

11. Ibid., 223.

12. Juhasz, *The Bush Agenda*, 298.

13. Ibid.

14. Stringfellow, *An Ethic for Christians*, 127.

15. Olivia Ward, "Doomsday Clock Reset for an Alarming World," *Toronto Star,* Jan. 17, 2007.

16. Walter Wink, *Unmasking the Powers: The Invisible Forces That Determine Human Existence* (Philadelphia: Fortress Press, 1986), 55.

17. Guinness, *Unspeakable*, 67.

18. Stringfellow, *An Ethic for Christians,* 127.

19. Ken Butigan, "The Spiritual Journey of Christian Nonviolent Resistance," *Pace e Bene, Essays on Nonviolence,* http://www.paceebene.org/pace/node/362/print (accessed 3/5/07).

20. Wink, *Unmasking the Powers,* 106.

CHAPTER EIGHT: The Powers of This World

1. William Stringfellow, *An Ethic for Christians and Other Aliens in a Strange Land* (Waco: Word Books, 1974), 31.

2. John Wesley, quoted by Albert C. Outler, *Theology in the Wesleyan Spirit* (Nashville: Discipleship Resources-Tidings, 1975), 40.

3. Roger S. Gottleib, *A Spirituality of Resistance: Finding a Peaceful Heart and Protecting the Earth* (New York: Crossroad, 1999), 26–27.

4. Walter Wink, *Engaging the Powers: Discernment and Resistance in an Age of Domination,* (Minneapolis: Fortress Press, 1992), 54.

5. Homeless teenager, interviewed by Terry Gross, *Fresh Air,* NPR radio, Feb. 6, 2002.

6. William Stringfellow, quoted by Dr. Matthew McMahan, "Short Quotes on Wealth From Church History," http://www.apuritansmind.com/Stewardship/ShortQuotesOnWealth.htm (accessed 3/5/07).

7. Wink, *Engaging the Powers,* 42.

8. Walter Wink, *Unmasking the Powers: The Invisible Forces That Determine Human Existence* (Philadelphia: Fortress Press, 1986), 4.

9. Stringfellow, *An Ethic for Christians,* 77–78.

10. Ibid., 27, 78.

11. Wink, *Unmasking the Powers,* 5.

12. Ibid., 4.

13. Stringfellow, *An Ethic for Christians,* 81.

14. Ibid., 84.

15. Hendrik Berkhof, *Christ and the Powers* (Scottdale, Pa.: Mennonite Publishing House, 1977), 30.

16. When I speak here of myth, I mean it in the best and most powerful sense of the term. Just as the dreams of individuals can clarify personal issues and provide guidance, the dreams and visions of the peoples of the earth expressed as myths can also clarify and provide guidance for their lives. These myths, emerging as they do from the depths of the collective unconscious, provide societies with a common context, a cosmology, a framework through which to understand and approach the universe and the divine. In our postmodern world, we are able to examine myths as stories about reality, not as literal reality itself. This enables us

to explore their spiritual truths and to use myths as templates to overlay onto current reality, and allows us to reclaim, reinterpret, change the emphasis, or transform them in ways that express new insights.

17. Stringfellow, *An Ethic for Christians,* 84.

18. Ibid., 30.

19. Ibid., 29.

20. Ibid., 31.

21. Ibid., 88.

22. Ibid., 52.

23. Ibid., 119.

24. James W. Douglass, *Resistance and Contemplation: The Way to Liberation* (Garden City, N.Y.: Doubleday, 1972), 139, 41.

25. Ibid., 29.

26. Stringfellow, *An Ethic for Christians,* 34.

27. Wink, *Unmasking the Powers,* 51–52.

28. Wink, *Engaging the Powers,* 46.

29. David C. Korten, *When Corporations Rule the World,* 2d ed. (San Francisco: Berrett-Koehler, 2001).

30. Wink, *Unmasking the Powers,* 55.

31. Stringfellow, *An Ethic for Christians*

32. Walter Wink, *Naming the Powers: The Language of Power in the New Testament* (Philadelphia: Fortress Press, 1984), 25.

CHAPTER NINE: A Modern Parable

1. Berkhof, Hendrik, *Christ and the Powers* (Scottdale: Herald, 1977), 44.

CHAPTER TEN: Economic Insanity

1. Franz Hinkelammert, "Globalization as Cover-Up: An Ideology to Disguise and Justify Current Wrongs," in Jon Sobrino and Felix Wilfred, eds., *Globalization and Its Victims* (London: SCM Press, 2001), 28–29.

2. Edmund L. Andrews, "Snow Urges Consumerism On China Trip," *New York Times,* Oct. 14, 2005, C1, http://www.nytimes.com/2005/10/14/business/14yuan.html?ex=1286942400&en=f9 a9ed4137bd9177&ei=5090&partner=rssuserland&emc=rss (accessed 3/5/07).

3. Thomas L. Friedman, *The Lexus and the Olive Tree: Understanding Globalization* (New York: Farrar, Straus & Giroux, 2000), 328.

4. Lester Thurow, *Building Wealth: The New Rules for Individuals, Companies, and Nations in a Knowledge-Based Economy,* audiocassette, John Cunningham, narrator (New York: HarperAudio, 1999), side 1.

5. William Greider, *One World, Ready or Not: The Manic Logic of Global Capitalism* (New York: Touchstone, 1997), 11..

6. Ibid.,

7. Ibid, 12.

8. Anthony Giddens, *Runaway World: How Globalization Is Reshaping Our Lives* (New York: Routledge, 2000), 32.

9. Quoted by Gil Rendle in "Finding the Path in the Wilderness," http://www.congregationalresources.org/frontpage/mj/rendle.asp (accessed 3/5/07).

10. Harvey Cox, "The Market as God: Living in the New Dispensation," *Atlantic Monthly,* March 1999, 18

11. Ibid., 20.

12. Siddharth Mohandas, "Market Fundamentalism," *The Washington Monthly*, July-Aug. 2002, http://www.findarticles.com/p/articles/mi_m1316/is_2002_July-August/ai_90114020 (accessed 3/5/07).

13. Frederick H. Borsch, "Pry Loose the Cold, Hard Fingers of the Market's 'Invisible Hand,'" *Los Angeles Times*, Feb. 5, 2001, http://www.commondreams.org/views01/0205-01.htm (accessed 3/5/07).

14. Friedman, *The Lexus and the Olive Tree*, 102.

15. Ibid., 103.

16. Ibid.

17. Borsch, "Pry Loose the Cold, Hard Fingers."

18. Edward Chancellor, *Devil Take the Hindmost: A History of Financial Speculation* (New York: Farrar, Straus & Giroux, 1999), 346.

19. Roger Terry, *Economic Insanity: How Growth-Driven Capitalism is Devouring the American Dream* (San Francisco: Berrett-Koehler, 1995), 58.

20. Friedman, *The Lexus and the Olive Tree*, 109.

21. Emmanuel Todd, *After the Empire: The Breakdown of the American Order* (New York: Columbia University Press, 2002), 98.

22. Robin Hahnel, *Panic Rules: Everything You Need to Know About the Global Economy* (Cambridge, Mass.: South End, 1999), inside cover.

23. Giddens, *Runaway World*, 220.

24. Jürgen Moltmann, "Has Modern Society Any Future?" in Jürgen Moltmann and Johannes Baptist Metz, *Faith and the Future: Essays on Theology, Solidarity, and Modernity* (Maryknoll, N.Y.: Orbis Books, 1995), 168.

25. Ibid..

26. Johnson, *Blowback*, 213.

27. Friedman, *The Lexus and the Olive Tree*, 365.

28. Ibid., 366.

29. Johnson, *Blowback*, 213.

30. Friedman, *The Lexus and the Olive Tree*, 443–444.

31. Giddens, *Runaway World*, 213.

32. Dale Allen Pfeiffer, "ExxonMobile: The Shame, the Ideal, and the Practical," *Uncommon Thought Journal*, Feb. 3, 2006, http://www.uncommonthought.com/mtblog/archives/020306-exxonmobile_the_sha.php.

33. William Stringfellow, *An Ethic for Christians and Other Aliens in a Strange Land* (Waco: Word Books, 1974), 42.

34. Richard Barnet and John Cavanagh, "Electronic Money and the Casino Economy," in Jerry Mander and Edward Goldsmith, *The Case against the Global Economy and for a Turn to the Local* (San Francisco: Sierra Club Books, 1996), 361.

35. John Micklethwait and Adrian Wooldridge, "The Hidden Promise: Liberty Renewed," in Frank J. Lechner and John Boli, eds., *The Globalization Reader*, 2d ed. (Malden, Mass.: Basil Blackwell, 2003), 15.

36. John Micklethwait and Adrian Wooldridge, *A Future Perfect: The Challenge and Hidden Promise of Globalization*, (New York: Random House, 2003), epigraph.

37. Paul Hawken, *The Ecology of Commerce: A Declaration of Sustainability* (New York: HarperCollins, 1993), 181.

38. Cavanagh, John, and Jerry Mander, editors, *Alternatives to Economic Globalization: A Better World Is Possible, A Report of the International Forum on Globalization*, Second Edition (San Francisco: Berrett-Koehler, 2004), 199.

39. Ibid., 204–05.

40. Robert Goodland, Herman Daly, Salah El Serafy, and Bernd von Droste, eds, *Environmentally Sustainable Economic Development: Building on Brundtland* (New York: UNESCO, 1991), 98.

41. Kenneth Lux, *Adam Smith's Mistake: How a Moral Philosopher Invented Economics and Ended Morality* (Boston: Shambala, 1990), 9.

42. Hendrik Berkof, *Christ and the Powers* (Scottdale: Herald, 1977), 51.

CHAPTER ELEVEN: Of, By, and For the Corporations

1. Ignacio Peon Escalante, quoted in David C. Korten, *When Corporations Rule the World,* 2d ed. (San Francisco: Berrett-Koehler Publishers, 2001), 143.

2. Patti Lynn, "Infact Lifts Boycott of Philip Morris/Altria's Kraft Foods Citing Global Tobacco Treaty as Major Victory for People over Tobacco Giant's Profits," *In the News,* Infact Publications and Reports, June 23, 2003, http://www.infact.org/062303boy.html (accessed 3/5/07).

3. Joel Bakan, *The Corporation: The Pathological Pursuit of Profit and Power* (New York: Free Press, 2005), 8.

4. Steinbeck, John, The Grapes of Wrath, (New York: The Viking Press, 1967), 45.

5. Merriam-Webster's Collegiate Dictionary, Eleventh Edition, ed. Frederick C. Mish (Springfield, Mass.: Merriam-Webster, 2006), 279.

6. Bakan, The Corporation, 28.

7. Steinbeck, *The Grapes of Wrath,* 42–43.

8. Bakan, *The Corporation,* 72–73, 69.

9. Steinbeck, The Grapes of Wrath, 43

10. Bakan, *The Corporation,* 60.

11. Steinbeck, *The Grapes of Wrath,* 44.

12. Ibid.

13. Stringfellow, *An Ethic for Christians,* 28.

14. Steinbeck, *The Grapes of Wrath,* 44.

15. Barry C. Lynn, *End of the Line: The Rise and Coming Fall of the Global Corporation* (New York: Doubleday, 2005), 3.

16. Melissa Block, "US Faces Flu Vaccine Shortage," *All Things Considered,* National Public Radio, Oct. 6, 2004, http://www.npr.org/templates/story/story.php?storyId=4073505 (accessed 3/5/07).

17. Barry C. Lynn, "Breaking the Chain: The antitrust case against Wal-Mart," *Harpers,* July 31, 2006, http://www.harpers.org/BreakingTheChain.html (accessed 3/5/07).

18. Kerry A. Dolan, "Offshoring the Offshorers," *Forbes,* Apr. 17, 2006, 74, http://members.forbes.com/forbes/2006/0417/074.html (accessed 3/5/07).

19. Ibid.

20. William Greider, "A Globalization Offensive," *The Nation,* Jan. 29, 2007, 5, http://www.thenation.com/doc/20070129/greider (accessed 3/5/07).

21. John Cochran, "Greenspan, 'Rock Star of Economics' Bows Out Tuesday," ABC News, Jan. 23, 2006, http://abcnews.go.com/Business/story?id=1533647 (accessed 3/5/07).

22. Thomas L. Friedman, *The Lexus and the Olive Tree: Understanding Globalization* (New York: Farrar, Straus & Giroux, 2000), 184.

23. Ibid., 161.

24. Ibid., 183.

25. Bakan, *The Corporation,* 71.

26. Jerry Mander, quoted in *The Case Against the Global Economy and for a Turn to the Local*, ed. Jerry Mander and Edward Goldsmith (San Francisco: Sierra Club Books, 1996), 314.

27. Bakan, *The Corporation*, 158.

CHAPTER TWELVE: Unholy Trinity

1. David C. Korten, "The Failures of Bretton Woods" in Jerry Mander and Edward Goldsmith, eds., *The Case Against the Global Economy and for a Turn to the Local* (San Francisco: Sierra Club Books, 1996), 25.

2. Experts have estimated that El Salvador's debt would rise to $8,841,000,000 by mid-2006. See CIA-The World Factbook: Rank Order-Debt-external, on the CIA Web site at https://www.cia.gov/cia/publications/factbook/rankorder/2079rank.html (accessed 3/6/07).

3. "It is time to cancel the crushing debt burden of the world's most impoverished nations," Religious Working Group on the World Bank and IMF, http://www.sndden.org/rwg/ (accessed 3/6/07).

4. William Stringfellow, *An Ethic for Cristians and Other Aliens in a Strange Land* (Waco: Word Books, 1974), 82.

5. Korten, "The Failures of Bretton Woods," 21.

6. "World Bank Group" from Wikipedia online encyclopedia at http://en.wikipedia.org/wiki/World_Bank (accessed 3/6/07).

7. In the World Bank's quota system, the United States has 16.52 percent of the voting power, according to Jonathan E. Sanford ("RS20413: IMF and World Bank: U.S. Contributions and Agency Budget," National Library for the Environment, Dec. 9, 1999). In the IMF, the United States has 17.53 percent of the vote, far more than other industrialized nations such as Japan, with 6.04 percent, Germany with 5.9 percent, France with 4.87 percent, or Italy with 3.21 percent. This quota system leaves developing nations with little to say about policies: Guatemala has .11 percent, Ethiopia has .07 percent, and Haiti has .05 percent of the vote. See "IMF Members' Quotas and Voting Power, and IMF Board of Governors" from the International Monetary Fund Web site, Nov. 6, 2006, at http://www.imf.org/external/np/sec/memdir/members.htm (accessed 3/6/07).

8. John Cavanagh and Jerry Mander, eds., *Alternatives to Economic Globalization: A Better World is Possible* (San Francisco: Berrett-Koehler, 2004), 65.

9. Ibid., 67.

10. "World Trade Organization: The Whole World—In Whose Hands?" videotape produced by Women's Divisions, General Board of Global Ministries, The United Methodist Church, 2000, http://gbgm-umc.org/umw/wto.html (accessed 3/6/07).

11. "Facts Have Faces: Africa: In Bondage to Debt," Church World Service, http://www.churchworldservice.org/FactsHaveFaces/africafact.html#history (accessed 3/6/07).

12. David C. Korten, *When Corporations Rule the World,* 2d ed. (San Francisco: Berrett-Koehler, 2001), 108–09.

13. Ibid., 109.

14. "The Progress of Nations, 1999," UNICEF, http://www.unicef.org/pon99/debtdat2.htm (accessed 3/6/07).

15. Stringfellow, *An Ethic for Christians,* 88–89.

16. Jean Somers, "Debt: The New Colonialism" in Bill Bigelow and Bob Peterson, *Rethinking Globalization: Teaching for Justice in an Unjust World* (Milwaukee: Rethinking Schools Press, 2002), 79.

17. Ibid., 80.

18. Ibid., 81.

19. In 1980, Brazil's debt was $64 billion. After paying $148 billion between 1980 and 1989, the debt had risen to $121 billion. Spiraling up, by 2005 it stood at $188 billion. Efforts to raise funds to service the debt continue have driven the massive deforestation of the ecologically diverse Amazon rain forest and have led to hunger and poverty. In the Philippines, SAPs have had a devastating effect on the environment, causing deforestation, soil erosion, destruction of coastal habitats and fisheries. Unemployment is at 48 percent. By 2005, its debt stood at over $65 billion. See CIA-The World Factbook: Rank Order-Debt-external, on the CIA Web site at https://www.cia.gov/cia/publications/factbook/rankorder/2079rank.html (accessed 3/6/07).

20. "Facts Have Faces: Africa: In Bondage to Debt."

21. Jubilee USA Network, "Why Drop the Debt?" http://www.jubileeusa.org/truth-about-debt/why-drop-the-debt.html (accessed 3/6/07).

22. Ibid.

23. "President of Tanzania's message to debt campaigners," Jubilee Debt Campaign, March 2005, http://www.jubileedebtcampaign.org.uk/?lid=559&tmpl=jdcmainprint (accessed 3/6/07).

24. "African NGOs on 2005 debt proposals," Jubilee Debt Campaign, March 2005, http://www.jubileedebtcampaign.org.uk/?lid=554&tmpl=jdcmainprint (accessed 3/6/07).

25. Noreena Hertz, *The Debt Threat: How Debt Is Destroying the Developing World . . . and Threatening Us All* (New York: HarperCollins, 2004), 124.

26. Neil Watkins and Debayani Kar, "Jubilee US Encouraged by Apparent G-8 Agreement for 100% of IMF, Multilateral Debts," Jubilee USA Network, Washington, D.C., Global Exchange, http://www.globalexchange.org/campaigns/wbimf/3119.html (accessed 3/6/07). Many poor countries do not qualify for HIPC debt relief. Nigeria borrowed $5 billion, paid $16 billion, and still owes over $34 billion. Although 12 percent of its population will be infected with HIV by 2010, in 2002 it spent only $350 million on providing health care, but over $2.9 billion servicing its debt (Jubilee USA Network, "Why Drop the Debt?"). In Ecuador, more than 34 percent of people now live in extreme poverty, and the number continues to grow, while the government spends $29 out of every $100 on debt repayment, compared with $13 for education and social welfare. In Peru, 54.8 percent of the people live in poverty. In 2002, 17.5 percent of the government budget went for debt servicing, while 17 percent was spend on health and 9.3 percent on education. None of these three countries qualify for debt relief. See Hertz, *The Debt Threat,* 123–24.

27. Hertz, *The Debt Threat,* 124.

28. Somers, "Debt: The New Colonialism," 78.

29. Shridath Ramphal, "Debt Has a Child's Face," UNICEF, http://www.unicef.org/pon99/debtcom1.htm (accessed 3/6/07).

30. Hertz, *The Debt Threat,* 174.

31. UNCTAD, "UNCTAD and WTO: A Common Goal in a Global Economy," http://www.unctad.org/TEMPLATES/webflyer.asp?docid=3607&intItemID=2298&lang=1 (accessed 3/6/07).

32. Ibid.

33. Lori Wallach, "Slow Motion Coup d'Etat: Global Trade Agreements and the Displacement of Democracy," *Multinational Monitor* 26, nos. 1 & 2 (Jan./Feb. 2005), http://multinationalmonitor.org/mm2005/012005/wallach.html (accessed 3/6/07).

34. Sarah Anderson and John Cavanagh with Thea Lee and the Institute for Policy Studies, *Field Guide to the Global Economy* (New York: The New Press, 2000), 72–73.

35. Lori Wallach and Michelle Sforza, *Whose Trade Organization? Corporate Globalization and the Erosion of Democracy* (Washington, D.C.: Public Citizen, 1999), 19.

36. Ibid., 19–21.

37. Ibid., 21.

38. David Hartman, "What's Good for General Motors . . ." *Chronicles,* May 2002, http://www.chroniclesmagazine.org/Chronicles/May2002/0502Hartman.html (accessed 3/6/07).

39. Wallach and Sforza, *Whose Trade Organization?* 115–18.

40. Ibid., 22–25.

41. Ibid., 172.

42. Ibid.

43. United Methodist Church, "World Trade Organization: The Whole World—In Whose Hands?"

44. Wallach and Sforza, *Whose Trade Organzation?* 118.

45. The Working Group on the WTO/MAI, *A Citizen's Guide to the World Trade Organization* (Washington, D. C.: Public Citizen, July 1999), 3.

46: Debi Barker and Jerry Mander, Invisible Government: The World Trade Organization--Global Government for the New Millenium? A Primer (San Francisco: International Forum on Globalization, 1999), 1.

CHAPTER THIRTEEN: No More Mr. Nice Guy

1. Mark Lewis Taylor, *The Executed God: The Way of the Cross in Lockdown America* (Minneapolis: Fortress Press, 2001), 3.

2. "Ken Saro-Wiwa and 8 Ogoni People Executed: Blood on Shell's Hands," Greenpeace, http://archive.greenpeace.org/comms/ken/murder.html (accessed 3/6/07).

3. Thomas Friedman, "What the World Needs Now: A Manifesto for the Fast World," *New York Times Magazine,* Mar. 28, 1999, reprinted at Global Policy Forum, http://www.globalpolicy.org/nations/fried99.htm (accessed 3/6/07).

4. Taylor, *The Executed God,* 67.

5. Christian Parenti, "War On Crime," *San Francisco Bay Guardian,* Nov. 18, 1998, http://www.hartford-hwp.com/archives/45a/558.html (accessed 3/6/07).

6. Michael Powell, "NYC has seen crime decline," *The Union,* Grass Valley, Calif., Nov. 25, 2006, A8.

7. Angela Y. Davis, "Masked Racism: Reflections on the Prison Industrial Complex," *Colorlines,* Sept. 1, 1998, http://www.corpwatch.org/article.php?id=849?printsafe=1 (accessed 3/6/07).

8. Christian Parenti, "The Prison Industrial Complex: Crisis and Control," *Corpwatch,* Sept. 1, 1999, http://www.corpwatch.org/article.php?id=852&printsafe=1 (accessed 3/6/07).

9. Davis, "Masked Racism."

10. Prison Policy Initiative, "US Incarceration Rates by Race," Prison Policy Initiative, June 30, 2004, http://www.prisonpolicy.org/graphs/raceinc.html.

11. Davis, "Masked Racism."

12. Christian Parenti interviewed by Bob Libal, "Lockdown America Revisited: A Conversation with Christian Parenti on Prisons, Policing, and the War on Terror," *Z Magazine,* Dec. 9, 2005, http://www.zmag.org/content/showarticle.cfm?ItemID=9292 (accessed 3/6/07).

13. Taylor, *The Executed God,* 57.

14. Si Kahn and Elizabeth Minnich, *The Fox in the Henhouse: How Privatization Threatens Democracy (*San Francisco: Berrett-Koehler, 2005), 100.

15. John Biewen, "Corporate-Sponsored Crime Laws," Part I of Corrections, Inc., Minnesota Pubic Radio and NPR News, April 2002, at http://americanradioworks.publicradio.org/features/corrections/laws1.html (accessed 3/6/07).

16. Parenti, "The Prison Industrial Complex: Crisis and Control."

17. Kahn and Minnich, *The Fox in the Henhouse,* 75.

18. Parenti, "The Prison Industrial Complex."

19. Ibid.

20. John Ross, "Earning Millions from the Misery of the Poor: Slave Labor in Private Prisons" in *CounterPunch Newsletter,* Nov. 2, 2006, http://www.counterpunch.org/ross11022006.html (accessed 3/6/07).

21. Ibid.

22. Silja J. A. Talvi, "Follow the Prison Money Trail," *In These Times,* Sept. 4, 2006, http://www.inthesetimes.com/site/main/article/2797/ (accessed 3/6/07).

23. Davis, "Masked Racism."

24. Steven Staples, "The FTAA, School of Americas, and Militarism," Environmentalists Against War, Nov. 24, 2003, http://www.envirosagainstwar.org/know/read.php?itemid=803 (accessed 3/6/07).

25. Talvi, "Follow the Prison Money Trail."

26. Davis, "Masked Racism."

27. Taylor, The Executed God, 9.

28. Nancy Chang, *Silencing Political Dissent: How Post-September 11 Anti-Terrorism Measures Threaten Our Civil Liberties* (New York: Seven Stories Press, 2002), 43–66.

29. Ibid., 67–69.

30. Ibid.

31. *The Sunday Times/The Australian,* "USA: Private Jet Flies Men to 'Torture' Friendly Countries," Nov. 15th, 2004, reprinted in CorpWatch, http://www.corpwatch.org/article.php?id=11673 (accessed 3/6/07).

32. Earl Ofari Hutchinson, "Domestic Spying Is Old News," *Pacific News Service,* Dec. 21, 2005, http://www.alternet.org/story/29895 (accessed 3/6/07).

33. Jeremy Scahill, "Blackwater Down," *The Nation,* Oct. 10, 2005, http://www.thenation.com/doc/20051010/scahill (accessed 3/6/07).

34. Martin Niemöller, "Martin Niemoller: Communists, Socialists, and Jews," age-of-the-sage.org, http://www.age-of-the-sage.org/quotations/niemoller_jews_communists_socialists.html (accessed 3/6/07). This Poem is widely attributed to Martin Niemoller, (1892-1984) a German Lutheran pastor who was a Nazi Resister. He was imprisoned at Sachsenhausen and Dachau concentration camps during World War II. He survived to become an influential voice for peace and reconciliation.

CHAPTER FOURTEEN: The Iron Fist

1. Walter Wink, *Unmasking the Powers: The Invisible Forces That Determine Human Existence* (Philadelphia: Fortress Press, 1986), 51.

2. William Greider, *Fortress America: The American Military and the Consequences of Peace* (New York: PublicAffairs, 1998), 71.

3. Daniel Ellsberg, during a panel discussion at the Earl Lectures, First Congregational Church, Berkeley, California, Jan. 30, 2003.

4. Borger, Julian and David Teather "So Much for the Peace Dividend: Pentagon is Winning the Battle for a $400 Billion Budget," in *The Guardian/UK*, May 22, 2003, http://www.commondreams.org/headlines03/0522-01.htm.

5. Helen Caldicott, *The New Nuclear Danger: George W. Bush's Military-Industrial Complex* (New York: The New Press, 2002), 172.

6. Antonia Juhasz, *The Bush Agenda: Invading the World, One Economy at a Time* (New York: HarperCollins, 2006), 38.

7. Anup Shah, "Arms Trade—a major cause of suffering," *Global Issues*, Nov. 9, 2006, http://www.globalissues.org/Geopolitics/ArmsTrade/Spending.asp (accessed 3/6/07).

8. Ibid.

9. Shah, Anup, "The Bush Doctrine of Pre-emptive Strikes: A Global Pax Americana," Global Issues website, Updated: Saturday, April 24, 2004, http://www.globalissues.org/Geopolitics/Empire/Bush.asp. The document itself can be found at: http://www.newamericancentury.org/RebuildingAmericas Defenses.pdf.

10. Ibid.

11. Thomas Friedman, *The Lexus and the Olive Tree: Understanding Globalization* (New York: Farrar, Straus & Giroux, 2000), 443.

12. U.S. Air Force, "Vision for 2020," as quoted in Karl Grossman, "Weapons in Space: A Media Blackout," a printed copy of a presentation at Press Freedom Conference, San Francisco, April 28, 2001.

13. Greider, *Fortress America*, 132.

14. Greg Goldin, "Selling War: How the military's ad campaign gets inside the heads of recruits," *LA Weekly*, March 6, 2003, http://www.laweekly.com/general/features/selling-war/3068/ (accessed 3/6/07).

15. Karl Grossman, "Space Corps: The dangerous business of making the heavens a war zone," *CovertAction*, April-June 2001, 32.

16. Gary Hart, quoted by Glenn Harlan Reynolds, "It Takes a Militia," *Reason*, May 1999, http://www.reason.com/news/show/30980.html (accessed 3/6/07).

17. Eisenhower, Dwight D., "Farewell Address to the American People," January 17, 1961, Eisenhower Presidential Library and Museum website, administered by the National Archives & Records Administration, http://www.eisenhower.archives.gov/farewell.htm.

18. Brad Knickerbocker, "Return of the 'military-industrial complex'?" *Christian Science Monitor*, Feb. 13, 2002, http://www.csmonitor.com/2002/0213/p02s03-uspo.html (accessed 3/6/07).

19. Grossman, "Space Corps," 32.

20. Caldicott, *The New Nuclear Danger*, 31.

21. Juhasz, *The Bush Agenda*, 139.

22. Grossman, "Space Corps," 32.

23. William Stringfellow, *An Ethic for Christians and Other Aliens in a Strange Land* (Waco: Word Books, 1974), 93.

24. Ibid., 89.

25. B. Martin Pedersen, *Prayers for Peace* (Chicago: The Council for a Parliament of World Religions, 2001), 43.

26. Juhasz, *The Bush Agenda*, 237.

27. Greider, *Fortress America*, 133.

28. Bruce Gagnon, Space Alert, *Newsletter 18* (Winter 2007), 6.

29. Center for Responsive Politics, "Lockheed Martin, Client Summary, 2005," Lobbying Database, http://www.opensecrets.org/lobbyists/clientsum.asp?txtname=Lockheed+Martin&year=2005 (accessed 3/6/07).

30. Center for Responsive Politics, "Northrop Grumman, Client Summary, 2005," Lobbying Database, http://www.opensecrets.org/lobbyists/clientsum.asp?year=2005&txtname=Northrop+Grumman (accessed 3/6/07).

31. Center for Responsive Politics, "Defense: Top Contributors to Federal Candidates and Parties, Election Cycle 2006," http://www.opensecrets.org/industries/contrib.asp?Ind=D&Cycle=2006 (accessed 3/6/07).

32. Caldicott, The New Nuclear Danger, 32.

33. Bryan Bender, "Congress Said to Steer Military Funds to Pet Projects," *Boston Globe,* June 17, 2005, http://www.commondreams.org/headlines05/0617-07.htm (accessed 3/6/07).

34. Caldicott, *The New Nuclear Danger,* 32.

35. Greider, *Fortress America,* 91.

36. Ibid., 65.

37. World Policy Institute, "Corporate Welfare for Weapons Makers: The Hidden Costs of Spending on Defense and Foreign Aid," Aug. 17, 1999, http://www.bu.edu/globalbeat/usdefense/Hartung081799.html (accessed 3/6/07).

38. Caldicott, *The New Nuclear Danger,* 40.

39. Ibid., 38.

40. Ibid.

41. Juhasz, *The Bush Agenda,* 179–80.

42. Ibid., 181.

43. Ibid., 182–83.

44. Ibid.

45. Ibid., 7.

46. Ibid., 138.

47. Ibid.

48. Friedman, *The Lexus and the Olive Tree,* 443.

49. Juhasz, *The Bush Agenda,* 212.

50. Ibid., 293.

51. Ibid., 200.

52. Ibid., 201.

53. Jeff Leys, "Economic Warfare: Iraq and the I.M.F," Voices for Creative Nonviolence, Sept. 18, 2006, http://vcnv.org/economic-warfare-iraq-and-the-1-m-f (accessed 3/7/06).

54. Ibid., 5.

55. Juhasz, *The Bush Agenda,* 212.

56. Ibid., 217.

57. Leys, "Economic Warfare," 3.

58. Ibid., 2.

59. Juhasz, *The Bush Agenda,* 290.

60. Nancy Pelosi, "By the Numbers: The Iraq War & U.S. National Security," http://speaker.gov/issues/index_html?id=0012 (accessed 3/7/06).

61. Greider, *Fortress America,* 109.

62. Juhasz, *The Bush Agenda,* 266.

63. David R. Francis, "Economist tallies swelling cost of Israel to US," Christian *Science Monitor,* Dec. 9, 2002, http://www.csmonitor.com/2002/1209/p16s01-wmgn.html (accessed 3/7/06).

64. Mary Beth Sullivan, "The #1 US Export," in Gagnon, *Space Alert,* 7.
65. Helen Caldicott, speaking at the home of Eleanor Wassen in Santa Cruz, California, on Sept. 15, 2003.
66. Greider, *Fortress America,* 107.
67. Ibid., 109.
68. Thomas Berry, "The Great Community of the Earth." Yes! Magazine, Winter 2001, 45, http://yesmagazine.org/articale.asp?ID=385 (accessed 3/6/07).

CHAPTER FIFTEEN: The Triumph of God over the Powers

1. Matthew Fox, *Original Blessing: A Primer in Creation Spirituality* (New York: Jeremy P. Tarcher/Putnam, 2000).
2. Walter Wink, *The Human Being: Jesus and the Enigma of the Son of the Man* (Minneapolis: Fortress Press, 2002), 119.
3. Ibid., 11.
4. Matthew Fox, *Sins of the Spirit, Blessings of the Flesh: Lessons for Transforming Evil in Soul and Society* (New York: Three Rivers, 1999), 14.
5. Wink, *The Human Being,* 2.
6. Allen D. Callahan, "Jesus' Arrest and Execution," in *From Jesus to Christ: Jesus' Many Faces,* http://www.pbs.org/wgbh/pages/frontline/shows/religion/jesus/arrest.html (accessed 3/7/07).
7. L. Michael White, "Jesus in Jerusalem at Passover," in ibid. (accessed 3/7/07).
8. Marcus Borg, *Jesus, A New Vision: Spirit, Culture, and the Life of Discipleship* (San Francisco: HarperSanFrancisco, 1987), 183–84.
9. Ibid., 185.
10. Dietrich Bonhoeffer, *The Cost of Discipleship* (New York: Collier Books, 1961), 60.
11. William Stringfellow, *An Ethic for Christians and Other Aliens in a Strange Land* (Waco: Word Books, 1974), 119; italics in original.
12. Charles L. Campbell, *The Word before the Powers: An Ethic of Preaching* (Louisville: Westminster John Knox Press, 2002), 47.
13. Bonhoeffer, *The Cost of Discipleship,* 99.
14. Albert Schweitzer, *The Mysticism of Paul the Apostle,* with an introduction by Jaroslav Pelikan, trans. William Montgomery (Baltimore: Johns Hopkins University Press, 1998), 22.
15. "Jesus the Great Physician," adapted from Donald Senior, "Jesus the Physician: What the Gospels Say about Healing," and Barry D. Smith, "Jesus as Healer," Jesus Institute, http://www.jesus-institute.org/life-of-jesus-modern/jesus-physician.shtml (accessed 3/7/07).
16. Stringfellow, *An Ethic for Christians,* 60.
17. Rev. Ginger Gaines-Cirelli, "Magical Mystery Tour," sermon preached at Capitol Hill United Methodist Church, Washington, D.C., June 18, 2006, http://www.gbgm-umc.org/caphillumc/sermons/sermon2006/061806_magicalmysterytour.htm (accessed 3/7/07).
18. Donald B. Kraybill, *The Upside Down Kingdom* (Scottdale, Pa.: Herald Press, 2003).
19. Gustaf Aulén, *Christus Victor: A Historical Study of the Three Main Types of the Idea of the Atonement* (New York: MacMillan, 1969), 4.
20. Wink, *The Human Being,* 104.
21. Paul Ray and Sherry Anderson, quoted in David C. Korten, *When Corporations Rule the World,* 2d ed. (San Francisco: Berrett-Koehler, 2001), 325.

22. Walter Wink, *Naming the Powers: The Language of Power in the New Testament* (Philadelphia: Fortress Press, 1983); *Unmasking the Powers: The Invisible Forces That Determine Human Existence* (Philadelphia: Fortress Press, 1986); *Engaging the Powers: Discernment and Resistance in a World of Domination* (Minneapolis: Fortress Press, 1992).

23. Wink, *Unmasking the Powers,* 173.

24 Matthew Fox, *Sins of the Spirit, Blessings of the Flesh,* 14.

25. Ibid.

26. Dorothee Soelle, *Suffering* (Philadelphia: Fortress Press, 1975), 132.

27. James W. Douglass, *Resistance and Contemplation: The Way of Liberation* (Garden City, N.Y.: Doubleday, 1972), 57.

28. Schweitzer, *The Mysticism of Paul the Apostle,* 384.

29. Jürgen Moltmann, "Has Modern Society Any Future?" in *Faith and the Future: Essays on Theology, Solidarity, and Modernity,* ed. Jürgen Moltmann and Johannes Baptist Metz, (Maryknoll, N.Y.: Orbis Books, 1995), 171.

30. Jim Wallis, sermon at St. James Cathedral, Seattle, Washington, November 29, 1999.

31. James W. Douglass, *The Nonviolent Coming of God* (Maryknoll, N.Y.: Orbis Books, 1991), 58.

32. Alice Walker, *We Are the Ones We Have Been Waiting For* (New York: The New Press, 2006).

33. Mark Lewis Taylor, *The Executed God: The Way of the Cross in Lockdown America* (Minneapolis: Fortress Press, 2001), 124.

34. Soelle, *Suffering,* 177.

35. Taylor, *The Executed God,* 124.

36. Ibid., 126.

37. Douglass, *The Nonviolent Coming of God,* 58.

CHAPTER SIXTEEN: A Better World Is Possible

1. Thomas Berry, *The Great Work* (New York: Bell Tower, 1999), 159.

2. United Nations Department for Economic and Social Affairs: Division for Sustainable Development, "Rio Declaration of Environment and Development," http://www.un.org/documents/ga/conf151/aconf15126-1annex1.htm (accessed 3/7/07).

3. Kenny Bruno, "The Corporate Capture of the Earth Summit," *Multinational Monitor,* July 1992, http://multinationalmonitor.org/hyper/issues/1992/07/mm0792_07.html (accessed 3/7/07).

4. Earth Charter International, "The Earth Charter," The Earth Charter Initiative, Stockholm, http://www.earthcharter.org/ (accessed 3/7/07).

5. David C. Korten, *The Great Turning: From Empire to Earth Community* (San Francisco: Berrett-Koehler, 2006), 26.

6. John Cavanagh and Jerry Mander, eds., *Alternatives to Economic Globalization: A Better World Is Possible, A Report of the International Forum on Globalization,* 2d ed. (San Francisco: Berrett-Koehler, 2004), 31.

7 Ibid., 79-100.

8. Ibid.

9. Richard Bauckham, "Jürgen Moltmann," in *The Modern Theologians: An Introduction to Christian Theology in the Twentieth Century,* Volume I, ed. David E. Ford (Campbell, Mass.: Basil Blackwell, 1990), 299.

10. Rosemary Radford Ruether, "Ecological Crisis: God's Presence in Nature?" in Douglas John Hall and Rosemary Radford Ruether, *God and the Nations, The Hein-Fry Lectures* (Minneapolis: Fortress Press, 1995), 10304.

11. Walter Wink, *Engaging the Powers: Discernment and Resistance in a World of Domination* (Minneapolis: Fortress Press, 1992).

12. Cavanagh and Mander, eds., *Alternatives to Economic Globalization*, 267.

13. Ibid., 257.

14. Walden Bello, "Globalization in Retreat," *Foreign Policy in Focus*, Dec. 27, 2006, http://www.fpif.org/fpiftxt/3826 (accessed 3/7/07).

15. Amy Goodman, "150 Nigerian Women End Their Unprecedented Peaceful Protest against Chevron, Winning Major Concessions," *Democracy Now*, KVMR-FM, July 19th, 2002, http://www.democracynow.org/article.pl?sid=03/04/07/032255 (accessed 3/7/07).

16. Bello, "Globalization in Retreat."

17. Emily Wax, "Kenya's 'Green Militant' Wins Nobel Peace Prize," *Washington Post Foreign Service*, Oct. 9, 2004, A1.

18. Cavanagh and Mander, eds., *Alternatives to Economic Globalization*, 256–57.

19. Ibid., 258.

20. Ibid., 264.

21. Ibid., 255.

22. Ibid., 253.

23. Anthony Giddens, *Runaway World: How Globalization Is Reshaping Our Lives* (New York: Routledge, 2000), 37.

24. Ibid., 217.

25. Gil Rendle, "Polity Gridlock: Finding the Path in the Wilderness," http://www.congregationalresources.org/frontpage/mj/rendle.asp (accessed 3/7/07).

26. David Korten's *The Great Turning and The Post Corporate World: Life after Capitalism* (San Francisco: Berrett-Koehler, 2006) also give concrete suggestions for alternatives to our present institutions and systems.

27. David Korten, "Global Economics, Environmental Integrity, and Justice: Reflections of an ' Economic Missionary," presented at National Council of Churches event on June 20, 2003, http://www.davidkorten.org/Talks/talks_globaleco.htm (accessed 4/5/07).

28. Cavanaugh and Mander, *Alternatives to Economic Globalization*, 164.

29. Wheatley, Meg, "Restoring Hope to the Future through Critical Education of Leaders," 2001, as quoted at http://thegreatturning.net/PDF/MG_Overview.pdf.

30. David Cortright, "Civil Society: The Other Superpower," *Disarmament Diplomacy* 76 (March/April 2004), http://www.acronym.org.uk/dd/dd76/76dc.htm (accessed 3/7/07).

31. Korten, The Great Turning, 316.

32. Ibid., 316–18.

33. James W. Douglass, *Resistance and Contemplation: The Way of Liberation* (Garden City: Doubleday, 1972), 57.

CHAPTER SEVENTEEN: Faith–Led Resistance as a Way of Life

1. Roger S. Gottlieb, *A Spirituality of Resistance: Finding a Peaceful Heart and Protecting the Earth* (New York: Crossroad, 1999), 32.

2. Thomas Berry, *The Great Work: Our Way into the Future* (New York: Bell Tower, 1999).

3. Dietrich Bonhoeffer, *The Cost of Discipleship* (New York: Collier Books, 1961), 48–49.

4. Martin Luther, tr. Frederick H. Hedges, 1853.

5. Jürgen Moltmann, "Has Modern Society Any Future?" in Jürgen Moltmann and Johannes Baptist Metz, *Faith and the Future: Essays on Theology, Solidarity, and Modernity* (Maryknoll, N.Y.: Orbis Books, 1995), 177.

6. Thomas Berry, "The Great Community of the Earth," *Yes! A Journal of Positive Futures* (Winter 2001), 45, http://yesmagazine.org/article.asp?ID=385 (accessed 3/7/07).

7. Ronald Goetz, "The Karl Barth Centennial: An Appreciative Critique," Christian Century, May 7, 1986, 458. http://www.religion-online.org/showarticle.asp?title=1037 (accessed 3/7/07).

8. Karl Barth, quoted in Richard J. Foster, *Prayer: Finding the Heart's True Home* (New York: HarperCollins, 1992), 243.

9. James W. Douglass, *Resistance and Contemplation: The Way of Liberation* (Garden City, N.Y.: Doubleday, 1972), 68–69.

10. Ibid.

11. Walter Wink, *The Human Being: Jesus and the Enigma of the Son of the Man* (Minneapolis: Fortress Press, 2002), 125.

12. Ibid.

13. Ibid., 100.

14. Ibid.

15. Foster, Prayer, 247.

16. Richard J. Foster, *Freedom of Simplicity* (San Francisco: Harper & Row, 1981).

17. Hendrik Berkhof, *Christ and the Powers* (Scottdale, Pa.: Herald Press, 1977), 51.

18. Marcus Borg, *Jesus, A New Vision: Spirit, Culture, and the Life of Discipleship* (San Francisco: HarperSanFrancisco, 1987), 194.

19. Paul Jeffrey, "Chicago Congregation Offers Single Mom Sanctuary," *Response* 38, no. 10 (Nov.-Dec. 2006), 33.

20. Ibid., 34.

21. Ibid., 35.

22. Borg, *Jesus, A New Vision*, 195.

23. Ibid., 195.

24. Ibid.

25. Larry L. Rasmussen, "Creation, Church, and Christian Responsibility," in *Tending the Garden: Essays on the Gospel and the Earth*, ed. Wesley Granberg-Michaelson (Grand Rapids, Mich.: Wm. B. Eerdmans, 1987), 123.

26. Moltmann, "Has Modern Society Any Future?" 172.

27. Borg, *Jesus, A New Vision*, 196.

28. elmira Nazombe, "Globalization Times: Big Rapids, Michigan," in *Globalization and Its Impact on People's Lives*, 2006–2007 Mission Study (New York: General Board of Global Ministries, The United Methodist Church, 2005), 28–29.

29. Tikkun, "Network of Spiritual Progressives," http://www.tikkun.org/community/spiritual_activism_conference/document.2005-04-27.5780162886 (accessed 3/7/07).

30. Sojourners/Call to Renewal, "A Covenant for a New America," http://www.sojo.net/index.cfm?action=action.c4na&item=C4NA_main (accessed 3/7/07).

31. National Religious Campaign against Torture, "Torture Is a Moral Issue," http://www.nrcat.org/statement.aspx (accessed 3/7/07).

32. World Council of Churches, "'Spirituality of Resistance' key theme of WCC's contribution to World Social Forum," Jan. 21, 2003, http://www.eappi.org/pressreleasesen.nsf/index/pr-03-04.html (accessed 3/7/07).

33. Borg, *Jesus, A New Vision*, 197.

34. Foster, *Prayer,* 249.

35. Mark Lewis Taylor, *The Executed God: The Way of the Cross in Lockdown America* (Minneapolis: Fortress Press, 2001), 98.

36. Cynthia B. Astle, "Ava Lowery," *The Progressive Christian: Faith and the Common Good* 181, no. 1 (Jan./Feb. 2007).

37. Paul Jeffrey, "Tacoma congregation declares 'sanctuary' for war resisters," United Methodist News Service, June 20, 2006, http://www.umc.org/site/c.gjJTJbMUIuE/b.1802107/k.B1E4/Tacoma_congrega-tion_declares_sanctuary_for_war_resisters.htm (accessed 3/7/07).

38. Eileen Hanson, "CPT trainees arrested advocating for Guantanamo detainees," CPTnet, Jan. 17, 2007, http://www.cpt.org/archives/2007/jan07/0019.html (accessed 3/7/07).

39. Amy Goodman, "Video Broadcast of Kidnapped Members of Christian Peacemaker Teams that Helped Expose Abu Ghraib Prisoner Abuse Scandal," Democracy Now, Nov. 30th, 2005, http://www.democracynow.org/article.pl?sid=05/11/30/153252 (accessed 3/7/07).

40. Scott Peterson, "Christian Peacemakers Celebrate Release," *Christian Science Monitor,* Mar. 24, 2006, http://www.csmonitor.com/2006/0324/p07s02-woiq.html (accessed 3/7/07).

41. Hanson, "CPT trainees arrested."

42. Borg, *Jesus, A New Vision,* 139.

43. Martin Luther King Jr., "Letter from Birmingham Jail," in King, ed., *Why We Can't Wait* (New York: Harper & Row, 1963), 77–100, http://www.stanford.edu/group/King/popular_requests/frequentdocs/birming-ham.pdf (accessed 3/7/07).

44. Ken Butigan, "The Spiritual Journey of Christian Nonviolent Resistance," Pace e Bene Nonviolence Service, http://paceebene.org/pace/nvns/essays-on-nonviolence/the-spiritual-journey-of-christian-no (accessed 3/7/07).

45. Charles L. Campbell, *The Word before the Powers: An Ethic of Preaching* (Louisville: Westminster John Knox Press, 2002), 100–04.

46. William Stringfellow, *An Ethic for Christians and Other Aliens in a Strange Land* (Waco: Word Books, 1974), 7.

47. Ibid., 59.

48. Campbell, *The Word Before the Powers,* 79.

49. Ibid., 106.

50. Stringfellow, An Ethic for Christians, 143.

51. Wink, *The Human Being,* 259–60.

CONCLUSION: By the Power at Work within Us

1. Jamie Owens Collins, 1976 Bud John Songs, Inc., Nashville, Tennessee. "The Victor" from No Compromise (Sparrow Records, 1978). http://www.goldlyrics.com/song_lyrics/keith_green/no_compromise/the_victor/ (accessed 3/7/07).

2. Robert Zoellick, "Committed in Cancun," *Wall Street Journal,* Sept. 8, 2003, editorial page.

3. Marques Howard, "Public Servants Reject WTO Tactics," *Los Angeles Indymedia,* Sept. 21, 2003, http://la.indymedia.org/news/2003/09/83932.php (accessed 3/7/07).

4. Claire Melamed, "The Collapse of the WTO Talks," *Christian Aid,* Sept. 9, 2003, http://www.christian-aid.org.uk/cancun/030916feature.htm (accessed 3/7/07).

5. San Francisco Independent Media Collective (SF-IMC), "Cat and Mouse in Cancun: WTO Talks Crash to Ground! Victory in Cancun!!" Sept. 15, 2003, http://archives.lists.indymedia.org/imc-sf-newscopy/2003-September/000004.html (accessed 3/7/07).

6. Diego Cevallos, "WTO/Cancun: Future Uncertain after Collapse of Talks," *Inter Press Service,* Sept. 15, 2003, http://www.commondreams.org/headlines03/0915-01.htm (accessed 3/7/07).

7. Bob Marley, "Redemption Song," *Uprising* (Jamaica: Island Records, 1980), http://www.songfacts.com/detail.php?id=4431 (accessed 3/7/07).

8. Jürgen Moltmann, "Has Modern Society Any Future?" in Jürgen Moltmann and Johannes Baptist Metz, *Faith and the Future: Essays on Theology, Solidarity, and Modernity* (Maryknoll, N.Y.: Orbis Books, 1995), 174.

9. Guarionex Delgado, "Narrow Path, Steep Way," in *Being Human: Poems of Resistance and Renewal* (Nevada City, Calif.: Rim of Fire Publishing, 2001), 96.

INDEX